M000251907

"This is an important book for the chu[...] fully crafted and nuanced explanations and corrections to common misunder-standings about what the Old Testament teaches. It is not surprising that such an ancient text written in such a different place and cultural context could be difficult to understand in today's world, at least in some of its parts. Naturally, some readers might quibble about certain points, but the authors select the problems well and treat them in a fair, judicious, and helpful manner."

—Richard E. Averbeck, director, PhD in Theological Studies, professor of Old Testament and Semitic languages, Trinity Evangelical Divinity School

"Unfortunately 'urban legends' grow like weeds in the garden of biblical inter-pretation. In this volume the authors do some much-needed weeding. Using sound interpretive principles and insightful contextual exegesis, they expose forty common misconceptions about Old Testament passages. Each chapter is clearly written and concise. The epilogue to the book, though short, is espe-cially helpful. The authors here explain how interpretive misconceptions get started. In the process, they identify several key principles for proper biblical interpretation which, if followed, will go a long way toward weed prevention."

—Robert B. Chisholm, Jr., department chair, senior professor of Old Testament studies, Dallas Theological Seminary

"I have sometimes thought about writing a book called 'What the Bible Doesn't Teach,' but now I will forget the idea; David Croteau and Gary Yates have done it. This book is a magnificent debunking of forty mistaken ideas about the Old Testament. It will be great if pastors, Sunday school teachers, and Bible study leaders read it, causing some of these urban myths to die."

—John Goldingay, professor of Old Testament and David Allen Hubbard Professor Emeritus of Old Testament, Fuller Theological Seminary

"It is important to know what the Bible says, but it is also important to know what the Bible *does not* say. Croteau and Yates have produced a very informative and fascinating book to help us disentangle fact from fiction in a number of OT passages. This is an outstanding book and I highly recommend it; but—spoiler alert—be warned, you just may run into some of your own favorite [mis]interpretations here! That is all the more reason for all of us to read it."

—J. Daniel Hays, dean, Pruet School of Christian Studies,
professor of biblical studies Ouachita Baptist University

"As a veteran of battling poor thinking about Scripture on the front lines of the internet and in the classroom, it is hard to express how much this book is needed and how it succeeds in hitting the mark. The authors are seasoned Bible scholars and professors with a heart to nurture clarity and faithfulness to the biblical text among their students. Readers who find among its pages one of their own cherished myths about something the Bible "teaches" might be miffed. Others—and I count myself among them—will cheer its direct yet irenic and engaging rebuttals and debunkings. This book will be a recommended antidote to careless Bible study and the propensity to impart its flawed results to others."

—Michael S. Heiser, scholar-in-residence, Faithlife

"It's rare to come across a book that is as engaging as it is scholarly, and as fascinating as it is edifying. Whether read cover to cover or used as a reference book, *Urban Legends of the Old Testament* will serve casual readers, study groups, and scholars well."

—Karen Swallow Prior, professor of English, Liberty University

"The authors of this book have done a remarkable job of choosing just the right issues to address, and they have offered thoughtful, balanced, well-researched, and gracious suggestions to help us adjust our thinking. Leaving behind these 'urban legends' will aid us on our quest to be faithful interpreters of God's Word who are accountable to the inspired Scripture. Reading this book will help pastors, Bible study leaders, and Sunday school teachers avoid these traditional pitfalls. Laypeople will find it readable and practical. In short, I recommend this book for anyone who wants to become a better reader of the Old Testament."

—John Walton, professor of Old Testament, Wheaton College

URBAN LEGENDS
OLD
OF THE
TESTAMENT

URBAN LEGENDS OLD OF THE TESTAMENT

40 Common Misconceptions

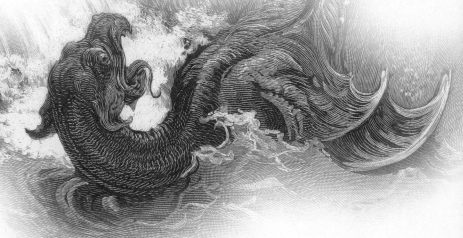

DAVID A. CROTEAU AND GARY E. YATES

ACADEMIC
NASHVILLE, TENNESSEE

Urban Legends of the Old Testament
Copyright © 2019 by David A. Croteau and Gary Yates

Published by B&H Academic
Nashville, Tennessee

All rights reserved.

ISBN: 978-1-4336-4832-8

Dewey Decimal Classification: 221.1
Subject Heading: BIBLE. O.T.--CRITICISM / BIBLE. O.T.--EVIDENCES, AUTHORITY,
ETC. / BIBLE. O.T.--HISTORY

Unless otherwise indicated, Scripture quotations are taken from The Christian Standard Bible. Copyright © 2017 by Holman Bible Publishers. Used by permission. Christian Standard Bible®, and CSB® are federally registered trademarks of Holman Bible Publishers, all rights reserved.

Scripture quotations marked NET are taken from the NET Bible®. Copyright © 1996–2006 by Biblical Studies Press, L.L.C. http://netbible.com. All rights reserved.

Scripture quotations marked NASB are taken from the NEW AMERICAN STANDARD BIBLE®. Copyright © 1960, 1962, 1963, 1968, 1971, 1972, 1973, 1975, 1977, 1995 by The Lockman Foundation. Used by permission.

Scripture quotations marked ESV are taken from the ESV® Bible (The Holy Bible, English Standard Version®). ESV® Text Edition: 2016. Copyright © 2001 by Crossway, a publishing ministry of Good News Publishers. The ESV® text has been reproduced in cooperation with and by permission of Good News Publishers. Unauthorized reproduction of this publication is prohibited. All rights reserved.

Scripture quotations marked NIV are taken from THE HOLY BIBLE, NEW INTERNATIONAL VERSION®, NIV® Copyright © 1973, 1978, 1984, 2011 by Biblica, Inc.® Used by permission. All rights reserved worldwide.

Scripture quotations marked NKJV are taken from the New King James Version®. Copyright © 1982 by Thomas Nelson. Used by permission. All rights reserved.

The web addresses referenced in this book were live and correct at the time of the book's publication but may be subject to change.

Cover design by Darren Welch. Cover illustration by Gustave Doré; sourced from Nicku/shutterstock.

Printed in the United States of America

1 2 3 4 5 6 7 8 9 10 VP 24 23 22 21 20 19

DAVID: To Ann, Danielle, and D. J.—may we all learn
to grow in the fear and knowledge of our Lord.

GARY: To my wife, Marilyn—her example of what it
means to live out the true message of God's Word has blessed
me and our children more than I could ever express.

Contents

Acknowledgments

FROM DAVE:

I want to thank several people who helped me in writing this book. First, Brian Gault and Ben Noonan were so gracious in talking with me and providing resource after resource, enabling me to provide much more informed research. To Nate Montgomery, who provided some aid in doing research that was very helpful. Also, to Columbia Biblical Seminary, John Harvey, and Jim Lanpher, for allowing me to take a sabbatical and work on this project. Finally, to Gary Yates, my coauthor, who read through every chapter I wrote and lovingly guided this New Testament scholar through this journey.

FROM GARY:

I first of all want to thank my coauthor, David, for the opportunity to work with this project. We first talked about this book at a coffee shop here in Lynchburg, and his fine work on *Urban Legends of the New Testament* convinced the editors at B&H that an Old Testament volume was a worthwhile project as well. I am also thankful to my Hebrew and Old Testament professors at Dallas Theological Seminary, who instilled in me a love for the Hebrew Scriptures and provided invaluable training for how to read and interpret the Old Testament. I hear their voices often in my own teaching, even if I often fall short of the high standards they modeled. Last, I want to thank my colleagues in the School of Divinity at Liberty University for the opportunity to teach the Bible for the past sixteen years and for the students in my classes whose questions over the years have helped me to dig deeper into many of the passages discussed in this book.

Prologue

Did George Washington say to his father "I cannot tell a lie" while confessing to chopping down a cherry tree? Did he also skip a silver dollar across the Potomac River? Did Patrick Henry really shout, "Give me Liberty, or give me Death!"? Finally, did Benjamin Franklin propose that the Great Seal of the United States contain a turkey? All of these are popular myths. An urban legend is a commonly circulated myth that is not true, but is repeated throughout the culture as common knowledge.[1]

In this book, we will discuss forty passages in the Old Testament that are commonly misunderstood. These carefully selected passages are not the only commonly circulating misinterpretations, but they represent a cross section of different issues involved in interpretation across the Old Testament. There is no desire to be "nit-picky" on our disagreements, because most of these misinterpretations are serious misunderstandings of what the original authors were attempting to communicate to the original audience.

Our hope is that through reading this book, you will see modeled careful interpretation and will not only learn the reasons for the misconceptions, but also learn how to interpret Scripture more accurately yourself. In discussing these forty passages, we have attempted to reflect sound hermeneutical approaches, but also engage larger issues related to biblical theology and how believers today read and apply the Old Testament as Christian Scripture.

---

[1] See David A. Croteau, *Urban Legends of the New Testament: 40 Common Misconceptions* (Nashville: Broadman & Holman, 2015), xiii.

The title of each chapter is the legend itself, not the correct interpretation of the text(s) at hand. Each chapter will begin with a presentation of the legend, presented *as if* we believe it. Then we will try to prove to you that it is an invalid interpretation of the passage. Finally, we will explain what the text does mean.

CHAPTER 1

In the "Gap" between Genesis 1:1 and 1:2, Satan Fell

Genesis 1:1–2

The Legendary Teaching on the "Gap Theory" in Genesis 1

The fall of Satan occurred in the "gap" between Gen 1:1 and 1:2. After the creation of the universe, Satan led a heavenly rebellion and was cast out of heaven and down to Earth. God judged the earth after Satan took up his residence there, reducing the planet to a condition of ruin and chaos. Genesis 1:2 should be read, "And the earth *became* formless and empty." God's work of re-creation (or restitution) of the ruined earth begins in Gen 1:3 and continues throughout the six days of creation recounted in the rest of the chapter. The gap theory provides an explanation of when Satan fell, and the undetermined time of the gap between Gen 1:1 and 1:2 explains how the universe can be millions or billions of years old even with the literal six-day creation portrayed in Genesis 1.[1] Geological strata indicating an old Earth belong to this original creation.

Countering the Legendary Teaching

The gap theory fails for various reasons. The syntax of the opening verses in Genesis 1 does not allow for the translation "And the earth *became* form-

---

[1]   The *Scofield Reference Bible* (1917) states that the expression "without form, and void" in Gen 1:2 demonstrates "that that the earth had undergone a cataclysmic change as the result of divine judgment. The face of the earth bears everywhere the marks of such a catastrophe. There are not wanting imitations which connect it with a previous testing and fall of angels."

less." The insertion of a satanic fall and divine judgment into Gen 1:1–2 is pure speculation, and the Hebrew Bible offers no clear account of the fall of Satan.[2] There is also nothing in the Bible to suggest that God judged the earth itself when Satan fell, and the reasons for such a judgment are not clear.

The gap theory is reflective of a problem with many contemporary readings of Genesis 1–2. In these readings, concerns with how the biblical account comports with modern scientific theories about the origin of the universe become the focal point rather than discovery of the theological message of the text itself. The particular question of the age of the universe has often dominated evangelical discussion of Genesis 1–2; although this issue has importance, we must first remember that this text is to be read as an ancient creation account, not a modern scientific one.

"Formless and Empty": An Indication of Divine Judgment?

Proponents of the gap (or restitution) theory propose that the expression translated in the King James Version as "without form, and void" (*tohu webohu*; CSB: "formless and empty") offers proof that catastrophic judgment resulting from the heavenly rebellion led by Satan has occurred between Gen 1:1 and 1:2. The term *tohu* has the meaning of "wasteland," "emptiness," or "nothingness."[3] It refers to a desert or uninhabited city (see Deut 32:10; Job 12:24; Ps 107:4; Isa 24:10), the "nothingness" of idols (1 Sam 12:21; Isa 41:29; 44:9), and futile words or deeds (Isa 29:21; 49:4). The term *bohu* ("void, waste") appears only with *tohu*, and the two words joined by a conjunction likely convey a single idea of utter or complete emptiness.

This word pair *formless and empty* (*tohu webohu*) appears elsewhere in the Old Testament only in Isa 34:11 and Jer 4:23. In these passages, the condition of something being "formless and empty" is the result of judgment. The fact that divine judgment is the cause of *tohu webohu* in Isaiah 34 and Jeremiah 4 does not, however, necessitate the same cause for this condition in Genesis 1. The chaos in Gen 1:2 merely reflects that God has either not begun or completed his work of creation.[4] Isaiah 45:18 states that God did not create the world to be a "wasteland" (*tohu*), and the specific

---

[2]   See chap. 32 for further discussion.
[3]   Ludwig Koehler and Walter Baumgartner, *Hebrew and Aramaic Lexicon of the Old Testament Study Edition*, trans. M. E. J. Richardson (Leiden: Brill, 2001), 2:1688–90.
[4]   John H. Walton, *Genesis*, New International Version Application Commentary (Grand Rapids: Zondervan, 2001), 74.

purpose of God's work in the six days of Genesis 1 is to bring order out of this chaos. There are multiple possible causes for a condition of *tohu webohu*, just as there could be multiple reasons for a jigsaw puzzle to be in a state of disorder. It could be that I have just taken the puzzle pieces out of the box or that I slammed my fist into the puzzle out of frustration. If the narrator's intent was to indicate that divine judgment was the cause of the condition of the chaos in Gen 1:2, it seems that the text would more explicitly reflect that idea.

The Gap Theory and the Grammatical Structure of Genesis 1:1–3

Proper understanding of the expression "formless and empty" eliminates the necessity of a gap between the pristine creation of Gen 1:1 and the chaos of 1:2. The syntax and structure of Gen 1:1–3 effectively rule out even the possibility of such a gap. Verse 2 begins with the conjunction *waw* ("and, but, now") attached to the noun *earth*. This type of circumstantial clause introduced by a *waw* + nonverbal form (referred to as a *waw*-disjunctive) is not an independent clause and does not denote sequence, which prevents the progression required by the gap theory: "and the earth *became* formless and empty." The other two clauses in verse 2 ("darkness covered the surface of the watery depths" and "the Spirit of God was hovering over the surface of the waters") are also *waw*-disjunctive clauses and provide background information prior to the first specific creative act that begins with "Then God said" in verse 3.

While the gap theory is ruled out, two possibilities remain for how to understand the relationship between the verses in Gen 1:1–3. One is the traditional view that Gen 1:1 describes God's first act of creation with the six days that follow in the chapter portraying how God brings order out of the initial chaos.[5] The second option is the precreation chaos view, which reads Gen 1:1 as the title for the chapter and views the chaos described in 1:2 as conditions that exist prior to God's actual work of creation that begins in 1:3.[6]

---

[5]   See Mark F. Rooker, "Genesis 1:1–3: Creation or Re-Creation? Parts 1 and 2," *Bibliotheca Sacra* 149 (1992): 316–23, 411–27.

[6]   See Bruce K. Waltke, "The Creation Account in Genesis 1:1–3—Part 3: The Initial Chaos Theory," *Bibliotheca Sacra* 132 (1975): 216–28; and the translation notes on 1:1–3 in the NET Bible.

Traditional View
Gen 1:1—God's initial act of creation
Gen 1:2—Conditions resulting from God's initial act of creation
Gen 1:3—"Then God said" (God's creative work resumes)

Precreation Chaos View
Gen 1:1—Title for chapter
Gen 1:2—Conditions that exist prior to God's work of creation
Gen 1:3—"Then God said" (God's first creative act in the chapter)

There are several key issues dividing these two readings, but, unlike the gap theory, both are viable readings of Gen 1:1–3.[7] The same basic structure for Gen 1:1–3 proposed by the precreation chaos view also appears in the opening verses of the complementary creation account found in Gen 2:4–7.[8] One implication of the precreation chaos view would be that Genesis 1 does not portray an *ex nihilo* ("out of nothing") creation. This understanding of creation is affirmed elsewhere in the Bible (see John 1:3; Col 1:16; Heb 11:3) but would not be the point of Genesis 1 itself. In contrast, the traditional view affirms creation *ex nihilo*, and the larger biblical teaching on creation raises questions as to why Gen 1:1 would affirm the existence of preexistent chaos that lies outside of God's creative activity.

The takeaway from this discussion is that there are viable arguments for both the traditional and precreation chaos views, and the details of Gen 1:1–3 do not fully resolve the issue of young Earth versus old Earth that gave rise to the gap theory. The syntax of Gen 1:1–3 can accommodate an old-Earth creation but also allows for a young Earth view if read in connection with a literal

---

[7] These issues include whether 1:1 is an independent or subordinate clause, whether 1:2 is to be read as subordinate to verse 1 or verse 3, and whether the noun *beginning* (*rēʾshit*) should be read as a construct ("in the beginning of" or "when God began to create") or absolute ("in the beginning") noun. The precreation chaos view treats *rēʾshit* as a construct noun, which is the form in which this word appears in forty-nine of its other fifty occurrences in the OT. The noun *rēʾshit* is also a construct noun in the four other times where the expression "in/at the beginning" appears (Jer 26:1; 27:1; 28:1; 49:34), but another noun appears with *bereʾshit* in these passages, which is not the case in Gen 1:1. In support of the traditional view, the noun *rēʾshit* does appear as an absolute noun in Isa 46:10 in the statement that God declares "the end from *the beginning*."

[8] For Gen 2:4–7, there is also (1) title (2:4), (2) series of *waw*-disjunctive clauses providing background information, and (3) main verb ("and God formed") as the first action. Nevertheless, the parallel between the two sections is not exact, in that 1:1 contains a finite verb ("created") and 2:4 does not.

six-day creation in the rest of the chapter.[9] Faithful readers of Scripture have read Genesis 1 in both ways. For young-Earth creationists, the narrative genre, the numbering of the days, and the references to morning and evening support a literal six-day creation. Other commentators acknowledge these details but read the narrative in more figurative or analogical ways.[10]

The Message and Purpose of the Creation Account in Genesis 1

Like other ancient Near Eastern creation accounts, Genesis 1 pictures creation out of a watery chaos. The narrative in Genesis 1 particularly resembles Egyptian creation accounts, which also begin with a watery chaos and then attribute the creation to the spoken word of Atum.[11] Recognition of such parallels helps contemporary readers to appreciate more fully the message of Genesis 1 in its ancient literary context. These parallels do not indicate that the biblical text has borrowed from these pagan texts or has adopted their mythological worldview. These parallels merely reflect common conceptual understandings from the ancient world that the biblical writer (and the Holy Spirit) employed to convey his message in an understandable way to his audience. The purpose of biblical revelation was not to correct ancient cosmogony or to provide advanced scientific understanding of how the world was created. The biblical writer also employed parallels with ancient Near Eastern creation accounts to polemicize against the false beliefs reflected in the pagan myths and stories of creation.[12]

The biblical account stresses that the one true God is the sole actor in the creation process. The sun, moon, and stars that were deified in other cultures are simply identified in Genesis as "the greater light," "the lesser light," and markers of the seasons (1:14–17).[13] There is no cosmic battle with the forces of chaos as God creates solely through the power of his word (Gen 1:3, 6, 8–11, 14, 20, 22, 24, 26). God is both separate from his creation and distinct from

---

[9]   Michael S. Heiser, "Creation, Evolution, Intelligent Design, and the Replicating Universe: What Does the Hebrew Text of Genesis 1 Allow?" accessed November 15, 2017, www.michaelsheiser.com/Genesis%201%20and%20creation.pdf, 7.

[10]   See J. Daryl Charles, ed., *Reading Genesis 1–2: An Evangelical Conversation* (Peabody, MA: Hendrickson, 2013).

[11]   See further Johnny V. Miller and John M. Soden, *In the Beginning . . . We Misunderstood: Interpreting Genesis 1 in Its Original Context* (Grand Rapids: Kregel, 2012), 77–112.

[12]   For more on the relationship between the Old Testament and ancient Near Eastern myth, see John N. Oswalt, *The Bible among the Myths: Unique Revelation or Just Ancient Literature?* (Grand Rapids: Zondervan, 2009).

[13]   Miller and Soden, *In the Beginning,* 180.

the forces of nature. The radical differences between Genesis and other ancient Near Eastern creation accounts are far more striking than the similarities.

Application

Genesis 1–2 does not directly address our contemporary and scientific questions about creation, but the text informs our Christian worldview and is foundational to our understanding of the one true God. Yahweh, the God of Israel, is the Creator of the world and every living thing. The Lord is transcendent over all of his creation, and every human being lives under his sovereign rule. The manner in which God creates by his word reminds us as well of the power of God's Word and its importance as the source of life and blessing. The good and powerful God who has created the universe is worthy of our worship and obedience.

Annotated Bibliography

BOOKS

Charles, J. Daryl, ed. *Reading Genesis 1–2: An Evangelical Conversation.* Peabody, MA: Hendrickson, 2013. Overview of major evangelical views on how to interpret Genesis 1–2.

Walton, John H. *The Lost World of Genesis One: Ancient Cosmology and the Origins Debate.* Downers Grove, IL: IVP Academic, 2009. Thoughtful discussion of how reading Genesis 1 in its ancient Near Eastern context impacts contemporary understandings of origins issues.

COMMENTARIES

Hamilton, Victor P. *The Book of Genesis, Chapters 1–17.* New International Commentary on the Old Testament. Grand Rapids: Eerdmans, 2010. Scholarly evangelical commentary with excellent discussion of the interpretive issues surrounding Gen 1:1–3.

ARTICLES

Rooker, Mark. "Genesis 1:1–3: Creation or Re-Creation? Parts 1 and 2." *Bibliotheca Sacra* 149 (1992): 316–23, 411–27. Defends the traditional view of Gen 1:1–3 and argues against the precreation chaos theory.

Waltke, Bruce K. "The Creation Account in Genesis 1:1–3, Parts 2 and 3." *Bibliotheca Sacra* 132 (1975): 25–36. Offers a solid refutation of the gap theory.

WEBSITES

Heiser, Michael S. "Creation, Evolution, Intelligent Design, and the Replicating Universe: What Does the Hebrew Text of Genesis 1 Allow?" accessed November 15, 2017. www.michaelsheiser.com/Genesis%201%20and%20creation.pdf. Helpful discussion of key differences between the major views on Gen 1:1–3.

CHAPTER 2

The Trinity Is Directly Taught in Genesis 1:26

Genesis 1:26

The Legendary Teaching on Genesis 1:26

The use of the plural pronouns *we* and *our* when God expresses his intention to create humanity ("Let us make man in our image") in Gen 1:26 is the Bible's first statement on plurality in the Godhead. The internal dialogue within the Godhead demonstrates specifically a plurality of personhood. This plurality is also supported by the fact that the Hebrew word for *God* (*'elohim*) itself is plural in form. The Trinity is taught in the very first chapter of the Bible.

Countering the Legendary Teaching

The interpretation of Gen 1:26–28 requires both a historical and canonical understanding. In its historical context, Gen 1:26–28 is not teaching the plurality of the Godhead. As Michael Heiser has noted, "The triune godhead idea is never transparently expressed in the Old Testament."[1] The author of Genesis and his Hebrew audience would have more likely understood the "us" and "our" of Gen 1:26 as referring to God's interaction with the members of his heavenly council. Allen Ross explains that the plurals in Gen 1:26 "do not explicitly refer to the triunity of the Godhead but do allow for that doctrine's development throughout the progress of revelation."[2] We see the concept of Trinity from a canonical perspective, but we should avoid using Gen 1:26 itself as a proof text for the Trinity.

---

[1] Michael S. Heiser, *The Unseen Realm: Recovering the Supernatural Worldview of the Bible* (Bellingham, WA: Lexham Press, 2015), 39n1.

[2] Allen P. Ross, *Creation and Blessing: A Guide to the Study and Exposition of the Book of Genesis* (Grand Rapids: Baker, 1988), 112.

Does the Word *'Elohim* Reflect Plurality in the Godhead?

The plural form *'elohim* when used with reference to the singular God of Israel is an example of what is called a plural of majesty or an honorific plural.[3] Rather than indicating plurality of personhood, the plural of majesty for *'elohim* reflects the abstract quality of deity or is a honorific title for Yahweh emphasizing his special status and supreme authority.[4] As Bruce Waltke explains, these kinds of plurals are employed for a singular individual who is "so thoroughly characterized by the qualities of the noun that a plural is used."[5]

The plural *'elohim* is used even for singular foreign gods such as Chemosh (Judg 11:24; 1 Kgs 11:33), Dagon (1 Sam 5:7), or Baal (1 Kgs 18:24) and reflects their status as national deities, not a plurality of personhood.[6] We see a similar use of the plural of majesty when applied to humans. In Judges 19, the plural form of "lord/master" (*'adon*) is used for the Levite to signify his authority over his servant and concubine (vv. 11–12, 26–27). David refers to Saul as "your lord" (plural of *'adon*) to convey Saul's authority over Israel's armies (1 Sam 26:15–16).[7] In light of this evidence, we can conclude that the plural ending for *'elohim* in Gen 1:26–28 does not reflect plurality in the Godhead. This plural of majesty is attested elsewhere in the Hebrew Bible only with reference to nouns and not with pronouns such as the "us" and "our" found in Gen 1:26, so we will address the reasons for these plural pronouns below.

Lack of Clear Old Testament Evidence for the Trinity

Two aspects central to the trinitarian theology of the New Testament are not as clearly developed or revealed in the Old Testament: the deity of the promised Messiah as the Son of God and the distinct personhood of the Spirit of God. The promised Messiah is primarily depicted in the Old Testament as a

---

[3]   See Bruce K. Waltke and M. O'Connor, *An Introduction to Biblical Hebrew Syntax* (Winona Lake, IN: Eisenbrauns, 1990), 122 (par. 7.4.3b); and H. F. W. Gesenius, *Gesenius' Hebrew Grammar*, 2nd English ed., ed. E. Kautzsch and A. E. Cowley (New York: Oxford, 1910), 396–98 (par. 124). An example would be the use of the plural Behemoth used for the creature portrayed in Job 40:15–16, 19, because it represents the greatest of its species.

[4]   W. Randall Garr, *In His Own Image and Likeness: Humanity, Divinity, and Monotheism*, Culture and History of the Ancient Near East (New York: Brill, 2001), 2.

[5]   Waltke and O'Connor, *Introduction to Biblical Hebrew Syntax*, 122 (par. 7.4.3a).

[6]   Robert B. Chisholm Jr., "Some Dead End Streets: Misusing the Old Testament to Deny or Support the Concept of the Trinity" (Unpublished paper presented at the Evangelical Theological Society National Meeting, San Antonio, TX, November 15, 2016), 1.

[7]   Chisholm, "Some Dead End Streets," 2.

human descendant of David. The passages that speak of any Davidic king as the "son" of God (see 2 Sam 7:13–14; Ps 2:7) refer to the king's adoption as God's vice-regent rather than to his divine nature. Some key passages in the Old Testament indicate that the Messiah would be more than human (see Ps 110:1; Isa 9:6; Dan 7:13–27), but it is only in the New Testament that we clearly see Messiah as both man and God.

The Holy Spirit as a distinct person within the Godhead is also not as clearly revealed in the Old Testament as in the New. The Spirit of God is more an aspect of God's own person than a separate person. The Lord's presence among his people (Exod 33:14) is equivalent to God placing his Spirit among them (Isa 63:7–14), meaning essentially that the Spirit is the Lord's "alter ego" (see Hag 2:5).[8] Like the Greek word for "spirit" (*pneuma*) in the New Testament, the Hebrew word for "spirit" (*ruah*) refers to "wind" or "breath." The Spirit is the agent of God's dynamic activity and power at creation (Gen 1:2). The Spirit is also the means by which God empowers individuals to do his will (see Exod 31:3–4; Judg 3:10; 6:34; 14:6; 1 Sam 16:13; 2 Sam 23:2; Isa 61:1). The statement in Isa 63:10 that the wilderness generation "grieved" the Spirit with their rebellion is moving toward the more personal view of the Spirit found in the New Testament (see Eph 4:30). Ultimately the Old Testament revelation concerning the Holy Spirit does not contradict the New Testament but also is not as fully developed.

Genesis 1:26–28 and the Divine Council

When arguing for divine plurality in Gen 1:26, some interpreters have read the "let us" language as "self-deliberation" or "self-exhortation" reflecting internal dialogue within the Godhead. W. Randall Garr has noted, however, that other examples of such language are not attested elsewhere in the Hebrew Bible.[9] The explanation of "us" and "our" in Gen 1:26 that best fits with the explicit teaching of the Old Testament and the culture of the ancient Near East is that God announces his intention to create humanity to the members of the divine council, the powerful heavenly beings who administer the creation under his authority.[10] This view does not require one to understand that humans are created in

---

[8]   M. V. Pelt et al., "חוּר" in *New International Dictionary of Old Testament Theology and Exegesis*, ed. W. A. VanGemeren (Grand Rapids: Zondervan, 1997): 4:1075.

[9]   Garr, *In His Own Image and Likeness*, 18–19.

[10]   For discussion of this council, see Heiser, *Unseen Realm*, 23–28; "Divine Council," *Lexham Bible Dictionary*, ed. J. D. Barry et al., (Bellingham, WA: Lexham Press, 2016); E. Theodore Mullen Jr., "Divine Assembly," *Anchor Bible Dictionary*, ed. David Noel Freedman (New York: Doubleday, 1992): 2:214–17.

the "image of angels" or anything less than the "image of God." Genesis 1:27 clearly indicates that God alone does the work of creation and that the heavenly beings with God are only spectators at the creation of humanity, just as they were when God first created the earth (see Job 38:7).[11] The verb *to create* (*bara*) appears three times in verse 27 in the third person singular, and the verse also explicitly states that humans were created "in his [God's] own image."[12]

Support for the view that the first person plurals in Gen 1:26 refer to members of the divine council is found in Gen 3:5 and 22. In tempting Eve to eat from the forbidden tree, the serpent tells her, "You will be like *'elohim*, knowing [plural] good and evil." If *'elohim* here referred to the one true God, we would expect the participle *knowing* to be singular. The use of the plural for "knowing," however, suggests that *'elohim* refers to the members of the divine assembly. God appears to be further addressing this divine council in verse 22 when he states, "The man has become like one of us." Another reference to the divine council likely appears in the story of the Tower of Babel in Gen 11:7 when God states, "Let's go down there and confuse their languages so that they will not understand one another's speech."

The divine council in ancient Near Eastern religions outside of Israel consisted of a pantheon of gods presided over by the chief god. In Canaanite mythology, the high god El presided over the assembly. The members of this heavenly assembly are referred to in the Old Testament as "the sons of God" (*bene 'elohim* in Gen 6:2; Job 1:6; 2:1; 38:7; *bene 'elim* in Pss 29:1; 89:6) and "the council/assembly of the holy ones" (Ps 89:5, 7). We see one of the clearest references to the heavenly assembly in Ps 82:1, which states that God (*'elohim*) takes his stand "in the divine assembly" (*'adat-'el*) and pronounces judgment "among the *'elohim*." The plurality of *'elohim* here clearly has nothing to do with the Trinity.

Because of its monotheistic perspective, Israelite theology conceived of the divine assembly in distinctive ways from the polytheistic cultures around them. The Lord's authority over this council is absolute (see Ps 89:7; Dan 7:10). On the basis of the preferred reading of Deut 32:8 in the Greek Septuagint (and the Dead Sea Scrolls—4QDeut), which states that God "divided mankind . . . according to the number of the sons of God" (ESV), it appears that the members of the heavenly council were delegated authority and guardian-

---

[11]   Heiser, *Unseen Realm*, 40.
[12]   Heiser, *Unseen Realm*, 40.

ship over the nations (compare Dan 10:13, 21).[13] We also know from Gen 6:1–4 that there was a rebellion among the "sons of God" that likely took place in connection with the fall of the figure known from later revelation as Satan. Psalm 82 pronounces judgment on these rebellious "sons of God" for how they have abused their authority and promoted injustice among the nations.

There are additionally at least three passages in the Old Testament that associate the heavenly assembly with the prophets and prophetic activity. In Jer 23:18–23, Jeremiah claims that his prophetic opponents offer false assurances of security to the people of Judah because the Lord has not "sent" them and they have not stood in the Lord's "council" to receive their messages. A true prophet had access to the deliberations of the heavenly assembly and then was called to proclaim God's words and plans to the people. We see the message of a prophet who has stood in the Lord's council in 1 Kgs 22:19–22. The prophet Micaiah reports that the Lord has determined to punish Ahab by having him die in battle and that one of the members of the heavenly assembly has offered put a lying spirit within the prophets who encourage Ahab to fight. The prophet Isaiah also interacts with the heavenly council at his commissioning in Isaiah 6. The Lord asks on behalf of the council, "Who should I send? Who will go for us?" (v. 8). Isaiah responds, "Here I am. Send me." The Lord then commissions Isaiah to the difficult task of proclaiming judgment to an obstinate nation (vv. 9–12).

In conclusion, reference to the divine council provides the best explanation of the plural "us" and "our" in Gen 1:26 when we consider this passage in its historical context. This concept is attested in the Old Testament in ways that the Trinity is not. From a larger canonical perspective, we can see an anticipation of the later biblical doctrine of the Trinity in Gen 1:26 in the plural language but not a clear and explicit revelation of the Trinity.

Application

Genesis 1:26–28 reflects the exalted role of humanity in God's creation. God announces that humans would serve as his images by exercising dominion over

---

[13]   The Hebrew Masoretic Text (MT) of Deut 32:8 reads that God divided humankind into nations "according to the number of the sons of Israel." The reading "sons of Israel" was likely a secondary theological interpretation of the original "sons of God." Verse 9 also clarifies that Israel was distinct from the other nations in that it was the Lord's own inheritance. The logic of why the number of nations would correspond to the number of Jacob's sons is not clear. For a more detailed discussion of this textual issue, see Michael S. Heiser, "Deuteronomy 32:8 and the Sons of God," *Bibliotheca Sacra* 158 (2001): 52–74.

the creation. This exalted status is a reminder of our own worth to God, and a starting point for Christian ethics is the belief that all humans have infinite value in the eyes of God. The way in which Yahweh relates to his divine council in the Old Testament also reflects his uniqueness as the only eternal Creator God. The Lord's rule over creation extends even over the powerful heavenly beings who help to administer his kingdom rule. Rather than compromising monotheistic faith, a proper understanding of the Old Testament teaching on the divine council provides further confirmation of the Lord's absolute sovereignty as "King of kings and Lord of lords."

Annotated Bibliography

BOOKS
Heiser, Michael S. *The Unseen Realm: Recovering the Supernatural Worldview of the Bible.*
    Bellingham, WA: Lexham Press, 2015. Accessible study of the divine council and the key
    passages relevant to this discussion.

COMMENTARIES
Walton, John H. *Genesis*. New International Version Application Commentary. Grand Rapids:
    Zondervan, 2001. Comments on Gen 1:26 argue against reading this passage as referring
    to plurality in the Godhead.

WEBSITES
Taylor, Justin. "Is 'Let Us' in Genesis 1:26 a Reference to the Trinity? Tom Schreiner on
    Authorial Intent and Canonical Reading." The Gospel Coalition (blog). January 27, 2015.
    https://www.thegospelcoalition.org/blogs/justin-taylor/is-let-us-in-genesis-126-a-reference-
    to-the-trinity-tom-schreiners-on-authorial-intent-and-canonical-reading/. Argues for a
    canonical reading that sees a reference to the Trinity in Gen 1:26.

CHAPTER 3

———

Women Were Created Inferior to Men
Genesis 2:18–20

The Legendary Teaching on Genesis 2:18–20

After God created Adam, he demonstrated his dominion over the animals by naming them. But there was no suitable companion for Adam among the animals. Then God created a helper out of Adam's side. We know that this woman was inferior to Adam, because she is referred to as a "helper" (Gen 2:18). A helper is someone who comes under a superior to assist the superior in a job or duty. Merriam-Webster's dictionary says a helper refers especially to "a relatively unskilled worker who assists a skilled worker."[1]

Countering the Legendary Teaching

In Gen 2:18, God declared that it was not good for Adam to be alone, so he decided to "make a helper corresponding to him." The English word *helper* can have different connotations. But the definition of the English word, particularly the connotation it can have in certain contexts, is fairly irrelevant for understanding the original text. Therefore, we will study the Hebrew word translated as "helper" (*'ezer*) in several contexts to discover if it conveys a negative or inferior nuance.

---

[1]   *Merriam-Webster's 11th Collegiate Dictionary*, s.v. "helper."

13

When God Is the "Helper"

Although the Hebrew word *'ezer* ("helper") occurs too many times in the Old Testament to study each use, five uses will be examined to get a sense of the use of this word in reference to God as a helper. Outside of Gen 2:18 and 20, the next use occurs when Jacob is blessing Joseph in Gen 49:25a: "by the God of your father who helps you, and by the Almighty who blesses you with blessings of the heavens above." In this passage, God is referred to as the one who helps Joseph. The text is not attempting to communicate that Joseph is superior to God in any way.

In Exod 18:4, Moses named his son Eliezer because the God of his father was his helper. Again, Moses is not placing himself in a superior position to God. In speaking about the tribe of Judah, Moses asks God to "be a help" against Judah's foes (Deut 33:7). But Moses is not placing God in an inferior to position to Israel. The use in Deut 33:26 might need a little extra explanation: "There is none like the God of Jeshurun, who rides the heavens to your aid, the clouds in his majesty." The God of Jeshurun refers to the God of the upright, a loving way of referring to Israel. Moses refers to God riding upon the heavens, which was a way of describing God as superior to all other gods, as "unique and solitary."[2] This is a powerful way to refer to God and is especially helpful for our study since God is referred to as aiding (*'ezer*) them. Finally, in Deut 33:29, God is the shield of Israel's help, again referring to God as a helper with connotations of power: "Happy are you, O Israel! Who is like you, a people saved by the Lord, the shield of your help, and the sword of your triumph! Your enemies shall come fawning to you, and you shall tread upon their backs" (ESV).[3] All of these five uses are evidence that the word for "helper" in the Hebrew did not inherently contain a reference to inferiority.[4]

---

[2] Eugene H. Merrill, *Deuteronomy*, New American Commentary (Nashville: Broadman & Holman, 1994), 447.

[3] Other references to God as "helper" include 1 Sam 7:12; Pss 33:20; 115:9–11; 121:2; 124:8; 146:5–6.

[4] It is interesting to note that the Septuagint (LXX, the translation of the Hebrew Old Testament into Greek) uses the word βοηθός ("helpful, helper") to translate *'ezer* in Gen 2:18, 20 and many times about God in the Septuagint. The translators could have used words such as δοῦλος (typically translated as "slave" or "servant," many times with negative connotations), διάκονος ("servant"), or ὑπηρέτης ("helper, assistant," which frequently refers to helping in a subordinate way). The word used, βοηθός, does not contain a hint of the connotation of inferiority. For more information on this word in the LXX and the Greek New Testament, see Moisés Silva, ed., "βοηθέω," in *New International Dictionary of New Testament Theology and Exegesis* (Grand Rapids: Zondervan, 2014), 524–25.

Other References to "Helper"

There are many other references to "helpers" in the Old Testament. Joshua 1:14 says that the Israelite warriors (specifically referring to men only) must help other Israelites in conquering the land. In Josh 10:3, the king of Jerusalem sent a message to the kings of Hebron, Jarmuth, Lachish, and Eglon and asked for their help in attacking Gibeon since they were at peace with the Israelites. When the Gibeonites were being attacked, they asked Joshua to help them and save them from the Amorite kings (Josh 10:6).[5] There are many references throughout the Old Testament to "help" in warfare, both from those who were victorious and those who were defeated.[6]

Interpreting Genesis 2:18 and 20

What does it mean that woman was a "helper" and "complement" to man? The word translated "corresponding to" (CSB) or "suitable" (NIV) refers to being "in front of." Figuring out what it means in Genesis 2 has been tricky. Famed Old Testament scholar Driver said it means "corresponding to him, [that is] adequate to him . . . capable of satisfying his needs and instincts."[7] Michael Rosenzweig referred to the last part of that definition as "Driver's drivel."[8] The Hebrew word (*kenegdo*) does not indicate that women were created to satisfy the needs of man. Instead, it refers to "a correspondence between the man and the woman."[9] The equality found between man and woman was not found with the beasts. As man named the animals, he is portrayed as a social being, created for relationship.[10] And no relationship with any of the animals was sufficient. Therefore, God made woman. The reference to the woman being a complement means that man and woman are equal in dignity and worth,[11] that she was created as a suitable partner to be in relationship with man. Unlike the animals, and like the man, she was created in the image of God, sharing with the man in the work of dominion (Gen 1:26–28).

---

[5]   In this reference, if anything, the one needing help is implying inferiority. Though this should not be taken too far.

[6]   Two other examples are 2 Sam 8:5 and 18:3.

[7]   Cited in Michael L. Rosenzweig, "A Helper Equal to Him," *Judaism* 35, no. 3 (1986): 277.

[8]   Rosenzweig, "Helper," 278.

[9]   Kenneth A. Mathews, *Genesis 1–11:26*, New American Commentary (Nashville: Broadman & Holman, 1996), 213.

[10]   Derek Kidner, *Genesis: An Introduction and Commentary*, Tyndale Old Testament Commentaries (Downers Grove, IL: InterVarsity Press, 1967), 70.

[11]   Rosenzweig, "Helper," 280.

The reference to woman as man's helper does not lessen this equality. As God was a helper to Israel, so woman was to help man. As Kenneth Mathews writes, she "will play an integral part, in this case, in human survival and success. What the man lacks, the woman accomplishes."[12] The uses of "helper" described above place a special dignity on the role, rather than any connotation of inferiority. When the word is used, there is typically an element of cooperation between the helper and the one being helped, especially when the strength of the one being helped is insufficient.[13]

Some interpreters, like Augustine, have proposed that woman is a helper in the sense of "begetting of descendants."[14] Although the context of Gen 1:28 may refer to procreation, no explicit reference to her as a childbearer is stated in Genesis 2. She is not valued for what she can give Adam, but "for herself alone."[15]

Application

Recently I (Dave) received a phone call from a woman who found my name online. She contacted me because she had come to some "radical conclusions," and she wanted to ask someone who knew the Bible what they thought. Her conclusion: women were *not* inferior to men! I asked her where she had heard the concept of women being inferior. She said she had learned it in church, and she referenced Genesis 2. Although I am not sure how she came to the conclusion that this was wrong, she said she was scared to say anything because she thought she might be alone in her thinking. Wrong teaching on this verse has been very detrimental to women, impacting the way they view themselves and how many men view them.

Woman was made as a suitable helper for man. Genesis 2 does not contain a reference to woman as inferior. Instead, she is portrayed as the appropriate complement to support man. There is no excuse for using this verse to denigrate women. Instead, women should be treated with dignity and respect. Men should treat them honorably. If a man is married, he should not take his role as head of the household (see Eph 5:22–23) as an excuse to display his power, but as an opportunity to love and serve her. Women were created in the image

---

[12]   Mathews, *Genesis 1–11:26*, 214.
[13]   Ernst Jenni and Claus Westermann, "עזר," in *Theological Lexicon of the Old Testament* (Peabody: Hendrickson, 1997), 872.
[14]   Claus Westermann, *Genesis 1–11*, A Continental Commentary (Minneapolis: Fortress, 1994), 227.
[15]   Kidner, *Genesis*, 70.

of God and were put on this earth to help man. One scholar says that being an *'ezer* ("helper") means to have a godlike quality.[16] This is true if one understands this concept the way Jesus did: "For even the Son of Man did not come to be served, but to serve, and to give his life as a ransom for many" (Mark 10:45). We should all seek opportunities to help and serve each other. Supporting one another is truly a "godlike quality." Viewing women as inferior to men is antithetical to Scripture. We have all been created in the image of God.

Annotated Bibliography

COMMENTARIES
Mathews, Kenneth A. *Genesis 1–11:26*. New American Commentary. Nashville: Broadman & Holman, 1996, esp. 213–16. Mathews provides some helpful comments to navigate through these verses.

ARTICLES
Rosenzweig, Michael L. "A Helper Equal to Him." *Judaism* 35, no. 3 (1986): 277. Rosenzweig comes from a nonevangelical perspective but has some insight on the meaning of "helper" and "suitable" that aid in interpreting the passage accurately.

WEBSITES
Mowczko, Marg. "Three Scholars with Two Views on Eve's Role as Helper." *Marg Mowczko* (blog). October 26, 2017. https://margmowczko.com/eve-as-helper-genesis-2/. Coming from an egalitarian perspective, this blog post summarizes three perspectives on woman as helper and provides a balanced conclusion.

---

[16] Rosenzweig, "Helper," 280. He does point out that men have the same trait.

CHAPTER 4

———

The Virgin Birth Was Prophesied in Genesis
Genesis 3:15

The Legendary Teaching on Genesis 3:15 and the "Seed of the Woman"

Genesis 3:15 is known as the *Protoevangelium* ("the first preaching of the gospel"); more than that, Gen 3:15 is an explicit prophecy concerning Jesus Christ as "the seed of the woman." This reference to the "seed" (KJV) of the woman further reflects that the future savior would be born of a virgin.[1] Genesis 3:15 is the first of more than 300 explicit Old Testament prophecies fulfilled by Jesus as Messiah and Savior.

Countering the Legendary Teaching

The virgin birth of Jesus (Matt 1:18–25; Luke 1:27–34) is a central tenet for the Christian faith, but the virgin birth of Jesus is not explicitly prophesied in Gen 3:15. Genesis 3:15 points more indirectly to a future savior, and we ultimately need the full biblical canon to understand how Jesus Christ would bring about the ultimate defeat of sin, death, and Satan.

"Seed" of the Woman: Indication of a Virgin Birth?

References to the "seed" of a woman elsewhere in the Old Testament argue against reading Gen 3:15 as a prophecy of a virginal conception. The phrase

---

[1]   The note on Gen 3:15 in one study Bible reads: "The 'seed of the woman' can only be an allusion to a future descendant of Eve who would have no human father. Biologically, a woman produces no seed, and except in this case Biblical usage always speaks only of the seed of men. This promised Seed would, therefore, have to be miraculously implanted in the womb." Henry M. Morris, *The Defender's Study Bible* (Grand Rapids: World Publishing, 1995), 13.

"seed of the woman" (KJV) is merely identifying Eve as the mother of all living and the progenitor of the human race. Eve herself reflects this understanding when she announces in Gen 4:25 that the Lord has "given me another offspring/child/seed (*zera'*)" when Seth is born. Seth is Eve's "seed/offspring" even though he was born in a natural way. When Abram sends Hagar away with her son Ishmael, the Lord appears to Hagar and promises her, "I will greatly multiply your offspring (*zera'*)" (Gen 16:10).[2] These texts are the same as someone having a conversation with my wife and referring to our children as "her" children or offspring. In Gen 24:60, Rebekah's sisters pronounce a blessing upon her as she leaves home to marry Isaac, expressing the desire that her "offspring" (*zera'*) will possess the gates of their enemies.[3]

We see references to the woman's seed as a natural way of referring to a mother and her children outside the book of Genesis as well. Leviticus 22:13 makes provisions for a priest's daughter who is a widow and has no "children/offspring" (*zera'*), allowing her to return to her father's house. In the story of Samuel's birth, his mother Hannah vows that if the Lord will give to her *zera'*, then she will devote the child to the Lord (1 Sam 1:11). Eli the priest would later pray that the Lord would give to Elkanah, Samuel's father, *zera'* by Hannah to replace the child she had given to the Lord (1 Sam 2:20–21).

In Isaiah 54, Zion is portrayed as a barren woman who was forsaken by the Lord her husband when he sent her away into exile. Nevertheless, the Lord would take his wife back, and this once-barren woman would have more children than she could imagine when the people of Israel returned to the land. Isaiah 54:3 refers to these children as the "seed" (*zera'*) of the woman. Finally, in Isa 57:3, the prophet refers to the people of Israel as "offspring [*zera'*] of an adulterer and a prostitute" because of their pagan worship practices.

The term *zera'* appears more than 250 times in the Old Testament; when referring to children or offspring, it more commonly refers to the "offspring" of the father, but there are enough references to the "offspring" coming from the woman to demonstrate that this also is a normal way of referring to children. The expression "seed of the woman" in Gen 3:15 (KJV) offers no evidence for seeing a reference to the virgin birth of a promised child, even if it might be suggestive of later canonical developments.

---

[2]   Jack P. Lewis, "The Woman's Seed (Gen 3:15)," *Journal of the Evangelical Theological Society* 34 (1991): 299–300.
[3]   Lewis, "The Woman's Seed (Gen 3:15)," 300.

The Collective Nature of the "Seed" in Genesis 3:15

Reading Gen 3:15 as a prophecy of the virgin birth is further unlikely in that the expression "seed of the woman" refers to multiple descendants and not to Jesus alone. John Calvin explains that a personal Savior is not directly promised in Gen 3:15 but that it is ultimately in Christ that this prophecy has "attained its completion."[4] The Hebrew word for *seed* (*zera'*) is a collective noun that appears in the singular when referring to either a single descendant or multiple offspring.[5] Eve employs the term in the individual sense at the birth of Seth in Gen 4:25 when she states, "God has given me another child (*zera'*) in place of Abel." The term *zera'* refers to an individual son and immediate descendant elsewhere in Genesis as well (see 15:3; 17:7; 21:2, 13).[6] More often, however, *zera'* refers to multiple descendants, as when God makes a covenant with Noah and all of his descendants (Gen 9:9) or when God promises to multiply Abraham's "offspring" like the stars in the sky or the sand on the seashore (Gen 13:16; 15:5; 16:10; 22:17; 26:4; 28:14; 32:12).[7] In some passages, there are not clear indicators in the context whether "seed" refers to a single child or multiple descendants (e.g., Gen 12:7; 13:15; 15:18; 22:18; 24:7), and the same ambiguity is present in the reference to the woman's "seed" in Gen 3:15. The following singular pronoun *he* and the singular verb *will strike* that refer to the woman's "seed" do not resolve the issue, because singular pronouns and verbs are also used elsewhere when multiple descendants are in view (Gen 16:10; 22:17; 24:60).[8] Bruce Waltke offers the likely solution that Gen 3:15 merges the concepts of immediate, distant, and multiple descendants for the woman.[9]

In light of how the curse passage in 3:14–16 describes conditions that would exist from that point forward, the enmity between the serpent's offspring and the woman's offspring refers to a conflict that has existed from the time that Adam and Eve sinned in the garden. The "seed/offspring of the woman" then refers to Eve's offspring in general and not exclusively to Christ.

---

[4]   John Calvin, *Commentary on the Pentateuch*, trans. Henry Downing (Edinburgh: T&T Clark, 1860), 43.
[5]   Herbert W. Bateman IV, Darrell L. Bock, and Gordon H. Johnston, *Jesus the Messiah: Tracing the Promises, Expectation and Coming of Israel's King* (Grand Rapids: Kregel Academic, 2012), 39.
[6]   Bateman, Bock, and Johnston, *Jesus the Messiah*, 39–40.
[7]   Bateman, Bock, and Johnston, *Jesus the Messiah*, 39.
[8]   See Walton, *Genesis*, 225n3 (see chap. 1, n. 4). For the opposing view that an individual "seed" is in view in Gen 3:15, see Jack Collins, "A Syntactical Note (Genesis 3:15): Is the Woman's Seed Singular or Plural?" *Tyndale Bulletin* 48 (1997): 139–48.
[9]   Bruce K. Waltke, with Cathi J. Fredericks, *Genesis: A Commentary* (Grand Rapids: Zondervan, 2001), 93.

Genesis 3:15 and the Messianic Hope

Although Gen 3:15 provides the initial anticipation of a future salvation for fallen humanity, the text is ambiguous regarding the ultimate triumph of the seed of the woman over the serpent-seed. Many English versions reflect this idea of triumph with the translation that the seed of the woman would "crush" the head of the serpent-seed, while the serpent-seed would "bruise" the heel of the seed of the woman.[10] The same verb (*sup*), however, is used to describe the attack of both seeds against each other. There is not a distinction between "crushing" and "bruising," because both seeds are portrayed as "striking at" each other, and the imperfect (iterative) verb forms suggest a continual and ongoing struggle.[11] Humans striking the heads of serpents and serpents striking at the heels of humans are both potentially lethal blows, but humans appear to have the advantage.[12] It is difficult to see how the order of human striking the serpent and then serpent striking the human reflects the ultimate defeat of the serpent-seed, but perhaps this order reflects the primacy of the lethal strike administered to the serpent.[13] The fact that Gen 3:15 appears in a curse on the serpent also suggests that the text anticipates more than the two sides fighting to a draw.[14]

There is hope for Adam and Eve in the context of sin and cursing in Genesis 3. The serpent is cursed, and the first couple would not die. Adam and Eve would also have offspring that would cause the human race to continue. The Lord's provision of clothing to cover their nakedness was an act of grace in response to their disobedience (Gen 3:20–21). We need the fuller revelation of the Bible, however, to see how Jesus would ultimately bring about the complete triumph over death and Satan. In Genesis, we begin to see the emergence of a godly seed through Seth and then through Noah, who would "bring us

---

[10]   Some interpreters have seen the reference to enmity in 3:15 as nothing more than the perpetual hostility and conflict between humans and snakes. This element is certainly present in the text, but a talking snake who lures the first couple into disobeying the word of God seems to also represent some type of evil spiritual being—one that is later identified with Satan in the progress of revelation. Serpents represent malevolent spiritual beings throughout the ancient Near East. For supportive evidence, see Gordon J. Wenham, *Genesis 1–15*, Word Biblical Commentary (Waco, TX: Word, 1987), 72–73. Identifying the serpent-seed from this text is problematic, but the larger canon of Scripture would clarify that this seed includes the spiritual powers of evil, as well as sinful humanity that rejects the Lord and opposes his rule (see John 8:44; Rom 16:20; 2 Cor 11:3; Rev 12:9; 20:2).

[11]   Wenham, *Genesis 1–15*, 79.

[12]   Wenham, *Genesis 1–15*, 80.

[13]   John D. Currid, "Genesis," in *A Biblical-Theological Introduction to the Old Testament: The Gospel Promised*, ed. M. V. VanPelt (Wheaton, IL: Crossway, 2016), 34.

[14]   Wenham, *Genesis 1–15*, 80.

relief from the agonizing labor of our hands, caused by the ground the LORD has cursed" (Gen 5:29). Then through Noah's son Shem would come Terah, Abraham, Isaac, and ultimately Jesus.

Christian interpreters have often assumed a detailed understanding of the future Messiah in the early chapters of Genesis that simply is not present. Some have read Gen 4:1 to say that Eve believes she has just given birth to the promised Messiah or even that her child is the Lord himself. Rather than Eve simply saying, "I have gotten a man *with the [help of] the LORD*," they read the text to say: "I have gotten a man, *the LORD*." Both translations are possible because the Hebrew *'et* that comes after "man" and before "the LORD" could either be the preposition "with" or the Hebrew marker of the accusative, which is not translated in English but is used to indicate the direct object of the verb. Both forms look exactly the same, but there is no indication that Adam or Eve understood that any future "seed" of theirs would be God in the flesh. Eve is simply saying that she has given birth to a child with the Lord's help in fulfillment of his earlier promise of offspring. To suggest that Eve is expressing the hope with the birth of Cain (Gen 4:1), and later Seth (Gen 4:25), that God has provided the single descendant that would crush the head of the serpent is reading more into these passages than is there.

Application

The sin of Adam and Eve did not take God by surprise, and Gen 3:15 begins to reveal God's plan to redeem fallen humanity. The Lord would raise up a godly (and royal) seed through Seth and through Abraham that would ultimately become a source of blessing to all peoples in spite of the reality of sin and death. Through later revelation, we learn that the coming Messiah would decisively defeat Satan through his death on the cross for sinners. Paul, alluding to Gen 3:15, can confidently state that God would "soon crush Satan" under the feet of God's people (Rom 16:20). Believers share in the victory of Jesus over sin, evil, and death.

Annotated Bibliography

BOOKS

Alexander, T. Desmond. "Messianic Ideology in the Book of Genesis." In *The Lord's Anointed: Interpretation of Old Testament Messianic Texts*, edited by P. E. Satterthwaite, R. S. Hess, and Gordon H. Wenham, 19–39. Grand Rapids: Baker, 1995. This chapter develops Gen 3:15 in the context of the larger messianic theology in Genesis.

COMMENTARIES

Walton, John H. *Genesis*. New International Version Application Commentary. Grand Rapids: Zondervan, 2001. Lengthy discussion of Gen 3:15 makes a compelling case for the "seed of the woman" having a collective reference in this text.

Wenham, Gordon J. *Genesis 1–15*. Word Biblical Commentary. Waco, TX: Word, 1987. Scholarly commentary defending a messianic reading of Gen 3:15.

WEBSITES

Keathley, J. Hampton III. "Prophecies of the Birth of Christ." *Bible.org*. May 28, 2004. www.bible.org/article/prophecies–birth–christ. Discusses Gen 3:15 in the context of other Old Testament messianic prophecies.

CHAPTER 5

——

Radical Islam Has Inherited
Ishmael's Violent Spirit
Genesis 16:12

The Legendary Teaching on Ishmael and His Descendants

Abraham's lack of faith and patience that led to the birth of Ishmael through Hagar is the cause of the perpetual conflict between Arabs (the descendants of Ishmael) and Jews (the descendants of Isaac) in the Middle East today. The Bible informs us that the conflict between Ishmael and Isaac would be never-ending. Arabs, as the descendants of Ishmael, have inherited his rebellious ("like a wild donkey") and violent qualities (Gen 16:12), and the existence of radical Islam and violent jihadism is proof that "the spirit of Ishmael" still exists among Arab peoples today.

Countering the Legendary Teaching

The portrayal of Ishmael as a "wild donkey" conveys a positive message that even resembles the portrayal of the twelve tribes of Israel in Genesis 49. The Bible never prophesies a perpetual conflict between the sons of Isaac and Ishmael, and Ishmael's descendants even have a vital role in the working out of salvation history and a share in the covenantal blessings given to Abraham and extended through Isaac.

Birth Announcement and Hope for an Oppressed Woman

The declaration that Ishmael would be "like a wild donkey" in Gen 16:12 appears in the context of a birth announcement designed to offer hope and encouragement to a beleaguered slave. Tony Maalouf explains, "Having been the recipient of a special revelation from the 'God who sees' everything and cares for everyone, it would become much easier for Hagar to accept her circumstances."[1] The angelic announcement concerning Ishmael in Gen 16:10–12 was a positive message concerning the future of Hagar's son.

Readers today understandably read "like a wild donkey" as an insult. Referring to someone in this way in our culture would likely cause an angry reaction. Comparing someone to a donkey might seem to convey the qualities of stupidity, stubbornness, or contentiousness. As part of this comforting announcement to Hagar, however, the image likely is a promise that Ishmael and his descendants would enjoy the freedom and independence of living as roving nomads, in spite of the difficulties that such a lifestyle would also entail.

The term *wild donkey* (*pere*) appears only ten times in the Hebrew Bible. It is not always clear whether the connotations associated with the wild donkey are positive or negative. The prevailing ideas associated with this animal appear to be "freedom, isolation, and wilderness habitat."[2] Gordon Wenham states that the wild donkey is a figure for "an individualistic lifestyle untrammeled by social convention."[3] The wild donkey lives in barren areas (Job 24:5; Isa 32:14; Jer 14:6; Hos 8:9). In Job 39:5–8, the wild donkey lives in the wilderness and laughs at the noise of the city and, unlike his domesticated counterpart, never has to endure the abusive commands of a taskmaster.

The second statement about Ishmael in Gen 16:12 does refer to hostilities that would exist between Ishmael (and his descendants) and surrounding peoples. The Hebrew reads, "hand-to-hand with everyone and everyone hand-to-hand with him" and is somewhat ambiguous in meaning because of the lack of a verb. Nevertheless, in twenty-seven of the thirty-three instances in which the noun *hand* (*yad*) is followed by the preposition *be* ("in, on, upon, against") that has a person, people, or inhabited area for its object, the sense is adversarial and denotes conflict (e.g., Exod 7:4; Josh 2:19; 1 Kgs 11:26–27).[4] The NET Bible even reads, "He will be hostile to everyone, and everyone will be hostile to him." A people at perpetual odds would seem to be disagreeable and violent, but this

---

[1]   Tony Maalouf, *Arabs in the Shadow of Israel: The Unfolding of God's Prophetic Plan for Ishmael's Line* (Grand Rapids: Kregel Academic, 2003), 65.

[2]   R. Christopher Heard, *Dynamics of Dislection: Ambiguities in Genesis 12–36 and Ethnic Boundaries in Post-exilic Judah*, Semeia Studies 39 (Atlanta: Society of Biblical Literature, 2001), 69.

[3]   Gordon J. Wenham, *Genesis 16–50*, Word Biblical Commentary (Grand Rapids: Zondervan, 2015), 11.

[4]   Heard, *Dynamics of Dislection*, 69–70.

statement needs to be read in light of the surrounding context. We have two other important uses of "hand" in this context that inform our understanding here. In Gen 16:6, Abram says to his disgruntled wife Sarai concerning Hagar, "Your slave is in your hands" (*be* + *yad*) and says she could do with Hagar as she wished. Sarai then mistreats Hagar so that she flees from Abram's household. In verse 9, the angel of the Lord instructs Hagar to return to Sarai and to submit "to her authority" (*tahat* + *yad*; lit. "under her hand").

The statement in verse 12 about Ishmael's "hand" being against everyone should then be understood at least in part as a promise of the reversal of Hagar's powerlessness in verse 9. Ishmael would not be subjugated to others in the way that Hagar was to Sarai, and he would have the strength to stand up to others when wronged. Maalouf explains, "Constant roaming of the bedouin tribes in the desert, with no established legal system and clear civil law code, put them in a state of conflict with each other, and set others against them for fear of their raids, since nomads dislike the settled life."[5] The point is that Ishmael would be able to contend for himself in these disagreements and confrontations.

The final statement concerning Ishmael in verse 12 that he would "settle near ('*al pene*) all his relatives" is also open to interpretation. Because '*al pene* does have an adversarial sense in other passages (e.g., Job 1:11; 6:28), some English translations (NIV, NRSV, NLT) view this statement as also referring to perpetual conflict between Ishmael and his neighbors. The NIV reads that Ishmael "will live in hostility toward all his brothers." The preposition '*al pene* more often has a spatial nuance and likely refers in Genesis 16 to how Ishmael would live away from other peoples because of his Bedouin lifestyle. The fact that '*al pene* has this spatial meaning in Gen 25:18 with reference to Ishmael's descendants suggests the same meaning is intended here.[6] This last description of Ishmael says nothing about violence or hostility.

The announcement that Ishmael would be like a wild donkey parallels the depiction of a number of the tribes of Israel in Jacob's blessing of his sons in Genesis 49. Judah is like "a young lion" (v. 9), Issachar "a strong donkey" (v. 14), Dan "a viper" (v. 17), Naphtali "a doe set free" (v. 21), and Benjamin "a wolf" (v. 27). The portrayals of Judah and Benjamin as a lion and wolf are violent in nature and would seem to depict these tribes as violent—predators tearing apart their prey (vv. 9, 27). Judah would subjugate his enemies so that the nations would give obedience to him (vv. 8, 10), and this prom-

---

[5]   Maalouf, *Arabs in the Shadow of Israel*, 72.
[6]   Heard, *Dynamics of Dislection*, 72.

ise ultimately points to the dominion of the house of David and the future Messiah. Under attack from archers, Joseph's bow would be strong and agile (v. 23).[7] Military strength would be essential for Israel's survival and security as a nation in the violent world of the ancient Near East. These portrayals, however, do not infer that Israel was a vicious, warmongering people, and we should avoid drawing similar conclusions about Ishmael and his descendants on the basis of Gen 16:12. We would not suggest from Genesis 49 that the "spirit of Judah" or "spirit of Benjamin" is responsible for the present-day conflicts in the Middle East.

Isaac and Ishmael in Perpetual Conflict?

Christopher Heard notes that, contrary to popular opinion, the Old Testament never prophesies perpetual animosity between the descendants of Ishmael and Isaac.[8] The two brothers are never in conflict as adults and join to bury their father in Gen 25:9. Isaac subsequently lives near Ishmael, suggesting cordial relations between the two. Joseph's brothers sell Joseph into slavery to a caravan of Ishmaelite traders who take him to Egypt (Gen 37:25–29), but Joseph's own brothers are the ones who act in hatred. Only two passages in the Old Testament refer to Ishmaelites committing acts of violence against Israel. Ishmaelites carry out raids against Israel during the time of Gideon (Judg 8:24), and Ishmaelites and Hagrites are mentioned as enemies that conspire against Israel in Ps 83:6. Heard writes, "Although Christians commonly claim that Isaac's and Ishmael's descendants have fought constantly since Isaac's birth, it is hard to sustain that claim with biblical evidence."[9]

God's Blessing of Ishmael and His Descendants

Ishmael is not the promised child through whom God's covenant promises to Abraham would be fulfilled, but this fact does not minimize God's blessing of Ishmael or negate his redemptive concern for Ishmael's descendants. The

---

[7]   A strong case can be made for an alternate reading of Gen 49:22 that translates the verse as depicting Joseph as the "son of a donkey" (*ben porat*) in a manner that recalls the depiction of Ishmael "like a wild donkey" (*pere' 'adam*) (rather than "a fruitful vine"). The noun *son* (*ben*) is never used with a plant elsewhere in the Hebrew Bible but does appear with animals (Gen 18:7; Ps 29:6). See S. Gevirts, "Of Patriarchs and Puns: Joseph at the Fountain, Jacob at the Ford," *Hebrew Union College Annual* 46 (1975): 35–49.

[8]   Christopher Heard, "On the Road to Paran: Toward a Christian Perspective on Hagar and Ishmael," *Interpretation* 68 (2014): 276–77.

[9]   Heard, "On the Road to Paran," 279.

circumcision of Ishmael in Gen 17:23 demonstrates that he was included in the blessings of the Abrahamic covenant. The name Ishmael ("God hears") is testimony to how God had been attentive to the cries of Hagar when she was alone in the wilderness after Sarai sent her away when Hagar was with child (Gen 16:11). The promise that Ishmael would have many descendants (Gen 16:10) parallels the promises to Abraham that he would have numerous offspring (Gen 15:5; 17:20; 22:17).

The blessing of Ishmael would in fact help to bring fulfillment of specific covenant promises to Abraham—that he would be the father of many nations (Gen 17:4–5) and that all nations would be blessed through Abraham (Gen 12:3; 18:18; 22:18). Isaiah 60:6–8 specifically mentions the inclusion and participation of Ishmael's descendants (Midian, Kedar, Nebaioth; compare Gen 25:13; 28:9; 37:28) in the future kingdom when the nations stream to Zion to worship the Lord. Ishmael's descendants will bring their wealth as tribute to the Lord and their flocks and herds for sacrifices to the Lord.

Other literary features in Genesis point to favorable and sympathetic readings of the characters Hagar and Ishmael. The birth announcement from the angel concerning Ishmael is the first of such annunciations in Scripture, and similar annunciations in the Old Testament anticipate the birth of a special or promised child (including Isaac, Samson, and Samuel). Hagar's experience when God intervenes to deliver Ishmael from death in Genesis 21 parallels Abraham's as he prepares to offer Isaac in Genesis 22.[10] Both Hagar and Abraham take a journey to a desolate place, and both hear an angel from heaven announcing God's intervention on behalf of their sons (Gen 21:17; 22:11–12).

The depiction of Ishmael in Genesis also invites comparison with Joseph in that both are expelled from their home because of their master's wife.[11] Sarah expels Ishmael because she observes him "laughing" (mocking?) (*tsahaq*) at the feast for Isaac's weaning (Gen 21:8–10), and Potiphar's wife falsely accuses Joseph of attempting to rape her and thus "mocking" (*tsahaq*) his master's house (Gen 39:14–17). In spite of their unfair treatment, both young men prosper because God is "with" them (Gen 21:20; 39:2, 21). These favorable comparisons with other individuals who are part of the covenant people of God suggest that we should also view Hagar and Ishmael as positive characters, not as the ancestors of Israel's perpetual enemies.

---

[10]   For fuller development of the Hagar-Abraham parallels, see S. Nikaido, "Hagar and Ishmael as Literary Figures: An Intertextual Study," *Vetus Testamentum* 51 (2001): 221–29.

[11]   Nikaido, "Hagar and Ishmael," 232–41.

Application

Christians have often used wrong interpretations or simplistic readings of Scripture to justify prejudice or hatred toward specific groups of people. Identifying the mark of Cain in Gen 4:15 or the curse of Ham in Gen 9:25 as the curse of black skin or equating Native Americans with the Canaanites to justify their extermination are prominent examples of such readings. Attributing the conflict in the Middle East to "the spirit of Ishmael" or the lack of evangelical compassion toward Arab refugees in our current environment reflects a similar misreading of the Bible. The genealogical relationship between Ishmael and present-day Arabs is complex to begin with, and the statement that Ishmael would be "like a wild donkey" in Gen 16:12 does not characterize Arab peoples as violent. Ishmael plays a strategic role in the working out of God's plan to bless all nations through Abraham (Gen 12:3), and the descendants of Ishmael will be among the people of God "from every tribe and language and people and nation" (Rev 5:9). Loving the descendants of Ishmael is a reflection of the heart and character of God himself.

Annotated Bibliography

BOOKS
Maalouf, Tony. *Arabs in the Shadow of Israel: The Unfolding of God's Prophetic Plan for Ishmael's Line*. Grand Rapids: Kregel Academic, 2003. Helpful treatment from an Arab Christian of the role of Ishmael and Arab peoples in the working out of God's kingdom purposes.

COMMENTARIES
Wenham, Gordon J. *Genesis 1–15 and 16–50*. Word Biblical Commentary (Grand Rapids: Zondervan, 2017). Scholarly evangelical commentary with two volumes on Genesis, here presented as one volume.

ARTICLES
Heard, Christopher. "On the Road to Paran: Toward a Christian Perspective on Hagar and Ishmael." *Interpretation* 68 (2014): 270–85. Argues for a more charitable Christian reading of the figure of Ishmael.

WEBSITES
Rishmawy, Derek. "I Am Not Abraham's Mistake." *Patheos, Christ and Pop Culture* (blog). February 27, 2013. http://www.patheos.com/blogs/christandpopculture/2013/02/i–am–not–abrahams–mistake/. Argues that popular evangelical theology about Arabs often contradicts biblical teaching.

CHAPTER 6

———

The Angel of the Lord Refers
to the Preincarnate Jesus

Genesis 18:1–13

The Legendary Teaching on the Angel of the Lord as Jesus

God often appears in human form in the Old Testament (e.g., Gen 18:1–13; 32:24–32; Josh 5:13–15; Isa 6:1–10; Ezek 1:4–28; Dan 3:28–29). Because the Second Person of the Trinity is the One who took on humanity in the incarnation, we can conclude that the Lord Jesus is also the One who appears in these visible manifestations of God in the Old Testament. The most common of these "Christophanies" are the appearances of the angel of the Lord to various individuals (Gen 16:7–13; 22:11–14; Judg 2:1–5; 6:11–24; 13:2–23; Zech 3:1).[1] The angel who appears to Moses at the burning bush in Exodus 3 is referred to both as "Yahweh" (vv. 2, 4, 5, 7, 16, 18) and "God" (vv. 4–6, 11, 16, 18). Moses and others who met this angel actually encountered the preincarnate Christ.

Countering the Legendary Teaching

The angel of the Lord is both identified with God and distinct from God. Rather than anachronistically reading New Testament trinitarian ideas into

---

[1]   The identification of the angel of the Lord with Christ goes back to Justin Martyr and was the view of the early church fathers. For discussion of the history of interpretation on the angel of the Lord, see William G. MacDonald, "Christology and 'the Angel of the Lord,'" in *Current Issues in Biblical and Patristic Interpretation: Studies in Honor of Merrill C. Tenney Presented by His Former Students*, ed. G. F. Hawthorne (Grand Rapids: Eerdmans, 1975), 325–28.

the text, the better explanation is that the angel of the Lord is identified with God as his messenger and representative. The angel so fully identifies with the One who has sent him that seeing and hearing him is the same as having an encounter with God himself. Identification of the angel of the Lord with Jesus also runs the risk of minimizing the uniqueness of the incarnation, in which God the Son does not merely appear in human form but fully takes on humanity apart from a sin nature. The true humanity of Jesus in the incarnation demands that "his human nature had a temporal beginning and continuous existence."[2] The evidence also suggests that the title "angel of the Lord" does not describe one single figure.

The Interchangeability of the Angel and the Lord

The interchangeability of the angel of the Lord and Yahweh is reflected in a number of passages in the Old Testament. The angel of the Lord often speaks and acts as God. In Genesis 16, the angel of the Lord appears to Hagar and speaks as God in both the first and third persons (vv. 10–11). At the conclusion of this episode, the narrator states that the Lord had appeared to Hagar and that she had called him "the God Who Sees," while affirming that she had seen "the One who sees me" (vv. 12–13). In Judg 2:1–4, the angel of the Lord speaks as God in the first person, declaring that he was the one who had brought the people out of Egypt. The angel's voice is also that of the Lord when he accuses the people, "You have not obeyed me," and threatens not to drive out the Canaanites before them.

Douglas Stuart states that the story of the burning bush in Exodus 3 is "perhaps the strongest of all passages for identifying the 'Angel of the Lord' as the Lord himself."[3] Angelic messengers, including the angel of the Lord, are referred to as "the LORD" in other texts as well (Gen 12:7; 17:1; 18:1). In Exod 23:20–23, the angel of the Lord is the one who would bring Israel into the Promised Land, who had the authority to forgive sins or withhold forgiveness, and who would destroy the enemies of Israel when they conquered the land of Canaan. Individuals who encounter the angel of the Lord or other angelic figures often recognize these figures as God (Gen 16:13; 31:11–13; 48:15–16)[4] and respond to these figures as if they were God or give them

[2]   MacDonald, "Christology and 'the Angel of the Lord,'" 325.
[3]   Douglas K. Stuart, *Exodus*, New American Commentary (Nashville: Broadman & Holman, 2006), 112.
[4]   Stuart, *Exodus*, 112.

worship that should only be accorded to God. Gideon presents a meal as a gift/offering to the angel of the Lord (Judg 6:18–21), and both Gideon and Samson's parents fear that they are going to die after seeing this angel (Judg 6:22–23; 13:22; compare Exod 33:20).

The Angel of the Lord Distinguished from God

Despite the close identification of the angel of the Lord and God, there are also a number of passages that clearly distinguish the angel from the Lord, and these passages are determinative in demonstrating that the angel himself is not Yahweh or the preincarnate Christ.[5] In Exodus 32–33, the Lord tells Moses that the Lord would send his angel ahead of the people of Israel to protect them and deliver them from their enemies (32:32–34; 33:2). The Lord states that he himself will not accompany Israel because he is likely to destroy them on the way because of their rebelliousness (33:3). In response to Moses's intercession, the Lord reverses his decision and promises that his presence would go up with Israel to the land (33:12–16). The distinction between the angel going up with the people and the Lord himself going up with the people is specifically what motivates the prayer of Moses.

When David sinned against the Lord by conducting a military census, the Lord determined that he would bring a plague upon Israel and sent out the angel of the Lord to execute the punishment (2 Samuel 24; 1 Chronicles 21). The angel killed 70,000 men, but at the moment he was prepared to destroy Jerusalem, the Lord commanded the angel to withdraw his hand (1 Chr 21:14–15; compare 2 Sam 24:16). The Lord is the sovereign King who determines the nature and extent of the judgment; the angel of the Lord is merely the agent who executes the judgment.[6]

When the angel of the Lord appears and speaks to Gideon in Judges 6, the text alternates between the angel speaking as the Lord (vv. 12, 20) and the Lord himself speaking (vv. 14, 16, 18). In verse 21, however, the angel vanishes from the scene, while the Lord continues to speak to Gideon in verse 23. When Samson's father, Manoah, wishes to prepare food for the angel of the Lord, the angel instructs him to present a burnt offering to the Lord instead

---

[5]   Robert B. Chisholm Jr., *A Commentary on Judges and Ruth*, Kregel Exegetical Library (Grand Rapids: Kregel, 2013), 137n66.

[6]   René A. López, "Identifying the 'Angel of the Lord' in the Book of Judges: A Model for Reconsidering the Referent in Other Old Testament Loci," *Bulletin for Biblical Research* 20 (2010): 15–16.

(Judg 13:16). The angel explicitly distinguishes himself from the Lord.[7]

There are other texts in which the angel of the Lord speaks in the first person while still identifying the Lord as the source of his message. In swearing an oath to Abraham following his willingness to offer Isaac as a sacrifice, the angel states, "I swear by myself, declares the Lord" (NIV) as preface to the divine promise (Gen 22:15–16; compare Zech 3:6–10). By speaking for the Lord in this way, the angel functions in essentially the same role as the prophet as a human messenger of God.

The Angel of the Lord as God's Appointed Messenger

In light of these passages that distinguish the angel of the Lord from the Lord himself, we should understand that the angel is not the Lord in a personal sense but rather that he is identified with the Lord as his representative and messenger. In the culture of the ancient Near East, a royal messenger or envoy of the gods had the same authority as the master and had the authority to speak personally for the king. John Walton explains, "Since such messengers represent, they do not speak for themselves but only for God. It is therefore not unusual for them to use the first person." When the angel is identified with the Lord, it indicates "the source and authority behind the message."[8]

When Joseph's messenger speaks to Joseph's brothers, he alternates between third and first person, speaking for Joseph but also warning that the one who had stolen Joseph's cup would become "my slave" (Gen 44:3–9). Moses speaks as the Lord's messenger in Deut 29:2–6, first declaring that the Lord had performed great and miraculous acts in bringing Israel out of bondage from Egypt but then switching to first person when he states, "I led you forty years in the wilderness . . . so that you might know I am the Lord." Bruce Waltke notes that we see the equation of sender and messenger in passages such as Judg 11:13; 2 Sam 3:12; and 1 Kgs 20:2–6 as well.[9] The same convention likely applies in the Old Testament texts in which the angel of the Lord speaks on behalf of the Lord. In the historical context of the Old Testament, the messenger/representative view of the angel of the Lord provides a more plausible explanation than the Christological view.[10]

---

[7]   Walton, *Genesis*, 466 (see chap. 1, n. 4).

[8]   Walton, *Genesis*, 465.

[9]   Bruce K. Waltke, with Charles Yu, *An Old Testament Theology: An Exegetical, Canonical, and Thematic Approach* (Grand Rapids: Zondervan, 2007), 362.

[10]   Rather than one specific angelic figure who was the preincarnate Christ, the term *mala'ak yhwh* likely refers to various messengers (angelic and human) who served in this role at different times. The

Application

The God of the Old Testament is transcendent and holy but also active and present in this world. The appearances of God represented in human form reflect the degree to which God condescends to make himself known and the depth of his involvement with his people. The ways in which God has made himself known gives us assurance of his presence in our lives and should also lead to our wholehearted seeking after him. The psalmist compares his passion for God to the deer's longing for the "flowing streams" (Ps 42:1–2).

Although the angel of the Lord is not to be identified with the preincarnate Christ or even viewed as a single figure in Scripture, the way in which this heavenly messenger visibly represents God anticipates and points forward to the incarnation of God in the person of Jesus as the perfect expression of the Word of God (see John 1:14–18).[11] The writer of Hebrews reminds us that God has spoken in various ways throughout history but has spoken finally and decisively through his Son Jesus (Heb 1:1). Indeed, the revelation given through God's Son demands even greater faithful attentiveness than what was conveyed through God's human and heavenly messengers in the Old Testament (Heb 2:1–4).

---

phrase *mala'ak yhwh* is what is known in Hebrew as a construct chain, which indicates that the word *angel* or *messenger* should be translated as a definite noun ("the angel of the Lord"). In such phrases, the construct noun (angel) never takes the definite article, and its definiteness in this expression is determined by the following absolute noun being a proper name (Lord). Nevertheless, the fact that a specific figure is in view does not indicate or necessitate that the same angelic figure is in view every time this expression appears. The Hebrew grammarian Gesenius (H. F. W. Gesenius, *Gesenius' Hebrew Grammar*, 2nd English ed., ed. E. Kautzsch and A. E. Cowley [New York: Oxford, 1910], 412) notes that there are exceptions to the construct noun being translated as definite noun when followed by a proper name (e.g., Exod 10:9 ["a feast of the Lord"]; Deut 7:25 ["an abomination to the Lord"]; 22:19 ["a virgin of Israel"]; and 1 Sam 4:12 ["a man of Benjamin"]). In Hag 1:13, even the human prophet is referred to as *mala'ak yhwh* ("the messenger of the Lord"), but this designation does not mean that Haggai is the only human prophet who functioned in this role. Chisholm (*Commentary on Judges and Ruth*, 137n66) compares the expression "angel of the Lord" to "the servant of the Lord" (see Deut 34:5; Josh 8:31), which is the same type of construction (construct noun + proper name). The "servant of the Lord" is a definite figure in each context it appears, but there are multiple figures identified by this expression throughout the Old Testament. Thus, we could potentially see the same with "the angel of the Lord" as well.

[11]   For how the manner in which Second Temple Jewish literature after the OT era increasingly tended to blur the distinction between the Lord and manifestations of the divine like the angel of the Lord helped to prepare the way for the recognition of Jesus the Messiah as a manifestation of God, see David B. Capes, *The Divine Christ: Paul, the Lord Jesus, and the Scriptures of Israel* (Grand Rapids: Baker Academic, 2018), 42–43.

Annotated Bibliography

BOOKS

MacDonald, William Graham. "Christology and 'the Angel of the Lord.'" In *Current Issues in Biblical and Patristic Interpretation: Studies in Honor of Merrill C. Tenney Presented by His Former Students*, edited by Gerald F. Hawthorne, 324–35. Grand Rapids: Eerdmans, 1975. Discusses the history of interpretation for the angel of the Lord in the Christian church and argues against identifying the angel as Christ.

COMMENTARIES

Chisholm, Robert B., Jr. *A Commentary on Judges and Ruth*. Kregel Exegetical Library. Grand Rapids: Kregel, 2013. Scholarly evangelical commentary with discussion of the appearances of the angel of the Lord in Judges.

Walton, John H. *Genesis*, New International Version Application Commentary. Grand Rapids: Zondervan, 2001. Discusses the appearances of the angel of the Lord in Genesis.

ARTICLES

López, René A. "Identifying the 'Angel of the Lord' in the Book of Judges: A Model for Reconsidering the Referent in Other Old Testament Loci." *Bulletin for Biblical Research* 20 (2010): 1–18. Argues for identifying the angel of the Lord as God's representative messenger rather than God himself or the preincarnate Christ.

WEBSITES

McBride, Louis. "Was 'the Angel of the Lord' an Appearance of the Preincarnate Christ?" *Baker Deep End Blog*. August 22, 2011. https://bbhchurchconnection.wordpress.com/2011/08/22/was-the-angel-of-the-lord-an-appearance-of-the-preincarnate-christ/. Provides a blog post summarizing the arguments of MacDonald and Walton.

CHAPTER 7

———

Taking the Lord's Name in Vain Refers to Using God's Name as a Curse Word

Exodus 20:7

The Legendary Teaching on Exodus 20:7

There are many ways in which Christians live in disobedience to Exod 20:7 by taking God's name in vain: "You shall not take the name of the LORD your God in vain, for the LORD will not hold him guiltless who takes his name in vain" (ESV). This verse refers to using God's name in a "vain" or "empty" way. People do this commonly when using "God" in an expression or idiom, but they aren't really referring to God. For example, many people will text someone the abbreviation OMG or say that phrase out loud. When someone says that, they are not really talking to God. They are using his name like a curse word. It is an "empty" use since it does not fully carry the sense of reverence required when referring to God. There are many more expressions that do this, but I won't repeat them here. God promises punishment to those who use his name like this, so we must be careful to avoid this sin.

Countering the Legendary Teaching

It is hard to know exactly where some of these legendary teachings began. This legend might be traced back to a Jewish practice. To avoid taking God's name in vain, Jews would avoid using his name altogether. From there, however, several steps have to be made to arrive at the popular understanding of this verse.

Although the word translated as "vain" can be translated as "empty," this could imply that the word is referring to using God's name with a lack of

37

reverence, in a way that trivializes it. Some translations have "misuse" (CSB, NIV) instead of "vain." *Misuse* seems to be a little closer to the meaning in this context and avoids the vagueness of the word *vain*. The word can also refer to falsehood or lying. It does not appear that the verse is simply referring to a tone of voice or a use of the word in a particular expression. Nor does it reference blasphemy (speaking sacrilegiously against God) or profanity.

Exodus 20:7 does not forbid misusing "the name of God," but says not to misuse "the name of the LORD your God." The word *God* refers to a category, not a name. The god of the Bible has a name and it is not "God." His name is usually translated as "LORD." According to Exod 3:14, his name is "I AM."[1] This fact also casts doubt on the idea that using the word *God* in an expression is the point of the verse, since that is not his name.

Another possible point of inquiry would be to study the concept of "profaning" his name. If profaning and taking his name in vain are the same, then verses such as Lev 18:21 and 19:12 would demonstrate that this is not simply a reference to speaking his name in an "empty" way.

Christians have weakened the Third Commandment by saying that it refers to using God's name in a saying or idiom. In fact, if using an expression like "OMG" would be considered breaking the Third Commandment, then what about the phrase "God bless you" after someone sneezes? It is a common courtesy to say that, but the vast majority of people who use it are not truly invoking a blessing from heaven down on to the person who sneezed. That would be similar to an "empty" use of God's name.

The Meaning of "Vain"

Some historical background of the ancient Near East is helpful in understanding this prohibition. The people of Canaan used the name of their gods to give authority to their statements. They might invoke the name of Baal or Marduk to claim that their prophecies would come to pass. Names of gods were also used for invoking magic spells to try to get the god to do the bidding of the one praying (see Jer 28:2). Knowing that this was common, God gives this command in Exod 20:7, at least in part, to warn the Israelites against using his name (Yahweh) to give authority to their words (when he has not actually given them the words to say) or to try to manipulate him to meet their request.

---

[1] That Yahweh is the accepted position by most scholars today, see Paul Joüon and T. Muraoka, *A Grammar of Biblical Hebrew*, 2nd ed., with Corrections (Rome: Gregorian and Biblical Press, 2011), 66. See also n. 1 on same page.

Does the Third Commandment prohibit using the name of God irreverently? Yes and no. No, in the sense that it does not refer to using the English word *God* in an idiom; yes, if someone says, "God said." All Christians should be very careful about beginning their sentences with "God said."

This interpretation becomes easier to see in the verse when the word *misuse* is in the translation. By misuse, it means "using the name of God to give our words authority," even though God did not say those words. Stuart says it means "to be invoking his name as guarantor of one's words."[2] The meaning of this verse probably finds its origin as a prohibition against perjury,[3] but in this context it is worded much more generically than that.[4]

How do some scholars find a reference to perjury in the Third Commandment?[5] The verb usually translated as "take" (as in "you shall not take the name," ESV) can refer to taking an oath.[6] Also, since the end of the verse refers to the idea of not finding someone guiltless (or not acquitting someone), this provides even more connotations of a legal setting. Commenting on the parallel version in Deut 5:11, Eugene Merrill says, "The meaning clearly is that one must not view the name as a counterpart of Yahweh and then proceed to take it in hand (or in mouth) as a means of accomplishing some kind of ill-advised or unworthy objective. This was typical of ancient Near Eastern sorcery or incantation where the names of the gods were invoked as part of the act of conjuration or of prophylaxis."[7]

The Importance of the "Name"

Exodus 20:7 also includes a reference to God's "name." The concept of protecting God's "name" is a reference to his reputation. For example, Eccl 7:1 says, "A good name is better than precious ointment, and the day of death

---

[2]   Douglas K. Stuart, *Exodus*, New American Commentary (Nashville: Broadman & Holman, 2006), 455.

[3]   Stuart, *Exodus*, 455.

[4]   See H. B. Huffmon, "The Fundamental Code Illustrated: The Third Commandment," in *Pomegranates and Golden Bells* (Winona Lake, IN: Eisenbrauns, 1995), 363–71; and Carl Meyers, *Exodus*, New Cambridge Bible Commentary (Cambridge: Cambridge University Press, 2005), 173.

[5]   Note that Daniel I. Block, *Deuteronomy*, New International Version Application Commentary (Grand Rapids: Zondervan, 2012), 163, appears to agree that this verse is not "a taboo on verbal profanities," but he does not appear to see a reference to perjury. Instead, he believes the verse is about the proper representation of Yahweh.

[6]   Meyers, *Exodus*, 174. Note that some believe it is parallel to the Ninth Commandment on not bearing false witness. See John H. Walton, "Deuteronomy: An Exposition of the Spirit of the Law," *Grace Theological Journal* 8, no. 2 (1987): 214, 221–23.

[7]   Merrill, *Deuteronomy*, 149 (see chap. 3, n. 2).

than the day of birth" (ESV). The word *name* is "a verbal symbol for a person or thing, and the ancients in particular obviously appreciated the way names connoted the very value, character, and influence of a person or thing."[8] Therefore, invoking God's name inappropriately would lead to the defamation of his character. This is why there is a stern warning against doing this at the end of Exod 20:7.

If using the name of God, that is, Yahweh, means to use it in a way in which it is not fully referencing God, then there are some difficult expressions to explain in the Old Testament. Two of the most common ways to refer to God in the Old Testament are by the Hebrew words for "Elohim" and "Yahweh." But several times those words are used as superlatives. For example, a phrase in Gen 23:6 could be literally translated "you are a prince god among us." However, the word for "god" (Elohim) is used as a superlative, hence the translation "You are a mighty prince" (NIV). Yahweh is sometimes abbreviated as "Yah" (יָהּ). A phrase in Jer 2:31 could be translated literally as "a land of Yah darkness." Since "Yah" is being used as a superlative, it should be translated as "a land of great darkness" (NIV).[9] The uses of these words for God in the Hebrew Old Testament demonstrate that someone can use "God" in an expression or idiom and not be breaking the Third Commandment.

Having the name of a deity in the ancient Near East meant you could use the name for your own purposes. The Third Commandment prohibits the use of Yahweh's name for self-interests. As Walton concludes, "His name was not to be thought of as a symbol with efficacious power that could be used to pursue one's own self-interests."[10]

Application

The Third Commandment is not emptied of application due to this interpretation, but explodes with different applications. Rather than simply avoiding the use of the word *God* in certain expressions, Christians are to be careful about putting words into God's mouth. This commandment is not directly a reference to using the word *God* in an offensive phrase. This does not give

---

[8]   Stuart, *Exodus*, 456.

[9]   See Brian P. Gault, "An Admonition against 'Rousing Love': The Meaning of the Enigmatic Refrain in Song of Songs," *Bulletin for Biblical Research* 20 (2010): 171 (see also n. 40). Other examples with "El/Elohim" include Gen 30:8; Exod 9:28; Pss 36:7, 65:9, 68:16, 80:10; Isa 14:13; Jonah 3:3; 1 Chr 12:23. Some examples with "Yah" include Jer 32:19; 1 Sam 26:12; Ps 118:5; Lam 3:66.

[10]   John H. Walton, "Interpreting the Bible as an Ancient Near Eastern Document," in *Israel: Ancient Kingdom or Late Invention?*, ed. Daniel I. Block (Nashville: Broadman & Holman Academic, 2008), 218.

Christians permission to "swear," however, as other verses need to be considered in that discussion.[11]

One popular but dangerous movement in America is prosperity theology. Preachers in this movement claim that God has promised that if people give them money, he will bless them. The blessing they claim God has promised includes a monetary blessing that will be 10 times or even 100 times the gift given. In this way, these preachers put words into God's mouth, claiming God's authority, yet they are spreading lies and defaming the name of God.

Some people in this movement, nicknamed "name it and claim it," use the name of Jesus in a magical way. They say that if you ask God for something in faith, and you say "in the name of Jesus," then God "has to" answer your request (if you have enough faith). This is using "Jesus" like a genie in a bottle, to command or manipulate him to give us what we wish. This is misusing Jesus's name, abusing it for selfish desire.

A much less insidious way that this commandment is not observed is in the common expressions "God told me to tell you" or "God said." Sometimes the person speaking will insert "I think" to temper the words, as in "I think God told me to tell you . . ." It is dangerous to refer to God to give authority to the words we speak. When we say "God said" we must be careful that God truly did say those words. Using these expressions can manipulate people into thinking that we are speaking for God when we are actually giving our own opinion.

Annotated Bibliography

BOOKS
Stuart, Douglas K. *Exodus*. New American Commentary. Nashville: Broadman & Holman, 2006. See 455–56. Stuart's commentary gives some brief but helpful comments clarifying the meaning of the Third Commandment.

COMMENTARIES
Meyers, Carl. *Exodus*. New Cambridge Bible Commentary. Cambridge: Cambridge University Press, 2005. See 173. Meyers's discussion is helpful and is similar to the conclusions here.

WEBSITES
Patton, C. Michael. "Taking the Lord's Name in Vain—What Does It Really Mean?" *CredoHouse* (blog). August 15, 2014. https://credohouse.org/blog/taking-the-lords-name-in-vain. This is a very helpful and readable article clearly explaining the common misinterpretation of the verse and providing application for today.

---

[11]   For example, see Eph 4:29. For a brief but helpful discussion on this, see Wayne Grudem, "Wayne Grudem on Offensive Language," *Desiring God*, January 15, 2007, https://www.desiringgod.org/articles/wayne-grudem-on-offensive-language.

CHAPTER 8

———

The Tabernacle Was an Elaborate Picture of Jesus
Exodus 25–40

The Legendary Teaching on Israel's Tabernacle

A popular Christian website offers this comment on the typological significance of the tabernacle:

> Is it any wonder then that each and every detail and Word about the tabernacle has spiritual significance? As we look to the tabernacle structure itself and its unique pieces of redemptive furniture there is great symbolism and typology found in them. Remember, everything was a finger pointing to the Messiah. The tabernacle, as a type, designed specifically and in detail by God, would point to the character and aspects of the ministry of Christ.[1]

Another study states concerning the tabernacle, "This holy unique construction speaks of Him in all of its details. Throughout we see the magnificent greatness of His wonderful person with wonder and amazement. At the same time, we also see how His perfect work of salvation is prophetically represented in the sacrificial acts."[2] The four colors of the curtain at the entrance portray the message of the Gospels (purple—Matthew and Jesus as Messiah; scarlet—Mark and Jesus as suffering servant; white—Luke and Jesus as sinless son of man; and blue—John and Jesus as the Son of God). The badger skins

---

[1]   "Good Reasons to Study the Tabernacle," *Bible History Online*, accessed December 29, 2017, https://www.bible-history.com/tabernacle/TAB4Reasons_for_Studying_the_Taberna.htm.
[2]   Paul F. Kiene, *The Tabernacle of God in the Wilderness of Sinai* (Grand Rapids: Zondervan, 1977), 12.

43

covering the Tent of Meeting provide a portrait of the humiliation of Jesus in his incarnation and a reminder that Jesus was vigilant like the badger. The ram skins point forward to Jesus providing an atoning sacrifice for sin. The table of the bread of presence and the lampstand picture Jesus as the bread and light of the world. The various sacrifices and offerings at the tabernacle anticipate the perfect sacrifice for sin that Jesus would make on the cross. The best way for Christians to study the details of the tabernacle provided in Exodus 25–40 is to explore every possible connection to the person and work of Jesus.

Countering the Legendary Teaching

The New Testament, and particularly the book of Hebrews, affirms the validity of noting typological correspondences between the tabernacle and Jesus (see John 1:14; Heb 9:1–10, 23–28; 10:1–4). Typology is also one of the primary tools for the New Testament writers in reading the Old Testament from a Christological perspective. The problem with the legendary approach to the tabernacle is not typology but the *excessive use of typology* in attempting to see Christological significance in every minute detail of the tabernacle. The purpose of biblical typology is not to detail historical coincidence but to explain the recurring patterns in redemptive history. Biblical typology notes the larger patterns of correspondence between the Old Testament type and the New Testament antitype and thus emphasizes how the presence of God in the tabernacle and the sacrifices there offered point forward to Christ. Finding Christological significance in every aspect of the tabernacle is more an allegorizing of the Old Testament than a reflection of the redemptive patterns that emerge from the text itself. As J. Daniel Hays has explained, "Just because there is a central storyline theological connection between Christ and the ancient tabernacle, we do not have the liberty to let our imaginations run wild and dream up prophetic connections about every little detail about the tabernacle."[3]

The primary message of the tabernacle for Israel was theological rather than Christological. The people of Israel had limited understanding of the future Messiah, especially in regard to his sacrificial death, and the primary purpose of the tabernacle was not to provide coded messages about the future Messiah that would have made little sense to the people at that time. The

[3]   J. Daniel Hays, *The Temple and the Tabernacle: A Study of God's Dwelling Places from Genesis to Revelation* (Grand Rapids: Baker, 2016), 60.

central message of the tabernacle was to communicate the reality of Yahweh's continual presence with his people and to provide instruction on how sinful people should approach, worship, and live in fellowship with a holy God.[4]

The Tabernacle/Temple in Its Ancient Near Eastern Setting

The Lord used specific cultural forms and symbols common to the ancient Near East to communicate his continual presence with his people. The tabernacle and temple reflected a shared ancient Near Eastern concept of sacred space, which viewed the gods as traversing and inhabiting specific locations. The tabernacle and temple were not merely the Old Testament place of worship like our church buildings; they were the actual dwelling places of Yahweh, where he lived and ruled among his people. The architecture and barriers limiting access to the presence of God protected the sanctity of the site and served as a constant reminder to Israel of how dangerous it was to enter the presence of a holy God.[5]

The pagan gods were believed to dwell on sacred mountains, and mountains often served as the meeting place between heaven and earth. Temples themselves symbolized cosmic mountains. Yahweh also revealed himself and met with his people on mountains; Zion as the site of the temple was portrayed as a lofty mountain (Ps 48:2). The tabernacle was a royal tent (note the lavish expense in its construction), and the temple was an earthly representation of God's heavenly throne. The word for "temple" and "palace" is the same in Hebrew (*hekal*), and Israel understood that as they worshipped at the temple, they were entering the presence of the sovereign King over all creation.

In the unfolding story of redemption, the Pentateuch particularly appears to develop key correspondences between the tabernacle and the garden of Eden. The point is that Yahweh is acting to restore what was lost at Eden, and the tabernacle becomes like an Eden in a fallen world where sinful individuals can still enjoy fellowship with God. These correspondences are reflected in the table below:[6]

---

[4]　See Tremper Longman III, *Immanuel in Our Place: Seeing Christ in Israel's Worship* (Philipsburg, NJ: Presbyterian & Reformed, 2001), 32–34.

[5]　See John H. Walton, *Ancient Near Eastern Thought and the Old Testament: Introducing the Conceptual World of the Hebrew Bible* (Grand Rapids: Baker Academic, 2006), 113–34.

[6]　See John H. Sailhamer, *The Pentateuch as Narrative: A Biblical-Theological Commentary* (Grand Rapids: Zondervan, 1992), 298–99.

Garden of Eden	Tabernacle
Access denied at east entrance (Gen 3:24)	Access granted at east entrance (Exod 27:13)
Place of service to God (Gen 2:15)	Place of service to God (Num 3:7)
God walks in the midst of the garden (Gen 3:8)	God walks in the midst of Israel (Lev 26:12)
Tree of life (Gen 2:9; 3:22, 24)	Lampstand as stylized tree of life (Exod 25:31–36)
Gold and onyx (Gen 2:12)	Gold and precious materials widely used in construction of tabernacle (Exod 25:3, 7, 11–13, 28–29, etc.)
Cherubim guarding entrance to garden (Gen 3:24)	Cherubim represented at the tabernacle (Exod 25:18; 37:9)

These details reflect the forward movement of redemptive history as God restores his presence among sinful humanity. Commenting on the significance of the tabernacle in redemptive history, Peter Enns explains, "The building of the tabernacle is more than simply a matter of building a worship site in the desert. It is a piece of heaven on earth."[7] In other words, the tabernacle and its furnishings would not have been understood by the original readers of the Hebrew Bible as hidden messages about the Messiah.

The tabernacle served as God's royal dwelling place, and the portability of the tabernacle stressed Yahweh's continual presence with Israel. While it may be natural for Christians to think of how the golden lampstand in the holy place of the tabernacle reminds us that Jesus is "the light of the world" or how the showbread helps us to see that Jesus is "the bread of life," the features and furnishings of the tabernacle likely convey a more basic message about God's presence; the tabernacle was God's home, and the people could look at the tabernacle and see the kinds of things one would expect to see if someone was actually living there. Richard Averbeck explains, "The combination of the daily lighting of the lampstand and associated burning of incense . . . plus the bread constantly on the table impresses one that the

---

[7]   Peter E. Enns, *Exodus*, New International Version Application Commentary (Grand Rapids: Zondervan, 2000), 506.

Lord had truly taken up residence in the tabernacle. If there is a lamp burning, incense burning and bread on the table, then someone is 'home.'"[8]

The Tabernacle and Christ

When we understand how the tabernacle demonstrated God's presence with his people in the Old Testament and what was required of his people as they came into his presence, we are better prepared to explore how the tabernacle points forward to Jesus. In the incarnation of Jesus, God's presence dwelled among humanity here on earth in the same way that God's presence resided among the people of Israel in the tabernacle and the temple. John 1:14 tells us, "The Word became flesh and dwelt among us. We observed his glory, the glory as the one and only Son from the Father." The Greek verb translated here as "dwelt" (*skanein*) is from the same root as the noun for "tabernacle" (*skana*) in the Septuagint, because the same Shekinah glory that was visible at the tabernacle could be seen in the person of Jesus Christ. In the transfiguration, the three disciples with Jesus actually saw the visible glory of God as the face of Jesus shined like the sun and his clothes became as white as light (Matt 17:2). The glory of God was now being revealed in Jesus, not the temple. In John 2:19–22, Jesus announced, "Destroy this temple, and I will raise it up in three days," referring to his own death and resurrection and how he personally had become the way into God's presence. In Matt 12:6, Jesus boldly declared with reference to himself that "something greater than the temple is here."

The daily sacrifices offered at the tabernacle and temple and the necessity of blood sacrifices for the atonement of sins in the Mosaic law (Lev 17:11; Heb 9:22) also prefigured the cross. Rather than offering animal blood that could never ultimately atone for sin, Jesus offered his own sinless body and life as the perfect sacrifice for sin (Heb 10:1–5). Animal sacrifices had to be offered over and over again, but Jesus had to die only once in providing atonement for sin (Heb 10:10–14). Rather than presenting his sacrifice at the earthly sanctuary, Jesus presented his blood at the heavenly sanctuary and thus opened a more perfect access into the presence of God (Heb 9:23–24).

---

[8]   Richard E. Averbeck, "Tabernacle," in *Dictionary of the Old Testament: Pentateuch*, ed. T. D. Alexander and D. E. Baker (Downers Grove, IL: InterVarsity Press, 2003), 815.

Application

The presence of God lost and then restored is a central theme in the story line of the Bible, and the tabernacle/temple and the person of Jesus are key aspects of that story. In the incarnation, Jesus replaced the temple, as the presence of God dwelled among humanity in a person. Through Jesus, God's people would worship God "in Spirit and in truth" without needing to come to a specific physical location (John 4:23–24). God's glory now tabernacles in the church as his people through the indwelling Spirit (1 Cor 3:16; 6:19–20; 1 Pet 2:4–5). The New Jerusalem is portrayed in Revelation 21–22 in ways that recall the garden of Eden in order to highlight that what was lost in the old creation will be restored in the new creation (Rev 22:1–3). God will dwell among his people for all eternity, and there will be no need for a temple because all of the redeemed will see God's face (Rev 21:22; 22:4–5). Through Christ, we have already gained access into the heavenly presence of God (Heb 12:22–24), and as we walk through this life in anticipation of eternity, we have God's promise that he will never abandon us (Heb 13:5).

Annotated Bibliography

Books

Hays, J. Daniel. *The Temple and the Tabernacle: A Study of God's Dwelling Places from Genesis to Revelation*. Grand Rapids: Baker, 2016. Develops the theme of temple/God's dwelling place in the Bible, highlighting important historical and theological issues.

Longman, Tremper, III. *Immanuel in Our Place: Seeing Christ in Israel's Worship*. Philipsburg, NJ: Presbyterian & Reformed, 2001. Helpful model for how to explain the typology of the tabernacle/temple in relationship to Christ.

Commentaries

Stuart, Douglas K. *Exodus: An Exegetical and Theological Exposition of Holy Scripture*. New American Commentary. Nashville: Broadman & Holman, 2006. Scholarly evangelical commentary with detailed exposition of Exodus 25–40.

Websites

Hyde, Daniel. "6 Reasons Christians Should Study the Tabernacle." *Ligonier*. October 5, 2012. https://www.ligonier.org/blog/6-reasons-why-christians-should-study-tabernacle/. Discusses important themes concerning the significance of the tabernacle in addition to its Christological significance.

CHAPTER 9

———

Unintentional Sin Is Inconsequential
Leviticus 4–5

The Legendary Teaching on Unintentional Sin

I was talking with a brother in our church this week. He had been wronged by a member of our congregation; he had been slandered. He referred to it as being sinned against. Being the pastor, I went to the "offending" person and asked him about it. When he gave his side of the story, it became obvious to me that the slander was unintentional. He did not realize when he was speaking that he was slandering, and his heart was not vindictive at all. I explained this to the man who had been slandered against, and he did not accept the reasoning. He wanted an apology and admission of guilt. However, he could not accept that since the slander was unintentional, he should just let it go.

Countering the Legendary Teaching

The issue in this legend does not involve the misinterpretation of a verse, but the lack of knowledge on scriptural teaching about the topic. The Bible distinguishes between intentional and unintentional sin, and we will see that God takes unintentional sin seriously. There are a few passages in the Old Testament that address this issue explicitly and one we will discuss in the New Testament. Sin is defined as a violation of God's law that leads to a rupture in the sinner's relationship with God.[1]

Making a few comments on the Old Testament law and the Christian

---

[1] For a very similar definition of sin, see Jay Sklar, "Sin and Atonement: Lessons from the Pentateuch," *Bulletin for Biblical Research* 22, no. 4 (2012): 468.

will help us orient ourselves. Although some people believe that the law was for Israel and has virtually no application to Christians today, we do believe this is a severe misunderstanding of the relationship between the old and new covenants. First of all, when Paul says, "All Scripture is inspired by God and is profitable for teaching, for rebuking, for correcting, for training in righteousness" (2 Tim 3:16), he was, at the very least, including the Old Testament; in fact, it was probably primarily about the Old Testament. If Paul believed the Old Testament was profitable or "useful" (NET), then we should as well. Second, while many of the specifics in the Old Testament law do not apply, one of the primary purposes of the law is to teach us more about the character of God. There are underlying principles of the laws that are eternal, as God's character never changes.

Leviticus 4–5: Unintentional Sin Is Forgivable

Leviticus 4:2 says, "When someone sins unintentionally . . ." We can now say with clarity that unintentional sins, as a category, do exist. Leviticus 4:3–31 describes what a priest (vv. 3–12), the whole community (vv. 13–21), a leader (vv. 22–26), and common people (vv. 27–31) must do when an unintentional sin occurs: an appropriate sacrifice must be made. When a common person has fulfilled the sacrificial requirements, "he will be forgiven" (v. 31). This entire chapter communicates the seriousness of unintentional sin. The fact that forgiveness is bestowed *after* the sacrifice has been completed provides compelling evidence that when someone commits an unintentional sin, God views that as a serious offense that needs forgiveness. An unintentional sin ruptures the sinner's relationship with God.

Leviticus 5 helps define unintentional sin. Verses 2–3 provide an example of someone touching something unclean without realizing it; this would be considered an unintentional sin. Verse 4 says that when someone makes a rash oath, and later realizes it, that would be an unintentional sin. These are some examples to help us understand the type of actions that would be considered unintentional sins.

Leviticus 5:5 states that when individuals realize they have sinned unintentionally, they need to confess that they have, in fact, sinned. Verses 6–13 explain the sacrifice that is necessary to receive forgiveness. The ending of Leviticus 5 discusses the seriousness of unintentional sin. Someone who commits an unintentional sin "will bear his iniquity" (v. 5). After the appropriate offering is given "for the error he has committed unintentionally . . . he will be forgiven" (v. 18). Before he makes that offering, "he is indeed guilty before the LORD" (v. 19). It appears fairly clear from Lev 5:18–19 that the person is not forgiven until restitution is made.

This summary of Leviticus 4–5 helps answer a few questions: unintentional sin is a valid category, and it is considered a serious offense that requires forgiveness. Jay Sklar concludes that "lack of intent does not mean the sinner is automatically excused."[2]

Leviticus 6: Intentional Sin Is Forgivable

Leviticus 6 appears to transition from unintentional sin to intentional sin. Examples of an intentional sin in Leviticus 6 include deceiving and defrauding your neighbor (v. 2). Then in verses 4–5, Moses says that "once he has sinned and acknowledged his guilt" he must make restitution for the sin he committed. After making restitution with the person he committed the sin against, he must make the appropriate offering (v. 6). Once that is completed, "he will be forgiven" (v. 7). This explains that an intentional sin can be forgiven as long as "the sacrifice was accompanied by confession of sin and a repentant heart."[3] The NET Bible concludes (when discussing Lev 4:2) that the phrase *unintentional sin* "refers to sins that were committed by mistake or done not knowing that the particular act was sinful."[4]

Numbers 15: Defiantly Intentional Sin Is Unforgivable

Numbers 15 discusses various offerings connected to the sacrificial system in the Mosaic law. Starting in verse 22, the topic of unintentional sin begins. Verses 22–29 summarize the laws discussed in Leviticus 4–5. Verse 30 turns to a related but different issue: defiantly intentional sin.[5] Some translations

---

[2] Sklar, "Sin and Atonement," 470.
[3] Sklar, "Sin and Atonement," 481n35. Leviticus 19:20–22 also discusses an intentional sin where the offending person can receive forgiveness with the appropriate offering. Note that Jacob Milgrom, *Leviticus 23–27*, Anchor Bible (New York: Doubleday, 2001), 2449, says that the "high-handed" or defiantly intentional sin described in Numbers 15 becomes reduced to unintentional when the sinner repents. For a reply, see Frank Crüsemann, *The Torah: Theology and Social History of Old Testament Law*, trans. Allan W. Mahnke (Minneapolis: Fortress, 1996), 318.
[4] NET Bible, note on Lev 4:2.
[5] While we understand three distinct categories for these sins, to explore an overview of competing interpretations, see Roy Gane, "Numbers 15:22–31 and the Spectrum of Moral Faults," in *Inicios, paradigmas y fundamentos: Estudios teologicos y exegeticos en el Pentateuco*, ed. Gerald Klingbeil, River Plate Adventist University Monograph Series in Biblical and Theological Studies 1 (Libertador San Martin, Entre Rios, Argentina: Editorial Universidad Adventista del Plata, 2004), 150–54.

keep the idiom from the Hebrew: sin with "a high hand" (*yad ramah*; ESV). Roy Gane defines defiant intentional sin as "disloyalty toward God and rebellious affront against his authority and covenant."[6] The defiance must be understood as in relation to God, whether it be committed publicly or not. If the text of Numbers 15 supports these definitions, it would be valid to view defiantly intentional, simply intentional, and unintentional sins differently.

Numbers 15:31 explains the consequence of defiantly intentional sin: "He will certainly be cut off . . .; his guilt remains on him." This is immediately followed with a narrative about a man gathering wood on the Sabbath. Connecting Old Testament narratives with the law prescribed in the context is helpful in interpreting that narrative and the law. It appears that the reason this narrative is placed right after the punishment for defiantly intentional sin is to provide an example of this type of sin.[7] There was no sacrifice for defiantly intentional sin in the Mosaic law. The man gathering wood was put to death. Jay Sklar concludes that a defiantly intentional sinner is "one who has completely rejected the covenant Lord himself. In short, it is the defiant sin of an apostate that is in view, sin for which no sacrificial atonement is possible."[8]

There are three categories for sin: unintentional sin (which is forgivable), simply intentional sin (which is forgivable), and defiantly intentional sin (which is unforgivable). The difference between simply intentional sin and defiantly intentional sin is an issue of attitude and the heart. It is not just the action that is committed, but the attitude and disposition of the sinner. Defiantly intentional sin is committed by someone who has rejected the covenant with God.[9]

Much of the sacrificial system was built upon the sins committed being unintentional. But unintentional and simply intentional (nondefiant) sins are dealt with in a very similar way. It is defiantly intentional sin that is different. Part of the reason for the sacrifices in the Mosaic law was to teach the Israelites about the seriousness of their sin. All three categories of sin were viewed as very serious offenses against a holy God, causing a rupture in relationship. It is valid to recognize the differences between these categories of sin, but nothing in the text validates viewing any category as dismissible.

---

[6]   Gane, "Numbers 15:22–31 and the Spectrum of Moral Faults," 155.

[7]   See Gane, "Numbers 15:22–31 and the Spectrum of Moral Faults," 156, who concludes: "This linkage between narrative and law reflects the fact that sins are not abstract theological constructs, but sad stories within relational contexts."

[8]   Sklar, "Sin and Atonement," 476.

[9]   Compare Lev 19:20–22 with Num 25:6–8 to see an example of this.

The Spectrum of Moral Faults[10]

Category	Unintentional		Simply Intentional	Defiantly Intentional
Description	Aware of the law, unaware they are breaking it	Unaware of the law and unaware their actions are wrong	Sin with knowledge that they are sinning	Open, bold rebellion against God's authority and the covenant
Forgiveness	Forgiveness through sacrifice		Forgiveness through sacrifice	No forgiveness through sacrifice

1 Samuel 14: An Example of Unintentional Sin

First Samuel 14 begins by explaining a battle that the Lord won for Israel. Using Jonathan, the Lord handed the Philistines over to Saul and his army. At verse 24, the story takes a fascinating turn. The Israelite troops were "worn out" because Saul had placed them under an oath: any man who ate food before evening was cursed. When the troops went into the forest, there was honey flowing on the ground, but none of them ate it because of the oath. Jonathan, however, "had not heard his father make the troops swear the oath" (v. 27), and he ate some honey. After the troops sinned by eating meat with blood still in it, and Saul made an altar and had animals sacrificed to atone for their sin (vv. 32–35), Saul decided he wanted to attack the Philistines and finish them off. The priest insisted that they consult God first. Saul inquired, but God did not answer. Therefore, Saul concluded that there must have been a sin that caused God not to answer. Saul declared that whoever sinned, even if it was his own son, that person must die (v. 39). Through casting lots, God selected Jonathan as the guilty individual. Jonathan admitted that he had eaten honey. Saul was ready to kill Jonathan, but the people convinced Saul not to kill him. So Saul did not pursue the Philistines.

Interestingly, Jonathan initially defended his action of eating honey (vv. 29–30) by saying that eating the honey would be helpful for the troops and they could have done much better in the battle with the energy given by the

---

10   Title taken from Gane's article "Spectrum of Moral Faults."

honey. But notice Jonathan's response when confronted: he quickly admitted to the action and then, in an expression of being contrite, humble, and repentant, said, "I am ready to die!" (v. 43). He took ownership for his sin.

The main point to take away from this story regarding unintentional sin is that God himself viewed the *sin* (v. 38) as being so serious that he did not respond to King Saul. This is an extreme example of "unintentional," as Jonathan could not have known that what he was doing was wrong. Yet God himself still held Israel accountable for the sin, though it was unintentional. God takes unintentional sin very seriously.

What about the New Testament?

There does not seem to be much discussion about intentional and unintentional sin in the New Testament. That does not mean the distinction is invalid, however. One of the clearest statements regarding unintentional sin was made by Peter in Acts 3:13–19.[11]

After God uses Peter to heal a crippled man at the Beautiful Gate, a crowd gathers. Peter decides that this is a great opportunity to preach, saying that they "denied the Holy and Righteous One and asked to have a murderer released to" them (v. 14). In verse 17, Peter declares, "I know that you acted in ignorance, just as your leaders also did." In other words, their sin was unintentional. Then Peter explains how they should respond: "repent and turn back, so that your sins may be wiped out" (v. 19). Unintentional sin continues to be a valid category, but it is never dismissed as inconsequential. Denny Burk concluded: "They are not excused by their ignorance."[12]

Application

The Bible does distinguish between defiantly intentional, simply intentional, and unintentional sin, in both the Old and New Testaments.[13] Unintentional sins do appear to be less significant, as the punishment for them was less severe than the punishment for defiantly intentional sin. However, they are still considered sin and therefore still significant. It appears that simply inten-

---

[11] Another possible passage, which has text critical issues, is Luke 23:34. See Denny Burk, "Is It Sin if It's Unintentional?" *Denny Burk: A Commentary on Theology, Politics, and Culture* (blog), February 4, 2010, http://www.dennyburk.com/is-it-sin-if-it%E2%80%99s-unintentional.

[12] Burk, "Is It Sin?"

[13] Possible New Testament references to defiantly intentional sin include Matt 12:22–32; Mark 3:22–30; Heb 6:4–8; 10:26–31; and 12:25–29.

tional sins and unintentional sins are more closely related to each other than defiantly intentional sins.

Just as God responds to unintentional sin differently than defiantly intentional sin, so should we. If someone intentionally sins against you, that is going to be a much more significant offense and more difficult to deal with emotionally. Forgiveness is still required when the offender repents, but you may find it difficult to forgive. If someone sins unintentionally against you, forgiving the offender is much easier. All you should need to hear is that the person is sorry and asks for forgiveness. Motives are important in relationships—both vertical and horizontal.

But what if I am sinned against, it was unintentional, and the person does not apologize, does not repent, and simply brushes it off as excusable because it was unintentional? I suggest that if a sin was unintentional and you point out the sin to the offender, you will likely get an immediate contrite response. If someone is not immediately contrite, the offense probably was not unintentional.

Denny Burk notes that the knowledge that we "commit unintentional sins should cause us to be humble in our relationships with others." His next comments are very insightful: "How many of us try to justify bad behavior with our spouses and friends on the basis of it being unintentional. '*I didn't mean to do it, so you shouldn't be hurt.*' Oftentimes, words like that reveal the very insensitivity that led to the *unintentional* sin. This is not to say that there's no moral difference between intentional sins and . . . unintentional ones. There is. It's just that in either case there is still an offense that must be dealt with."[14]

Annotated Bibliography

ARTICLES
Sklar, Jay. "Sin and Atonement: Lessons from the Pentateuch." *Bulletin for Biblical Research* 22 no. 4 (2012): 467–91. Sklar's article is extremely helpful in grasping the three categories of sin in the Mosaic law.
Gane, Roy. "Numbers 15:22–31 and the Spectrum of Moral Faults." In *Inicios, paradigmas y fundamentos: Estudios teologicos y exegeticos en el Pentateuco*, ed. Gerald Klingbeil, River Plate Adventist University Monograph Series in Biblical and Theological Studies 1. Libertador San Martin, Entre Rios, Argentina: Editorial Universidad Adventista del Plata, 2004. Gane helps to distinguish between defiantly intentional sins and simply intentional sins, providing various interpretations and critiques.

---

[14]   Burk, "Is It Sin?"

WEBSITES

Burk, Denny. "Is It Sin if It's Unintentional?" *Denny Burk: A Commentary on Theology, Politics, and Culture* (blog). February 4, 2010. http://www.dennyburk.com/is-it-sin-if-it%E2%80%99s-unintentional. Burk provides a short explanation of the seriousness of unintentional sin with some helpful applications.

Pierre, Jeremy. "Involuntary Sins." *Ligonier Ministries. Tabletalk.* June 1, 2016. https://www.ligonier.org/learn/articles/involuntary-sins. Pierre gives a brief explanation of unintentional/involuntary sins and explains how we should respond when we realize we have involuntarily sinned.

___

CHAPTER 10

The Mosaic Food Laws Were about Healthy Living
Leviticus 11

The Legendary Teaching on Clean and Unclean Foods

The primary purpose of the Mosaic laws distinguishing clean and unclean foods in Leviticus 11 and Deuteronomy 14 was to promote good health and hygiene for the people of Israel. Clean animals were those less likely to transmit diseases, while unclean animals were those that transmitted bacteria and other pathogens. For example, pork tended to transmit trichinosis, and shellfish were usually bottom-feeders and scavengers that carried more parasites than free-swimming fish.

The health benefits of the Mosaic food regulations extended to other purity laws in the Torah. For example, the requirement that the person with a skin disease live outside the camp (Lev 13:46) taught the concept of contagion. The requirement that soldiers cover their excrement in the camp (Deut 23:13) revealed an advanced understanding of sanitation that enabled Israel to be free from diseases like cholera, typhoid, and dysentery. The hygienic benefits of the purity laws demonstrate their divine origin, and ignoring the prohibitions against unclean foods, even today, could prove detrimental to one's physical health.[1]

---

[1]   One Christian blogger writes, "God clearly wants what is best for all the inhabitants of the earth—both man and creature as well as for the earth itself. These are all part of His creation. The laws are simple, rational and affirmed by modern science. God truly knows what is best and indicated this long before mankind was able to investigate disease-causing microorganisms, the life cycles of parasites or issues of environmental concern. God revealed principles to our ancient forefathers that would protect all that He made if we would be willing to follow the rules." See Susan Patterson, "God's Dietary Laws: Are They for Today?" *Off the Grid News,* accessed April 24, 2018, https://www.offthegridnews.com/off-grid-foods/gods-dietary-laws-are-they-for-today.

Countering the Legendary Teaching

The Old Testament never gives the preservation of health as the reason for the food and purity laws. Even with the laws that had potential health benefits, none of them mention good health as the motive for obedience. The express purpose of the Mosaic food laws was to remind Israel of their special status as the Lord's chosen people and also to remind the people of their need to maintain ceremonial purity as they lived constantly in the Lord's presence (Lev 11:43–45). Distinguishing between clean and unclean animals would recall how God had graciously chosen Israel from among the nations to be his separate and holy people; Israel as the chosen people would have to make those same kinds of distinctions in their diet.[2] Any health benefits of these food laws were secondary to their central purpose.

Various peoples in the ancient Near East distinguished between clean and unclean foods, but the animals belonging to these categories varied from people to people. For example, the camel was unclean in Israel but a delicacy among Arab peoples. The categories would likely have remained consistent if health issues were the focal point.[3] Health concerns would not necessarily apply to the unclean animals in the Mosaic law.[4] Pork was part of the diet of the peoples around Israel, and proper cooking of the meat removed the threat of trichinosis. There were potential health risks associated with clean animals as well. The ruminants of cud-chewing animals are hosts for parasites and bacteria.[5] Poisonous plants were also not included among the unclean foods, a significant omission if the regulations were for preserving health.[6] The laws teach nothing concerning contaminated drinking water, a major cause of the spread of disease.[7]

Israel's Special Status as God's Chosen People

In discussing how observance of the Mosaic food laws helped to teach and reflect Israel's unique status as God's chosen people, sociologist Mary Douglas

---

[2]   Allen P. Ross, *Holiness to the Lord: A Guide to the Exposition of the Book of Leviticus* (Grand Rapids: Baker Academic, 2002), 254.

[3]   Gordon J. Wenham, "The Theology of Unclean Food," *Evangelical Quarterly* 53 (1981): 6.

[4]   Wenham, "The Theology of Unclean Food," 6–7.

[5]   Joe M. Sprinkle, "The Rationale of the Laws of Clean and Unclean in the Old Testament," *Journal of the Evangelical Theological Society* 43 (2000): 647.

[6]   Sprinkle, "The Rationale of the Laws," 647.

[7]   Thomas D. S. Key and Robert M. Allen, "The Levitical Dietary Laws in Light of Modern Science," *Journal of the American Scientific Affiliation* 26 (1974): 63a.

has suggested that clean animals were those that in their particular spheres (land, air, and water) represented what was whole.[8] Clean animals conformed to the norm for the various spheres in their characteristics and forms of motion. Cud-chewing animals with hooves were the norm for land animals, and fish with fins and scales were the norm for water creatures. This symbolism taught Israel that the Lord was the source of life and wholeness and that they were to reflect his perfection as his people even in their diet. Unclean animals that were scavengers or that fed on carrion were possibly prohibited because of their associations with death, which was antithetical to Israel's relationship with the living God.

The provision in Deut 14:21 that the Israelites were not to eat the meat of any animal that had died of natural causes but they could give these animals to resident aliens or sell them to foreigners reflects that the observance of these laws was specifically for Israel. If hygiene was the major issue, then the Lord was unconcerned with the health of non-Israelites. This passage suggests that these food laws were not something that Israel was to pass on to other peoples.

The Presence of God and Ceremonial Purity

The common cultural conception of ceremonial purity in the ancient Near East was the Lord's way of teaching Israel both the blessings and responsibilities of living in his presence. The Lord required the priests and people to constantly distinguish between the holy and the common and the clean and the unclean as a way of teaching that every part of their lives was sacred to God (Lev 10:10; 11:44–45). The Lord required ceremonial purity of his people as they lived before him and came into his presence because of his actual physical presence among them. Richard Averbeck explains, "God was physically present with ancient Israel in the tabernacle; therefore, physical purity laws were important for the proper maintenance of the Lord's physical presence in their midst" (Exod 25:8; 2 Chr 34:8).[9] Something more important than hygiene was at stake in the observance of the purity laws.

Becoming ceremonially unclean in most cases did not involve doing something that was morally wrong, and all Israelites would have become unclean at some point through normal daily activities, such as having sexual

---

[8]   Mary Douglas, *Purity and Danger: An Analysis of Concepts of Purity and Taboo* (London: Routledge & Kegan Paul, 1966).

[9]   Richard E. Averbeck, "Clean and Unclean," in *New International Dictionary of Old Testament Theology and Exegesis*, ed. W. A. VanGemeren (Grand Rapids: Zondervan, 1997), 4:478.

relations, giving birth, or coming in contact with a corpse. Allen Ross clarifies that "when defilement was the reason for someone being unclean, then no sin was involved and so no forgiveness was required."[10] Nevertheless, the uncleanness had to be remedied in order for anyone appearing before the Lord at the sanctuary. Anyone who appeared before the Lord in an unclean state would die (Lev 15:31). One of the specific purposes of the Day of Atonement rituals was to purge the sanctuary of the uncleanness accumulated throughout the year so that Israel could continue to live in God's presence (Lev 16:16–19). The purity required of Israel was a religious issue, not one of hygienic cleanness.

Other supposed "health laws" had a spiritual or worship focus as well. Israel was not to eat animal fat, not in order to lower their cholesterol, but because the fat parts of the animal belonged to the Lord in sacrifice (Lev 3:16–17; 7:23–25). The Israelites were not to eat meat with blood in order to show respect for life (Lev 3:17; 17:10–14). They were to remedy skin rashes (Leviticus 13–14) and practice cleansing after coming in contact with a corpse (Numbers 19) as a means of preserving ritual purity. The prohibition of sex during menstruation was also a purity issue related to exposing the source of blood (Lev 18:19; 20:18). The people were to remove human excrement from the camp to prevent indecency that would be repulsive to the Lord as he walked among them (Deut 23:12–14).

"None of These Diseases"

The promise in Exod 15:26 that if Israel obeyed his commands the Lord would not inflict upon Israel any of the illnesses ("none of these diseases" KJV) he had inflicted on the Egyptians is not a promise related to specific laws that might have built-in health benefits for Israel; rather, it was connected to Israel's obedience to the Mosaic law as a whole. The Mosaic covenant stipulated that Israel would enjoy the blessings of long life and prosperity in the land if they kept the Lord's commands (Deut 4:40; 5:29–33; 6:1–3); it also warned of diseases and plagues that the Lord would bring against his disobedient people as covenant curses (see Lev 26:16, 21; Deut 28:22, 27, 35). The point of Exod 15:26 is that the obedient people of Israel would not have to fear the Lord afflicting them with plagues like the ones he had sent against the Egyptians. At various times in Israel's wilderness wanderings, disobedience

---

[10]   Ross, *Holiness to the Lord*, 244.

or rebellion against the Lord brought deadly plagues and maladies (Num 11:31–33; 21:4–9; 25:8–9).

The Setting Aside of Food Laws in the New Testament

From a canonical perspective, the most convincing reason that the food laws were not designed for health reasons is that they are set aside in the New Testament. When Jesus declared that what defiled a man was not food that entered his body but rather the evil thoughts of the heart, he was in effect cleansing all foods and rendering the distinctions between clean and unclean foods obsolete (Mark 7:14–23). Even though the primary point of Peter's vision of the sheet with clean and unclean animals was to teach him that all people were clean, the Lord's command to "kill and eat" the various animals also indicated the abolishment of the Mosaic food laws (Acts 10:9–16). The dietary laws in the Torah, along with circumcision and Sabbath observance, were the key boundary markers distinguishing Jew and Gentile, but maintaining Israel's distinct identity was no longer necessary under the new covenant because Jew and Gentile together now formed the people of God (Gal 3:28; Eph 2:11–21). The key pronouncement of the Jerusalem Council in Acts 15 was that Gentiles did not need to adopt a Torah-observant lifestyle in order to belong to God's people. The sacrificial death of Jesus for sin also provided an inward spiritual cleansing that transcended the ceremonial cleanness secured by the Mosaic purity laws (Heb 9:14). If physical health was the primary or even a major concern in the diet and purity laws of the Torah, it is hard to explain why God would remove this protection from his people. As Roy Gane has observed, "If God commanded the Israelites to do something for the sake of their health, it would make sense for us to observe that law for the same reason because their bodies function the same as ours."[11]

Application

Through his death for sinners, Jesus became the mediator of a new and better covenant. Christians are no longer under the Mosaic law. The food and purity laws served an important function in preparing for the coming of Messiah, but these laws reached their fulfillment in Christ and are no longer binding

---

[11]   Roy Gane, *Leviticus and Numbers*, New International Version Application Commentary (Grand Rapids: Zondervan, 2011), 210.

on believers today. At the same time, the Mosaic food and purity laws remind Christians of God's call to live holy lives as his chosen people (1 Pet 1:15–16) and to be separate and distinct from the world around them (1 John 2:15–16). Paul in 2 Cor 6:17 appears to allude to Leviticus 11 when exhorting believers not to "touch" unclean things as a way of encouraging the avoidance of sinful behavior.[12] Followers of Jesus no longer identify themselves as God's people by external purity but rather through a lifestyle of reflecting God's character to others that comes from an internal transformation of the heart. The food and purity laws covered all of life, and followers of Jesus are to live out their calling by reflecting God's holiness in every part of their lives as well.

Annotated Bibliography

BOOKS

McMillen, S. I., and David Stern. *None of These Diseases: The Bible's Health Secrets for the 21st Century*. 3rd ed. Grand Rapids: Revell, 2000. Updated version of a work that has argued for the health and hygiene rationale of the Mosaic food laws.

COMMENTARIES

Rooker, Mark F. *Leviticus*. New American Commentary. Nashville: Broadman & Holman, 2000. Scholarly, evangelical commentary with helpful discussion of Leviticus 11 that is accessible for the general reader.

WEBSITES

Key, Thomas D. S., and Robert M. Allen. "The Levitical Dietary Laws in Light of Modern Science," *Journal of the American Scientific Affiliation* 26 (1974): 61–64. Accessed July 2, 2017. https://faculty.gordon.edu/hu/bi/ted_hildebrandt/otesources/03-leviticus/text/articles/key-levdietary61a-asa.pdf. Examines the contribution of medical science to our understanding of the clean and unclean food laws.

Wenham, Gordon J. "The Theology of Unclean Foods." *Evangelical Quarterly* 53 (1981): 6–15. Accessed July 3, 2017. https://biblicalstudies.org.uk/pdf/eq/unclean-food_wenham.pdf. Analyzes the various views on clean and unclean foods with helpful explanation of the relevance of these laws in light of the New Testament.

---

[12]   Mark F. Rooker, *Leviticus*, New American Commentary (Nashville: Broadman & Holman, 2000), 181.

CHAPTER 11

———

The High Priest Wore a Rope
around His Ankle on the Day of Atonement
Leviticus 16

The Legendary Teaching on the High Priest
Wearing a Rope around His Ankle

Israel's high priest tied a rope around his ankle when he went into the holy of holies on the Day of Atonement (Yom Kippur) so that his body could be dragged out if he were struck down for violating the Lord's instructions when carrying out his duties on this sacred day. The rope was necessary because no other individual was allowed to enter the holy of holies, and even the high priest himself entered there only this one day of the year. The high priest also wore bells on his robes that indicated his movement in the sanctuary. If these bells stopped tinkling, the rope could be gently tugged to make sure that the high priest was still alive.

Countering the Legendary Teaching

The practice of Israel's high priest wearing a rope around his ankle as he entered within the holy of holies makes for an interesting sermon illustration but is never referred to in the Old Testament. This idea is based on a faulty understanding of why Exod 28:35 directs the high priest to wear bells on the hem of his robe[1] and further conflicts with instructions given in Leviticus 16

---

[1]   A note on Exod 28:35 from *The NIV Study Bible* (129) reads: "According to Jewish tradition, the end of a length of rope was tied to the high priest's ankle and the other end remained outside the tabernacle. If the bells on his robe stopped tinkling while he was in the Holy Place, the assumption that he had died could be tested by gently pulling on the rope."

on how the high priest was to dress when entering the holy of holies on the Day of Atonement. The custom of the high priest wearing a rope around his ankle is also never mentioned in any extant literature from the Second Temple period, including the Dead Sea Scrolls, the Apocrypha, the Jewish Pseudepigrapha, or the writings of the historian Josephus. The first known mention of this custom does not appear until the thirteenth century AD in a mystical commentary on the Torah called Zohar. In a section on the Day of Atonement, the commentary reads, "Rabbi Yitzchak said, 'A chain was tied to the feet of the High Priest, when he entered THE HOLY OF HOLIES, so that if he dies there they will take him out, SINCE IT IS FORBIDDEN TO ENTER THERE.'"[2]

When studying Jewish backgrounds for Bible study, it is always necessary to carefully distinguish between the beliefs and practices of biblical times and later legends or mishnaic and talmudic Judaism from the medieval period. The Mishnah mentions that some priests from the Second Temple period did die on the Day of Atonement (Yoma 8b–9a, 18a) but says nothing about the high priest wearing a rope in the event of his death.[3] Rabbinic teaching also suggests that individuals were likely granted exceptions to enter forbidden areas like the holy places in the temple normally restricted to priests for the purpose of construction or the removal of impurity (which would include the removal of a dead body).[4] The allowance of these types of exemptions also suggests that the high priest wearing the rope as a safeguard was both unknown and unnecessary.

Priestly Service and Deathly Danger

Being in the presence of a holy God was dangerous duty, and death was always a real possibility for the Israelite priests serving at the sanctuary (see Exod 20:18–19; 28:35, 43; 30:20–21). Roy Gane compares entering God's presence to coming close to a nuclear reactor.[5] We read in Leviticus 10 that Aaron's sons Nadab and Abihu even died on the day of the tabernacle's inauguration as the celebration of the Lord taking up residence in the sanctuary quickly turned into tragedy. After fire had come from the Lord to consume

---

[2]   For full translation of this paragraph, see http://www.yeshshem.com/zohar-emor-section-34.htm.

[3]   Ari Zivotofsky, "Tzarich Iyun: The Kohen Gadol's Rope," *Jewish Action*, Fall 2009, https://www.ou.org/torah/machshava/tzarich-iyun/tzarich_iyun_the_kohen_gadols_rope/.

[4]   Zivotofsky, "Tzarich Iyun."

[5]   Roy Gane, *Leviticus and Numbers*, New International Version Application Commentary (Grand Rapids: Zondervan, 2004), 188.

the initial sacrifices and offerings (9:23–24), fire consumed the two priests after they had "presented unauthorized fire before the Lord (10:1)."[6]

Nadab and Abihu were in the sacred precincts of the tabernacle when the Lord struck them dead, but their exact location is unclear. The expression "front of the sanctuary" in Lev 10:4 is imprecise, but the fact that the fire "came out" (v. 1, NIV) to consume them and that they are last seen in the courtyard of the tabernacle (9:18–20) suggests that they were not within the actual tent of the tabernacle in either the holy place or holy of holies.[7] Their cousins were sent to retrieve their bodies and to carry them "outside the camp" like the discarded portions of animal sacrifices. The high priest was to have no contact with a dead body (Lev 21:11), and other priests were not allowed to have contact with a corpse with the exception of a close relative (21:1–4). The priests were likely not allowed to remove the bodies of Nadab and Abihu because of their special consecration at the time of the tabernacle's inauguration.

The Rope Legend and the Day of Atonement

According to the legend, the rope around the leg of the high priest on the Day of Atonement provided for the safe removal of the high priest in case the Lord might strike him dead within the holy of holies. Even after the tragic deaths of Nadab and Abihu, however, the Lord gives no special instructions concerning precautions in the event of a priest's death within the sanctuary in Leviticus 10 or in the directives concerning the Day of Atonement in Leviticus 16. This omission is especially significant in that Lev 16:1 explicitly states that the death of Aaron's sons provided the occasion for the Lord's instructions concerning the Day of Atonement. If there was ever a time when the Lord might have given detailed instruction on what to do in case the priest died within the tent, this would have been it.

---

[6]   The exact nature of the young priests' transgression is unclear and beyond the scope of this chapter. The most likely possibilities are that they (1) offered incense using coals from a different fire ("strange fire") from the one that the Lord had just lit on the outer altar (Lev 16:12; Num 16:46); (2) offered incense that did not conform to the recipe given by the Lord (Exod 30:9); or (3) attempted to penetrate into the presence of God (note the references to coming "before the LORD" with fire and censors in Lev 10:1; 16:12). The prohibition against priests drinking intoxicating beverages in Lev 10:8 also suggests that Nadab and Abihu were likely drunk (perhaps from the celebration of the day) when they died. Gary Anderson argues that the text is purposely ambiguous as a reminder of the Lord's "utter transcendence" and the fact that he was not subject to human manipulation. See Gary Anderson, *Christian Doctrine and the Old Testament: Theology in the Service of Biblical Exegesis* (Grand Rapids: Baker Academic, 2017), 3–22.

[7]   Gane, *Leviticus and Numbers*, 189. See also Jacob Milgrom, *Leviticus 1–16*, Anchor Bible (New Haven: Yale University, 1998), 608.

The Day of Atonement was fraught with danger for the high priest as he would enter into the presence of the Lord within the holy of holies. The high priest entered this sacred area with the censor of burning coals so that the smoke would prevent him from seeing the fullness of God's glory (Lev 16:12–13). There was a sin/purification offering for both the priests and the people. The high priest would enter the holy of holies two separate times to sprinkle the blood of the two offerings (bull and goat) on the atonement lid of the ark of the covenant. Other rites, including the presentation of burnt offerings and the release of a live goat into the wilderness, were part of the Day of Atonement rituals that cleansed the sanctuary and removed Israel's sin and defilement from the camp.

The High Priest's Garments

The rope legend associated with the high priest and the Day of Atonement also reflects a misunderstanding of the priest's attire when he entered the holy of holies. The high priest did not wear his normal vestments when entering the holy of holies to present the blood of the sacrifices, which means that he was not wearing the bells that were supposed to indicate if he had died and needed to be removed by the rope tied around his ankle.

The beautiful and elaborate vestments of the high priest and the expensive materials they were made from reflected the dignity and holiness of the office. The hem of the high priest's robe was embroidered with pomegranates made of colored yarn and golden bells that were affixed to the robe. The bells would make a tinkling sound as the high priest carried out his duties inside the holy place. Various proposals have been offered for the purpose of the bells, but Exod 28:35 highlights that these bells are to be worn "before the LORD." More likely than indicating that the priest remained alive is the suggestion that the wearing of these bells reflects an ancient convention concerning the entry of a subject into a royal palace. The bells notified the Lord as king that the priest had entered into his presence. Nahum Sarna comments, "Just as one should not appear abruptly and unceremoniously before royalty, so the delicate sounds of the bell signal one's presence and intention."[8] The constant sounding of the bells would also remind the Lord that the priest was appearing before him as Israel's representative. The priest would die if his

---

[8] Nahum M. Sarna, *Exodus*, Jewish Publication Society Torah Commentary (Philadelphia: Jewish Publication Society, 1991), 183.

garments did not conform to the Lord's instructions. The purpose statement "so that he does not die" in Exod 28:35 refers to all the priestly vestments and not just the wearing of the bells.

When appearing before the Lord on the Day of Atonement, however, the high priest wore different clothing, donning a shirt, shorts, sash, and turban all made of linen. Gordon Wenham explains that in God's presence, "even the high priest is stripped of all honor; he becomes simply the servant of the King of kings, whose true status is portrayed in the simplicity of his dress."[9] The angels of heaven who are in the presence of God are also dressed in linen, symbolizing their purity and holiness (Ezek 9:2–3; 10:2; Dan 10:5–6). The legend taught that the priests outside the most holy place would pull on the rope if the bells on the robe stopped ringing, but the high priest actually did not even enter the holy of holies wearing the robe with the bells attached to it.

Application

The Lord blessed Israel with his continual presence at the tabernacle and temple, but direct access into God's presence was limited to the high priest on the Day of Atonement. The Day of Atonement was necessary every year so that the people could continue to live in God's presence. Any person who came into God's presence in an unclean state or tainted by sin was liable to death, and even Aaron's sons died while serving as priests because they approached God improperly. The rituals and sacrifices associated with the Day of Atonement were only shadows of the reality that is found in Christ. When he triumphed over death on the cross, the veil to the holy of holies was rent from top to bottom, signifying that access into God's presence was available to all who trusted in his atoning sacrifice for the forgiveness of their sins. Because of his perfect sacrifice, believers have direct access into the presence of God. The believer is no longer under the ritual requirements associated with entrance into the presence of God, but the enjoyment of God's presence still demands a lifestyle of holiness and obedience. The legend of the rope around the ankle may be repeated in an attempt to teach the fear of the Lord, a fully biblical concept. This concept, however, appears in other biblical texts (see Deut 4:24; Prov 1:7; Heb 12:14, 29). An appropriate understanding of

---

[9]   Gordon J. Wenham, *The Book of Leviticus*, New International Commentary on the Old Testament (Grand Rapids: Eerdmans, 1979), 230.

the fear of the Lord reminds us to reverence and honor the Lord in all that we do and to never presume upon his gracious presence in our lives.

Annotated Bibliography

COMMENTARIES

Gane, Roy. *Leviticus and Numbers*. New International Version Application Commentary. Grand Rapids: Zondervan, 2004. Focuses on the exposition and application of the text and has helpful discussions of both Leviticus 10 and 16.

Wenham, Gordon J. *Leviticus*. New International Commentary on the Old Testament. Grand Rapids: Eerdmans, 1979. Scholarly evangelical commentary with a helpful discussion of priestly garments and the Day of Atonement.

WEBSITES

Bolen, Todd. "The Rope around the High Priest's Ankle." January 13, 2009. http://blog. bibleplaces.com/2009/01/that-rope-around-high-priests-ankle.html. Concise argument of the reasons to view the rope around the ankle as legendary.

Zivotofsky, Ari. "Tzarich Iyun: The Kohen Gadol's Rope." *Orthodox Union*. From *Jewish Action*, Fall 2009. https://www.ou.org/torah/machshava/tzarich-iyun/tzarich_iyun_the_kohen_gadols_rope/. Rabbi demonstrates the legendary nature of the rope around the ankle practice for the Israelite high priest.

CHAPTER 12

———

Old Testament Saints Were Saved
by Keeping the Mosaic Law

Leviticus 18:5

The Legendary Teaching on Salvation
by Keeping the Law in the Old Testament

The Old Testament is a book of law; the New Testament is a book of grace. John 1:17 informs us that "the law was given through Moses; grace and truth came through Jesus Christ." Under the old covenant, the means of salvation was different from what it is today. People today are saved by faith in the finished work of Christ, but before Jesus provided atonement for sin through his death on the cross, people were saved by keeping the law God gave them through Moses.[1] As the Lord said, "Keep my statutes and ordinances; a person will live if he does them" (Lev 18:5; compare Ezek 20:11). Eternal life, in the Old Testament, came by keeping the law.

Countering the Legendary Teaching

The belief that salvation was by works and by keeping the Mosaic law in the Old Testament reflects a misunderstanding of the purpose of the law. Yahweh did not reveal the law to Israel in order to create a performance-based way of salvation. The law came only after Yahweh had made Israel his people by

---

[1]   Note the comment on John 1:17 in the *Scofield Reference Bible* that appears to reflect this perspective: "As a dispensation, grace begins with the death and resurrection of Christ (Rom. 3:24–26; 4:24, 25). The point of testing is no longer legal obedience as the condition of salvation, but acceptance or rejection of Christ, with good works as a fruit of salvation."

69

redeeming them out of their slavery in Egypt. When the people arrive at Mount Sinai, the Lord reminds them as a preface to giving his commandments, "You have seen what I did to the Egyptians and how I carried you on eagles' wings and brought you to myself" (Exod 19:4). Christopher Wright explains concerning the sequence of God redeeming and then giving the law to Israel: "The Israelites were not told to keep the law so that God might save them and they could be his people. He already had and they already were. He delivered them and made them his people and then called them to keep his law. Ethical obedience is a response to God's grace, not a means of receiving it."[2]

The fact that the Lord's relationship with Israel under the Mosaic law was based on grace and faith, not works, is further demonstrated by the way in which the Lord made provision for his people when they failed to keep his commandments through the sacrifices that offered atonement for sin. Wright notes that Israel's relationship with the Lord was "founded on his *redeeming* grace" and was "sustained by his *forgiving* grace."[3] The sin and guilt offerings provided atonement for individual sins (Leviticus 5–6), and the sacrificial rituals carried out on the Day of Atonement provided atonement for the nation so that the people of Israel could continue to live in the presence of a holy God (chap. 16). The constant slaughter of animals that occurred at the sanctuary was a reminder of the seriousness of sin. The gracious forgiveness and access into the presence of God provided by the animal sacrifices anticipated the cleansing from sin secured by the perfect sacrifice of Jesus (Heb 10:10–14).

Israel as a nation was the people of Yahweh because of his redeeming grace, and individual Israelites entered into a personal relationship with God by grace through faith in the same way as under the new covenant. The apostle Paul defends the idea of justification by faith from the Old Testament itself, using the example of Abraham who lived before the law (Romans 4) and David who lived under the law (Rom 4:6–8).[4] Genesis 15:6 states, "Abram believed the LORD, and he credited to him as righteousness." This passage does not reflect the moment that Abram entered into a relationship with the Lord, because he had responded in faith to the Lord's promises back in Genesis 12. Nevertheless, Genesis 15 marks the ratification of the covenant between Yahweh and Abraham, and the only thing required of Abraham to

---

[2]   Christopher J. H. Wright, *Old Testament Ethics for the People of God* (Downers Grove, IL: InterVarsity Press, 2004), 28.

[3]   Wright, *Old Testament Ethics*, 29.

[4]   Thomas R. Schreiner, *40 Questions about Christians and Biblical Law* (Grand Rapids: Kregel Academic and Professional, 2010), 29.

be considered a loyal covenant partner is a response of faith to the Lord's gracious initiatives. "Righteousness" in the Old Testament normally refers to moral behavior (see Gen 18:23; Isa 33:15; Ezek 18:5), but here Abraham does not practice righteousness but rather receives a righteousness that is "solely bequeathed by God's gracious declaration."[5]

Like Abraham, the people of Israel respond in faith to the Lord's saving initiatives at the beginning and end of their rescue from Egypt (Exod 4:31; 14:31). The purpose of God's revelation at Mount Sinai is so that the people would believe (Exod 19:9). The Lord's gracious forgiveness of David's sin demonstrates continuity in the means of salvation before and after the giving of the law. The Psalms and the Old Testament prophets further reveal how central faith was to the relationship between God and Israel (see Pss 7:1; 11:1; 107:2; Isa 7:9; Joel 2:32; Hab 2:4).[6] Paul's assertion that one cannot be justified by doing the works of the Law (see Rom 3:20–28; Gal 2:16; 3:10–14) is in line with the teaching of the Old Testament itself. Hebrews 11 also affirms that the exercise of faith was how the Old Testament saints pleased God.[7]

The object of faith for Old Testament saints was not Jesus Christ and his death, burial, and resurrection as the basis of their forgiveness for sin, but rather their faith rested in the person and promises of God as revealed at that time. Allen Ross notes, "It is most improbable that everyone who believed unto salvation consciously believed in the substitutionary death of Jesus Christ, the Son of God."[8] Israel trusted in God's gracious promise of the forgiveness of their sins (Ps 32:1–2), but the idea of a Savior-figure who would die for their sins only begins to emerge with Isaiah's teaching on the suffering Servant (Isa 50:4–9; 52:13–53:12).[9]

The Purpose of the Law: Instructing Israel How to Live

The purpose of the Mosaic law was not to provide a way for Israel to attain salvation but rather to instruct the nation on how to live out its special calling as God's people. The Ten Commandments taught the people their responsi-

---

5   Mathews, *Genesis 11:27–50:26*, 168.

6   Allen P. Ross, "The Biblical Method of Salvation: A Case for Discontinuity," in *Continuity and Discontinuity: Perspectives on the Relationship between the Old and New Testaments: Essays in Honor of S. Lewis Johnson, Jr.*, ed. John S. Feinberg (Westchester, IL: Crossway, 1988), 167.

7   Schreiner, *40 Questions*, 29–30.

8   Ross, "Biblical Method of Salvation," 170.

9   See Daniel I. Block, *For the Glory of God: Recovering a Biblical Theology of Worship* (Grand Rapids: Baker, 2014), 255.

bilities toward God (commands 1–4) and their responsibilities toward one another (commands 5–10). The law called for exclusive worship of Yahweh and provided instruction for the proper sanctuary, priesthood, and rituals that would reflect the Lord's holiness and distinguish Israel from the pagan peoples around them. The law informed the people of God's standards for moral and sexual purity so that they would be faithful to their marriage commitments and avoid the moral corruption that had caused the land itself to vomit out the Canaanites (Leviticus 18). Observance of the Mosaic law would also provide for the practice of legal and social justice in the land. The law commanded the Israelites to practice generosity toward the poor (Deut 15:7–11) and not to take advantage of the poor or deny them justice (Exod 23:6; Deut 24:15–18). Keeping the law would enable Israel to have a missionary presence among the nations. Israel would serve as a priestly nation mediating the presence of God to other nations (Exod 19:5–6). Israel's obedience to the Lord's commands would lead the nations to inquire concerning the source of Israel's righteous law and their unparalleled blessing (Deut 4:6–8).

The Demand for Obedience in the Old and New Covenants

The command in Lev 18:5 for the people to "do this and live" set forth a strict standard of obedience to the Mosaic covenant as the basis for Israel's blessing or cursing as God's people. The life promised in this verse was not eternal life but the covenant blessing of long life in the Promised Land. Punishment for disobedience to the Lord under the Mosaic covenant was often severe. A number of serious violations of the Mosaic law brought the death penalty or the punishment of being "cut off" from the people of Israel by excommunication or direct judgment from God. The entire generation that left Egypt, except Joshua and Caleb, died in the wilderness for various sins and rebellions against the Lord and did not enter the Promised Land. Israel's experience of the covenant curses warned of in Leviticus 26 and Deuteronomy 28 culminated with the destruction of Jerusalem in 586 BC.

In spite of these severe and exacting judgments, the Lord's grace guaranteed the continuation of his covenant relationship with Israel. Exodus 34:6–7 notes that after Israel worshipped the golden calf at Mount Sinai, the Lord revealed himself to be "a compassionate and gracious God, slow to anger and abounding in faithful love and truth, maintaining faithful love and truth." While God also would not "leave the guilty unpunished," his inclination to show grace was greater than his demand for justice. He would punish sin to "the third and fourth generation" but would maintain "faithful love to a thousand generations" by forgiving his people's sins. Even when bringing the judgment of exile upon Israel and Judah, the Lord expressed his abiding love for his people and promised to restore them by healing their apostasy and making a new covenant that would grant forgiveness for past sin and enablement for future obedience (Jer 31:2, 31–34; Hos 14:1–3). God's gracious forgiveness of Israel's sins stands at the center of his relationship with them as his people (see Ps 103:3, 8–12; Mic 7:18–20).

The relationship between faith and works is the same in both Old and New Testaments in that both affirm that obedience to God follows saving faith.[10] Abraham's faith is counted for righteousness, but this faith leads to righteous conduct (Gen 18:19). Deuteronomy teaches that obedience to the Lord's commands would characterize those who knew and loved the Lord (see Deut 6:5–9; 7:9–12; 11:1–3). Echoing Deuteronomy, Jesus teaches that those who love him are those who obey his commands (John 14:15–23). Those who obey are the ones who know God and abide in him (1 John 2:3–6; 3:24). Endurance to the end is a condition of future salvation (Matt 10:22; Rom 11:22; 1 Cor 15:1–2; Col 1:23; Heb 3:5–6). In the book of Revelation, those who "conquer" through their faith and obedience are the ones who receive eternal life (2:7, 11, 17, 26; 3:5, 12, 21; 21:7). Jesus warns that those who refuse to forgive others will not be forgiven by the Father (Matt 6:15). Faith and obedience are often used as "virtual synonyms" (2 Thess 1:8; 1 Pet 4:17; Rev 14:12), and obedience is seen as having faith as its source (Rom 1:5; 16:26).[11] James 2:14–26 teaches that faith without works is dead and cannot save. Believers do not earn their salvation by their works, because God is the One who enables and produces obedience in their lives. They are to "work out [their] own salvation" because God is working in them (Phil 2:12–13).[12]

Application

A godly life is the consequence of salvation and not its cause. The motivation for faithful Israelites to do good works and to serve the Lord was gratitude for his gracious redemption and faithfulness to his covenant promises (see Deut 6:20–25; 11:1–8; 26:1–11; Josh 24:16–18). Believers in the new covenant

---

[10] See Bradley Green, *Covenant and Commandment: Works, Obedience, and Faithfulness in the Christian Life*, New Studies in Biblical Theology (Downers Grove, IL: InterVarsity Press, 2014), 23–39.

[11] Green, *Covenant and Commandment*, 33–34.

[12] Green, *Covenant and Commandment*, 31.

have an even greater motivation to serve the Lord in light of the cross and the sacrifice of Jesus that has secured our forgiveness and salvation. Second Corinthians 5:14 reminds us that it is "the love of Christ" that "compels" us to please God and serve others. In both the Old and New Testaments, those who knew the Lord loved and obeyed him because he had first loved them and established a relationship with them based on grace and forgiveness.

Annotated Bibliography

BOOKS

Green, Bradley. *Covenant and Commandment: Works, Obedience, and Faithfulness in the Christian Life*. New Studies in Biblical Theology. Downers Grove, IL: InterVarsity Press, 2014. Discussion of the relationship between faith and works and how they are related within a covenantal relationship with God in both the Old and New Testaments.

Schreiner, Thomas R. *40 Questions about Christians and Biblical Law*. Grand Rapids: Kregel Academic and Professional, 2010. Helpful discussion clarifying justification by faith in the Old and New Testaments and various issues related to how the Mosaic law applies to believers in the new covenant.

COMMENTARIES

Stuart, Douglas K. *Exodus: An Exegetical and Theological Exposition of Holy Scripture,* New American Commentary. Nashville: Broadman & Holman, 2006. Scholarly evangelical commentary with thorough discussion of role and purpose of the Mosaic law.

WEBSITES

Feinberg, John S. "Salvation in the Old Testament." November 2005. http://www.ntslibrary. com/Salvation%20in%20the%20Old%20Testament.pdf. Scholarly discussion on the topic of salvation in the Old Testament. Reprinted from *Tradition and Testament: Essays in Honor of Charles L. Feinberg* (Chicago: Moody, 1981), 39–77.

CHAPTER 13

———

Using the Mosaic Law to Label Homosexuality as Sinful is Logically Inconsistent
Leviticus 18:22 and 20:13

The Legendary Teaching on Leviticus 18:22 and 20:13

Christians who believe that the prohibition of homosexuality in the book of Leviticus (18:22; 20:13) remains authoritative for the church, but who fail to observe other arcane laws in the Torah, are guilty of arbitrarily picking and choosing which parts of the Mosaic law they view as applicable for today. In a *West Wing* episode titled "The Midterms," President Jed Bartlet unravels the logic of those who view Leviticus as relevant for sexual ethics today by taking on a conservative talk show host who used Leviticus to teach that homosexuality was an "abomination." President Bartlet asks a series of loaded questions:

> "When I burn a bull on the altar as a sacrifice, I know it creates a pleasing odor for the Lord (Lev 1:9). The problem is my neighbors. They claim the odor is not pleasing to them. Should I smite them?
>
> I would like to sell my daughter into slavery, as sanctioned in Exodus 21:7. In this day and age, what do you think would be a fair price for her?"[1]

---

[1]   Quoted from "A Letter to Dr. Laura," David Mikkelson, "The Bartlet Letter," http://www.snopes.com/politics/religion/drlaura.asp. Published March 4, 2004. Updated May 25, 2016.

Countering the Legendary Teaching

President Bartlet expresses a form of what is known as the "shellfish argument," which asserts that the laws in Leviticus dealing with homosexuality are no more relevant to contemporary life than the prohibitions against eating shellfish in Lev 11:10–12. The supposition is that Christians who observe some Mosaic commands while ignoring others are logically inconsistent at best and hypocritical at worst. There is no question that ignorance of what the Bible teaches has often characterized discussions concerning same-sex practice, and many Christians have used the Bible as a weapon to bludgeon or self-righteously condemn others. Nevertheless, the key reason for viewing the prohibitions of homosexuality in Leviticus as having ongoing validity, while the prohibition against eating shellfish does not, is how the New Testament writers themselves applied the Mosaic law. They turned to the Mosaic law as an authoritative moral guide for new covenant believers, and the apostle Paul specifically formulated his opposition to homosexual practice in light of the laws in Leviticus.

The Context of Leviticus 18 and 22

The prohibition against same-sex behavior in Lev 18:22 and 20:13 seems straightforward. Both texts prohibit a man having sexual relations with another man "as with a woman." Nevertheless, revisionist views attempting to affirm same-sex practice have argued that only specific types of homosexual behavior are prohibited in these passages. Because of the reference to the practices of the Canaanites (Lev 18:3) and the subsequent prohibition against child sacrifice to the god Molech (v. 21), some have argued that Leviticus is prohibiting only same-sex practices related to cultic prostitution. Leviticus 18 as a whole, however, is clearly dealing with sexual sins of a more general nature. A specific connection between Molech worship and fertility rites of a sexual nature has not been established. In Leviticus 20, the prohibitions against child sacrifices to Molech (vv. 3–5) and homosexual practice (v. 13) do not appear together as they do in chapter 18. The most likely reason as to why a reference to sacrificing children to Molech is found in Leviticus 18 is that children are the product of the sexual act.[2] The strongest argument against seeing cultic or ritualistic sex in view in Leviticus 18 and 20 is that

---

[2]   See William J. Webb, *Slaves, Women, and Homosexuals: Exploring the Hermeneutics of Cultural Analysis* (Downers Grove, IL: InterVarsity Press, 2001), 197–99.

the term *qadesh* used elsewhere for "male temple/cult prostitute" (see Deut 23:17; 1 Kgs 14:24; 15:12; 22:46; 2 Kgs 23:7; Job 36:14) is not used in these texts.[3] Leviticus 18:22 and 20:13 more generally refer to a male having sexual relations with another male.

Same-Sex Behavior: An Issue of Purity or Ritualistic Taboo?

A second argument seeking to restrict the universality of Lev 18:22 is that the prohibition against same-sex activity is an issue related to boundary markers distinguishing Jews from Gentiles or simply a matter of ceremonial purity or ritualistic taboo. For example, Jacob Milgrom asserts that the prohibition in Lev 18:22 applied only to Jewish males living in the Promised Land. Leviticus 18:3, however, indicts the Egyptians and Canaanites for the practices mentioned in this chapter, and vv. 24–25 states that these practices are the specific reason why God was expelling the Canaanites from the land.[4] Other prohibited behaviors in Leviticus 18 include incest (vv. 6–18), sexual relations with a menstruating woman (v. 19), adultery (v. 20), child sacrifice (v. 21), and bestiality (v. 23). Of these actions, only sexual relations with a woman during her menstrual period would likely reflect a concern with ceremonial purity.

Some have argued for viewing the prohibition against homosexuality as an issue of ceremonial purity or ritualistic taboo on the basis of the characterization of same-sex activity as an abomination/detestable act (*to'ebah*) in both Lev 18:22 and 20:13. This term, however, is used in 18:26, 27, 29, and 30 to refer to all of the prohibited behaviors listed in this chapter, and the term actually indicates the serious nature of the violations in view here. This word specifically refers to something abhorrent and detestable.[5]

The term *to'ebah* does appear in some contexts relating to boundary markers or ceremonial purity. Based on the fact that the term *to'ebah* is connected with the eating of unclean animals (Deut 14:3), remarriage of a divorced woman (Deut 24:4), and the charging of interest on loans (Ezek 18:12), homosexual activist Matthew Vines observes that Christians "accept many Old Testament 'abominations' without controversy."[6] These issues relate to cultural taboos

---

[3]   Contemporary scholarship has also largely rejected the idea of cultic prostitution as part of the rituals associated with pagan fertility cults. For more on the issue, see Richard S. Hess, *Israelite Religions: An Archaeological and Biblical Survey* (Grand Rapids: Baker Academic, 2007), 332–35.

[4]   Jacob Milgrom, *Leviticus 17–22*, Anchor Bible (New York: Doubleday, 2000), 1788–90.

[5]   Rooker, *Leviticus* (see chap. 10, n. 12).

[6]   Matthew Vines, *God and the Gay Christian: The Biblical Case in Support of Same-Sex Relationships* (New York: Convergent Books, 2014), 85.

rather than binding moral laws.[7] Nevertheless, the overwhelming majority of references to "abomination" in the Old Testament are clearly ethical in nature. The term *to'ebah* appears in Leviticus only with reference to sexual sins and child sacrifice. Leviticus employs the synonym *sheqets* ("abhorrent/abhorrent thing") when referring to the eating of unclean animals (11:10–13, 20, 23, 41–43). In Deuteronomy, idolatry and pagan worship practices are "abominations" (*to'ebah*) (7:25–26; 13:14; 17:4; 27:15), as are the gods themselves (32:15–16). Pagan worship practices that are "abominations" include child sacrifice (12:31), prostitution (23:17–18), and occultism (18:9–14). The Lord views dishonest business dealings as an "abomination" (25:13–16).[8]

The word *abomination* appears more than forty times in the book of Ezekiel and refers both to idolatrous practices (e.g., 7:20; 8:9, 13, 15, 17; 16:36; 43:8), as well as to all of the sins that have made Judah guilty before God (9:4; 22:11; 32:16). The word *abomination* appears more than twenty times in Proverbs and has an ethical connotation in every instance (e.g., 3:32; 6:16–19; 8:7; 11:1, 20; 12:22; 15:8–9, 26; 20:10, 23; 21:27; 26:25; 28:9). Far from validating the idea that same-sex activity is simply an issue of ritualistic taboo, the overall usage of the term *to'ebah* strongly supports the argument that the commands in Lev 18:22 and 20:13 are moral in nature.

With the exception of sex with a menstruating woman, the prohibited sexual practices in Leviticus 18 have to do with the crossing of creational boundaries established by God in Genesis 1–3, rather than merely violations of ceremonial purity.[9] These fallen behaviors violate the ideal of Gen 2:24 in which a man is to leave his father and mother and be joined to his wife in a "one flesh" relationship. Same-sex intercourse violates the creational design of complementarity between male and female in the marriage and sexual relationship. The male and female come together as one in order to fulfill the creational mandate to "be fruitful, multiply" (Gen 1:28). God specifically creates the woman to be a "helper corresponding to" the man, so that together they complement and complete each other (Gen 2:18–19), and it is only the bringing together of man and woman that forms the unique one-flesh relationship involved in creational/covenantal marriage (Gen 2:23–25).

---

    [7]   The prohibitions against same-sex behavior in Leviticus would then be no different than Egyptian taboos against eating with foreigners, shepherding, and offering the types of sacrifices offered by the Hebrews (Gen 43:32; 46:34; Exod 8:26).

    [8]   For fuller discussion of this term, see Robert A. J. Gagnon, *The Bible and Homosexual Practice: Texts and Hermeneutics* (Nashville: Abingdon, 2001), 217–20.

    [9]   For this emphasis in Leviticus 18, see Nobuyoshi Kiuchi, *Leviticus*, Apollos Old Testament Commentary (Downers Grove, IL: InterVarsity Press, 2007), 330–38.

The emphasis on creation boundaries in Leviticus 18 further establishes the transcultural and universal nature of all of the prohibitions set forth in this chapter with the exception of verse 19.

The Authoritative Perspective of the New Testament

It is not arbitrary for Christians to believe that certain commands in the Mosaic law should continue to be observed, while others should not, because they are guided in such decisions by the authoritative revelation found in the New Testament. Paul teaches that the believer is no longer under the law of Moses (Rom 8:2; 10:4; Gal 3:25; 5:1, 6; Col 2:13–14). Christians no longer live under the Mosaic covenant and are no longer required to observe the 613 commands that were part of this covenant between God and Israel. The Old Testament food laws are rendered obsolete by the teaching of Jesus in Mark 7:19 and by Peter's vision regarding clean and unclean animals in Acts 10. These kinds of laws relating to ceremonial purity and Jewish boundary markers no longer apply to Christians today. In 1 Cor 7:19, Paul makes the shocking statement, "Circumcision does not matter and uncircumcision does not matter. Keeping God's commands is what matters." It was central to the gospel message that Gentiles did not have to become Jewish proselytes to become followers of Jesus (Acts 15). The book of Hebrews teaches that the Mosaic regulations concerning temple, priesthood, and the sacrificial system are no longer in effect because what they anticipated was fulfilled by Christ's atonement for sin (Heb 7:1–10:18).

At the same time, the Mosaic law as God's Word continues to serve as an authoritative moral guide for the believer today. Vines states concerning the Christian's relationship to the Mosaic law: "Paul said in Romans 7 that the law existed to expose our sin, revealing our need for a Savior. But once our Savior has come, we no longer need the law. We could compare it to the way drivers no longer need road signs once they arrive at a destination."[10] This perspective, however, is significantly at odds with New Testament teaching. Nine of the Ten Commandments are repeated in the New Testament. Much of the Mosaic law's sexual ethic, including the prohibition of same-sex intercourse, is reaffirmed in the New Testament. Paul in his epistles frequently reappropriates the Mosaic law to provide instruction and moral wisdom for the church (see 1 Cor 5:7, 13; 2 Cor 13:1; Eph 6:1–2) and even employs Moses's instruction on not muzzling

---

[10]   Vines, *God and the Gay Christian*, 80.

an ox while treading grain in teaching that the church is to pay its teachers and pastors properly (Deut 25:4; 1 Cor 9:9; 1 Tim 5:18).[11] The book of Leviticus is hardly irrelevant for Christians today. Two key Old Testament commands repeated in the New are for believers to "be holy because I am holy" (1 Pet 1:16) and to "love your neighbor as yourself" (Matt 19:19; 22:39; Mark 12:31; Rom 13:9; Gal 5:14; Jas 2:8), and both of these commands come directly from the book of Leviticus (19:2, 18; 20:7).[12]

With the exception of the prohibition of having sex with a woman during her menstrual period, the New Testament affirms the sexual ethic found in Leviticus. Adultery is prohibited (Matt 5:27–30), incest is viewed as morally unacceptable (1 Cor 5:1–2), and the general prohibition of *porneia* covers all sexual activity outside of God-ordained marriage (Matt 5:32; 15:19; 1 Cor 6:13, 18; Gal 5:19; Col 3:5). As Kevin DeYoung notes, "It would be strange for the prohibition against homosexual practice to be set aside when the rest of the sexual ethic is not, especially considering how the rejection of same-sex behavior is rooted in the created order."[13] Most important, Paul bases his apostolic prohibitions of same-sex intercourse in Rom 1:24–32; 1 Cor 6:9–10; and 1 Tim 1:10 on Levitical law. When Paul speaks of male with male sexual intercourse as a "shameless act" in Rom 1:27, he employs a term (*aschemousunen*) that appears forty-two times in Leviticus 18 and 20 in the Septuagint. When Paul states that "those who practice such things deserve to die" in Rom 1:32, he likely has the death penalty prescribed in Lev 20:13 in view.[14] One of the terms that Paul uses to describe same-sex intercourse in 1 Cor 6:9–10 and 1 Tim 1:10 is *arsenokoitai*. This term does not appear in Greek sources prior to Paul and was perhaps coined by him as a term combining the words *arsenos* and *koimao* that are used in the Greek Old Testament to translate the Hebrew "to lie with a male" (*shakav zakar*) in Lev 18:22 and

---

[11]   For more detailed discussion of the New Testament use of the Mosaic law, see Brian S. Rosner, *Paul and the Law: Keeping the Commandments of God*, New Studies in Biblical Theology (Downers Grove, IL: InterVarsity Press, 2013).

[12]   Kevin DeYoung, *What Does the Bible Really Teach about Homosexuality?* (Wheaton, IL: Crossway, 2015), 43–44.

[13]   DeYoung, *What Does the Bible Really Teach?* 46.

[14]   *New York Times* reporters Jeremy W. Peters and Lizette Alvarez have wrongly asserted that Paul is here calling for "the execution of gays." The people worthy of death in the context of Rom 1:24–32 include those guilty of all the sinful behaviors listed in this section, including slander, envy, disobedience to parents, and a lack of mercy. The death in view here in light of the larger context of Romans 1–3 is the spiritual death and separation from God that is remedied by the gospel of Christ (Rom 1:16). In 1 Cor 5:13, we see a specific passage in which the capital punishment or banishment prescribed by the Old Testament is replaced by excommunication from the church. See Peters and Alvarez, "After Orlando, a Political Divide on Gay Rights Still Stands," *New York Times*, June 16, 2016, http://www.nytimes.com/2016/06/16/us/after-orlando-a-political-divide-on-gay-rights-still-stands.html?_r=0.

20:13. The point is that Paul's sexual ethic and teaching on homosexual practice were clearly based upon the Mosaic law.

Application

Followers of Jesus are called to "speak the truth in love" (Eph 4:15) in all areas of life, and those who have experienced God's forgiveness in their own lives should be the first to extend mercy and compassion to others. A lack of Christian love has often hindered the church's witness to those who struggle with same-sex attraction or who are involved in same-sex relationships, and this failure to love our neighbors reflects that we have not truly recognized our own sexual brokenness. Loving and showing compassion to our neighbors also means courageously standing for the truth of God's Word against the tide of culture and public opinion. Our commitment to biblical authority means that we read Leviticus in the same way as the apostle Paul. Our goal in holding forth a biblical sexual ethic is not to condemn others or to win arguments, but rather to enable others to experience forgiveness, transformation, and the fullness of blessing that comes from living in accordance with God's creational design.

Annotated Bibliography

BOOKS
DeYoung, Kevin. *What Does the Bible Really Teach about Homosexuality?* Wheaton, IL: Crossway, 2015. Helpful overview of key texts and issues that is especially accessible for laypeople.
Gagnon, Robert A. J. *The Bible and Homosexual Practice: Texts and Hermeneutics*. Nashville: Abingdon Press, 2001. The definitive scholarly work defending the traditional Christian view on same-sex activity.

COMMENTARIES
Kiuchi, Nobuyoshi. *Leviticus*. Apollo Old Testament Commentary. Downers Grove, IL: InterVarsity Press, 2007. Scholarly, evangelical commentary with careful explanation of the sexual ethic reflected in Leviticus 18 and 20.

WEBSITES
Bock, Darrell et al. "Same-Sex Sexuality and the New Testament." Dallas Theological Seminary. February 28, 2017. https://voice.dts.edu/tablepodcast/same-sex-sexuality-and-new-testament/. Podcast of a panel discussion among professors at Dallas Theological Seminary on key New Testament texts related to the issue of homosexuality.
Bock, Darrell et al. "Same-Sex Sexuality and the Old Testament." Dallas Theological Seminary. February 21, 2017. https://voice.dts.edu/tablepodcast/same-sex-sexuality-and-old-testament/. Podcast of a panel discussion among professors at Dallas Theological Seminary on key Old Testament texts related to the issue of homosexuality.

Sprinkle, Preston. "Does the Bible Condemn Homosexuality?" *Eternity Bible College* (blog). August 22, 2013. http://archives.eternitybiblecollege.com/2013/08/22/does-the-bible-condemn-homosexuality/. The first in a series of twenty blogs dealing with the biblical teaching on homosexuality and related issues; this material subsequently appeared in his book *People to Be Loved: Why Homosexuality Is Not Just an Issue* (Grand Rapids: Zondervan, 2015).

CHAPTER 14

The Tithe in Ancient Israel
Was 10 Percent of Income
Leviticus 27:30–33

The Legendary Teaching on Leviticus 27:30–33

Many reasons are provided in Scripture for why Christians are required to tithe, that is, to give back to God 10 percent of their income. One of the more compelling reasons is that God's people have always given him 10 percent. Even in the Old Testament, God clearly commanded that 10 percent was to be given to him: "Every tenth of the land's produce, grain from the soil or fruit from the trees, belongs to the LORD; it is holy to the LORD" (Lev 27:30). Moses gave this command to Israel. The reason that the "land's produce" is the emphasis (as well as animals in v. 32) is that Israelites were primarily an agricultural society and did not deal with money very much. The Hebrew word sometimes translated as "tithe," here translated as "tenth," refers to giving 10 percent. That is what tithing is: giving 10 percent of one's income. It was commanded by God through Moses in the Old Testament, and it remains a command for Christians today.

Countering the Legendary Teaching

It is very honorable that many teachers of the Word of God exhort fellow Christians to be generous in giving. Many of these teachers are motivated by the hope of seeing the Great Commission funded so that missionaries can spread the gospel throughout the world. However, a few questions remain about the line of argumentation used above. Does the word *tithe* mean 10 percent? Does that necessitate that Jews living under the old covenant gave 10 percent of their income to God? What about income that was not derived from crops or cattle? Did Israelites tithe on that as well?

It is true that the word usually translated as "tithe" means 10 percent.[1] There is confusion among some Christians about the definition, but the Hebrew word, the Greek word, and the English word all refer to 10 percent. However, does that automatically mean that Israelites gave 10 percent of their income? To answer this question, an examination of a few passages about tithing in the Old Testament law is needed.

Leviticus 27:30–33: Incorporating a Cultural Practice into the Old Covenant

Leviticus 27 primarily deals with laws concerning vows (see v. 2). Both of the previous explicit references to tithing in the Old Testament were connected to vows: Abraham (Gen 14:18–22) and Jacob (Gen 28:20–22). A shift occurs in Lev 27:26 away from what *can* be vowed to what is *not* liable to vows.[2] The discussion on tithing occurs in this context.

Tithing was prevalent in the societies surrounding Israel.[3] Some of the vagueness of these verses is understandable since an introduction to the concept of tithing was unnecessary; Israelites would have been familiar with it. However, they would need to be instructed on how tithing was going to work in their particular situation, as it was expressed in the Mosaic law.

One of the interesting aspects of Leviticus 27 (and subsequent tithing passages) is that the products that are liable to tithing are all connected to the land of Israel. In Lev 27:30–33, Moses mentions grain, fruit, and animals from the herd or flock. He never mentions income earned from other enterprises, like those who worked with metal (see Gen 4:22) or those who were builders. Many Christians have stated correctly that Israel was primarily

---

[1] Note that Joseph M. Baumgarten, "On the Non-Literal Use of MA'ĂŚĒR/DEKATE," *Journal of Biblical Literature* 103 (1984): 245–51, argues that the Hebrew word can also refer to a religious offering without reference to an amount.

[2] See, e.g., John E. Hartley, *Leviticus*, Word Biblical Commentary (Dallas: Word, 1992), 487.

[3] Such pagan cultures as the Roman, Greek, Carthaginian, Cretan, Silecian, Phoenician, Chinese, Babylonian, Akkadian, Egyptian, Assyrian, Canaanite, Ugaritic, Moroccan, Persian, Lydian, Syrian, Sumerian, and South Arabian societies practiced tithing. For various lists, see J. M. P. Smith, "The Deuteronomic Tithe," *American Journal of Theology* 18 (1914): 119n1; Mark A. Snoeberger, "The Pre-Mosaic Tithe: Issues and Implications," *Detroit Baptist Seminary Journal* 5 (2000): 71; Marvin E. Tate, "Tithing: Legalism or Benchmark?" *Review and Expositor* 70 (1973): 153; and Ralph L. Smith, *Micah–Malachi*, Word Biblical Commentary (Waco, TX: Word, 1984), 333.

an agricultural society. However, being *primarily* agricultural does not mean *solely* agricultural.

The word *money* or *silver* occurs twenty-nine times in the book of Genesis. Even though the minting of coins did not begin until the late seventh century BC, money was available and used in trade much before this. In fact, Leviticus 25–27 contains a fascinating reference to money: "You are not to lend him your silver with interest or sell him your food for profit" (Lev 25:37). This is a reference to ancient banking rules. Therefore, Israelites used money before tithing is ever given as a command.[4]

One particular aspect of Lev 27:32 is highly problematic for those who want to use these verses as a command that Christians are required to give 10 percent of their income. Verse 32 says that the tenth animal that passes under the shepherd's rod must be tithed. In actual practice, it is unlikely that the person obeying this law would give 10 percent. If nine animals passed under the rod, zero would be given: zero percent. If nineteen animals passed under the rod, one would be given: about 5.3 percent. This also demonstrates that "firstfruits" and tithing were distinct, as the tithing of animals was the last animal under the rod, not the first.

Numbers 18:20–24: The Levitical Tithe

The Levites did not receive land the same way the rest of Israel did. Instead of land, they were to receive the tithe for serving at the temple. The Levites received the tithe as an inheritance, not a wage; it replaced the inheritance the rest of Israel received, which was land. The tithe commanded in Num 18:20–24 was mandatory for Israelites. The fact that there are not many specifics about the tithe in Numbers 18 is probably because tithing was already introduced in Leviticus 27. While Leviticus names the items liable to tithing, but provides no recipient, Numbers does not mention the items but does provide the recipients: the Levites.

Deuteronomy 12:17–19; 14:22–27: The Festival Tithe

Deuteronomy 12 introduces another tithe called the Festival Tithe. It is more fully explained in Deuteronomy 14. This is a distinct tithe from the Levitical

---

[4]   For more discussion on this, see David A. Croteau, *You Mean I Don't Have to Tithe? A Deconstruction of Tithing and a Reconstruction of Post-Tithe Giving* (Eugene, OR: Pickwick, 2010), 102–103.

Tithe of Numbers 18. In the latter, God gave the tithe as an inheritance to the Levites for their livelihood; in the former, those who bring the tithe to the festivals also are partakers of the tithe. Another difference is that in Num 18:31, the Levites could eat the tithe "anywhere," but, in Deuteronomy 14, the tithe had to be brought to Jerusalem. Moses clarified that these were two distinct tithes but reminded Israel in Deut 12:19 and 14:27 that they were not to neglect the Levites. See the table that summarizes the differences between the Numbers 18 tithe (the Levitical Tithe) and the Deuteronomy 12 and 14 tithe (the Festival Tithe).

	Levitical Tithe (Num 18)	Festival Tithe (Deut 12; 14)
Location	Eat anywhere (Num 18:31)	Jerusalem (Deut 14:23)
Recipients	Levites (Num 18:21)	All of Israel (Deut 14:26)
Owner	Levites (Num 18:24)	Original owner (Deut 14:26)
Purpose	Replace land inheritance (Num 18:24)	Teach fear of the Lord (Deut 14:23)
Redemption	Add 20% (Lev 27:31)	No mention of 20% (Deut 14:22–26)

Since this is another tithe, different from the Levitical Tithe, the Israelites were not giving 10 percent of their crops and cattle in tithes, but 20 percent, since there were two tithes. Therefore, 10 percent of their crops and cattle went to the Levitical Tithe and another 10 percent went to the Festival Tithe. But there is a third tithe described in Deuteronomy.

Deuteronomy 14:28–29: The Charity Tithe

Deuteronomy describes another tithe, which can be distinguished from the previous two tithes. The Charity Tithe was offered every third year, not every year. Also, it was intended for the Levite, foreigner, orphan, and widow. Although some have proposed that the Charity Tithe might replace either the Levitical or Festival Tithe every third year, that solution creates more problems than it solves.[5]

---

5   See Croteau, *You Mean I Don't Have to Tithe?*, 106, for more explanation.

Calculating the Tithe

Israel was supposed to function on a seven-year cycle. Each year in the first six years of the cycle, the people would give 20 percent of crops and cattle, 10 percent for the Levitical Tithe and 10 percent for the Festival Tithe. In years three and six, they would give another 10 percent for the Charity Tithe, totaling 30 percent in those years. In year 7, they were not required to tithe. The average they paid during the first six years of the cycle was 23-1/3 percent. However, this was not based on income; it was only from crops and cattle. In the New Testament period, artisans, fishermen, and tradesmen did not pay tithes on their income, and Jews who lived outside of Israel did not pay tithes on anything.[6] Therefore, it is an oversimplification of the Mosaic law (and factually incorrect) to say that Israelites gave 10 percent of their income to God.

Application

Hans Brandenburg says, "The entire Old Testament Law is but a shadow of that which is realized in Christ (Col 2:16–17)."[7] The same God who inspired the writing of the Old Testament inspired the writing of the New Testament; he does not change. Therefore, there are tangible lessons and principles that Christians can apply to their lives from the passages discussed above.

Deuteronomy 14:23 says that a purpose of the Festival Tithe was to teach Israel to fear the Lord. Fearing the Lord is commanded in many places in the Old Testament, as well as in the New Testament. This fear frequently references obedience. Therefore, the Festival Tithe was given to teach Israel to learn the fear of the Lord, which may be connected to teaching obedience. Christians also need to learn to fear the Lord. Acts 9:31 says that the church in Israel "had peace and was strengthened. Living in the fear of the Lord and encouraged by the Holy Spirit." Living in obedience to God is still an important concept in being a follower of Christ. In John 15 (see esp. vv. 10 and 14), Jesus makes the connection clear between loving him and obeying his commands.

The Charity Tithe teaches Christians about the importance that God places on taking care of the poor, such as orphans and widows. The New Testament continues this emphasis on taking care of others. First Timothy 5:3–10 discusses taking care of widows. Hebrews 13:2 mentions the importance of show-

---

[6]   F. C. Grant, *The Economic Background of the Gospels* (London: Oxford, 1926), 95n1.

[7]   Hans Brandenburg, *Die Kleinen Propheten II: Haggai, Sacharja, Maleachi (mit Esra und Nehemia)* (Basel: Brunnen, 1963), 153 (my translation).

ing hospitality to strangers. Jesus shows concern for the poor in many passages: Matt 6:2–3; 19:21; Luke 14:13, for example. James 2 heavily emphasizes taking care of the poor, and Paul says that when the leaders in Jerusalem asked that he remember the poor, he was very eager to do that (Gal 2:10). The collection that Paul discussed in several places (e.g., 1 Corinthians 16 and 2 Corinthians 8–9) was being taken up for the poor saints in Jerusalem. Followers of God in the Old Testament were supposed to take care of the poor; followers of God today should show at least the same concern.

Annotated Bibliography

BOOKS

Croteau, David A. *You Mean I Don't Have to Tithe? A Deconstruction of Tithing and a Reconstruction of Post-Tithe Giving*. Eugene, OR: Pickwick, 2010. See 99–111. This section gives a more comprehensive discussion and description of tithing in the Mosaic law.

ARTICLES

Köstenberger, Andreas J., and David A. Croteau. "'Will a Man Rob God?' (Malachi 3:8): A Study of Tithing in the Old and New Testaments." *Bulletin for Biblical Research* 16, no. 1 (2006): 53–77. https://digitalcommons.liberty.edu/cgi/viewcontent. cgi?article=1079&context=sor_fac_pubs. An article briefly summarizing all the significant passages that discuss tithing in the Old and New Testaments.

WEBSITES

Budiselić, Ervin. "The Role and the Place of Tithing in the Context of Christian Giving: Part 1." *ResearchGate.net*. October 14, 2014. https://www.researchgate.net/ publication/292629330_The_Role_and_the_Place_of_Tithing_in_the_Context_of_ Christian_Giving_Part_1. This online article helpfully summarizes several different viewpoints with similar conclusions to this chapter.

CHAPTER 15

The Old Testament Law Is Divided into Three Parts
Deuteronomy 6:1

The Legendary Teaching on Deuteronomy 6:1

The Old Testament contains three categories of laws: moral, civil, and ceremonial. Moral laws are timeless principles that apply to all people at all times. Civil laws relate to the legal system of the nation of Israel—those laws pertaining to the peaceful functioning of society. Ceremonial laws are connected to worship at the temple in Jerusalem. This tripartite distinction is taught in Deut 6:1: "Now these are the commandments, statutes, and ordinances that the LORD your God instructed me to teach you so that you may carry them out in the land where you are headed" (NET). Moses provides the three categories himself: "the commandments" refers to the moral laws; "statutes" refers to the ceremonial laws; "ordinances" refers to the civil laws. This distinction is not a modern invention but can be traced to Thomas Aquinas (d. 1274), and seeds of this thought can be seen in Origen (d. 254) and Augustine (d. 430).

This distinction is extremely important, since it is a primary way in which Christians can decide if an Old Testament law applies to them today or if it no longer functions authoritatively over their lives. If a law is moral, its functional authority continues. If a law is civil or ceremonial, a Christian no longer needs to keep that law. For example, adultery is prohibited in Exod 20:14. This is a moral law, so it still continues. Deuteronomy 15:1 says, "At the end of every seven years you must cancel debts." This is an example of a civil law. An example of a ceremonial law is Deut 16:13, which says, "You are to celebrate the Festival of Shelters for seven days when you have gathered in everything from your threshing floor and winepress." Neither the civil nor ceremonial laws apply today.

Unraveling the Tripartite Legend

Jonathan Edwards, perhaps the greatest theological mind America has produced, said, "There is perhaps no part of divinity attended with so much intricacy, and wherein orthodox divines do so much differ, as stating of the precise agreement and differences between the two dispensations of Moses and Christ."[1] This should cause interpreters to be very cautious when dealing with this topic. One of the problems with the tripartite categorization of the Mosaic laws is that it is not clear that anyone in the New Testament categorized them this way. The stance of Paul and other New Testament writers appears to be that the entire Old Testament law has been set aside since the coming of Christ. The Mosaic law was a unified covenant with Israel that is no longer in force for Christians. As Heb 8:13 says, "By saying a new covenant, he has declared that the first is obsolete. And what is obsolete and growing old is about to pass away."[2]

A second problem is trying to justify the categories exegetically. In looking at the argument from Deut 6:1, for example, it becomes difficult to conclude that three distinct categories of laws are in view. There are three Hebrew words being used: *mitsvah* (usually translated as "command"), *hoq* (usually translated as "statute"), and *mishpatim* (usually translated as "ordinances"). But the first word is singular, and the latter two are plural. That has led some Bible translation committees to view the latter two words as clarifying the first word. Notice how the two translations below render this phrase:

CSB: This is the command—the statutes and ordinances—the LORD your God has commanded . . .

ESV: Now this is the commandment—the statutes and the rules— that the LORD your God commanded . . .

---

[1]   Jonathan Edwards, *The Works of Jonathan Edwards*, rev. and cor. Edward Hickman (Carlisle: Banner of Truth, 1974), 1:465. Note John Wesley's statement: "Perhaps there are few subjects within the whole compass of religion so little understood as this," quoted in David A. Dorsey, "The Law of Moses and the Christian: A Compromise," *Journal of the Evangelical Theological Society* 34 (1991): 322.
[2]   See also Heb 10:15–17.

These two translations do not see three distinct categories of laws, but one category ("commands") with two subsets ("statutes" and "rules/ordinances"). It is important, as interpreters of Scripture, to allow the text to provide the categories that are used, not to import categories onto the text.[3]

A third problem with using this method to decide which laws continue and which do not is that it can be very difficult to distinguish between a law being in the "moral" category or the "ceremonial" or "civil" category. The Old Testament text does not list these laws separately. For example, Deuteronomy 22 contains many laws. Verse 12 says, "Make tassels on the four corners of the outer garment you wear." Although that verse is not considered to be a "moral" law in the tripartite law system, a few verses later the text explains that adultery is wrong and must be punished (v. 22). Although adultery is considered a moral law, there is nothing in the context to justify a switch from a "nonmoral" category to a moral category.

Furthermore, how could any of the laws in the Mosaic law not be considered "moral"? J. Daniel Hays says, "Because the Mosaic Law defined the covenant relationship between God and Israel, it was by nature theological. All of the Law had theological content."[4] Therefore, how could a law be "theological" yet not be moral? It seems that the Israelites would have viewed all of the laws as moral laws. Breaking any of them would be a "moral issue."

The issue of the applicability of the Sabbath to Christians is highly controversial in evangelicalism. Is keeping the Sabbath a moral issue or was it ceremonial or civil? The Sabbath was part of Israel's worship system; that would appear to make it ceremonial. However, many scholars would argue that its placement in the Ten Commandments automatically makes it a moral law. Numbers 15:35 says that someone who breaks the Sabbath is to be put to death. That makes the Sabbath appear to be a civil law. Because of these reasons, the distinctions between the categories appear to be arbitrary.

Christians Are under the New Covenant

The Mosaic covenant is not a functional covenant. It has no binding authority over Christians, as Hebrews 8–9 makes clear. This is not to say that the Mosaic covenant was bad. Instead, the author of Hebrews (see 8:13) says that the Mosaic laws are not valid because they are part of an obsolete

---

[3]   Note that the KJV, NIV, and NET could be read differently than the CSB and ESV.

[4]   J. Daniel Hays, "Applying the Old Testament Law Today," *Bibliotheca Sacra* 158 (January–March 2001): 23.

covenant. In Gal 3:24, Paul described the Mosaic law as a "guardian"; it was supposed to supervise Israel in its childhood. However, it had temporal limits, since it was the guardian "until" Christ—a word that refers to "up to the time" that something else occurs. Then he clarifies his conclusion in Gal 3:25: "But since that faith has come, we are no longer under a guardian." The law was a guardian, and we are no longer under the law. Paul himself did not distinguish between moral, ceremonial, or civil laws, but he referred to the law as a unified whole.

In Matt 5:17, Jesus says that he "did not come to abolish but to fulfill" the Law and the Prophets. That phrase, "the Law and Prophets," refers to the Old Testament Scriptures. Jesus was not doing away with all of Scripture. Instead, he was fulfilling Scripture. Notice that in Matt 11:13 Jesus says, "For all the prophets and the law prophesied until John." The Old Testament was prophetic, pointing to Jesus. The word *fulfill* in Matthew appears to refer to "setting out something's true meaning."[5] This can be seen in how Jesus uses the word in Matthew 5, explaining how Old Testament laws were understood, but then clarifying what they meant, providing the underlying, eternal principles of the Old Testament laws. Jesus was not saying that Christians have to keep the entire Old Testament law in the way that it was formulated for Israel under the old covenant.

Jesus fulfilled all the demands of the Mosaic law. By fulfilling it, he changed it. For example, when a prophecy is "fulfilled" in the New Testament, by nature the way that prophecy is read is changed. It no longer applies in the same way, because it has been fulfilled. That does not mean it was (or is) useless or bad, but the application changes because it was fulfilled. Sometimes Jesus simply restated Old Testament laws (see Matt 19:18–19); sometimes he modified laws (see Matt 5:31–32); sometimes he intensified laws (see Matt 5:21–22). Other laws were either changed significantly, like the discussion on oaths in Matt 5:33–37, or they were totally abrogated, like the food laws in Mark 7:15–19. Jesus did not declare that the entire Old Testament law was irrelevant; he also did not say that all the laws had to be kept. However, as Hays concluded, "The meaning of the Law must be interpreted in light of his coming and in light of the profound changes introduced by the new covenant."[6]

---

5   This is when the word is used in relationship to prophecy, not when referring to filling a container (as in Matt 13:48).

6   Hays, "Applying," 29.

What Approach Should Christians Take with the Old Testament Laws?

Instead of placing laws into categories that deem some as applicable and some as nonapplicable, Christians should side with Paul in saying, "All Scripture is inspired by God and is profitable for teaching, for rebuking, for correcting, for training in righteousness" (2 Tim 3:16). Included in "all Scripture" are the Old Testament laws. An appropriate approach, then, will find a way to interpret all the laws in a way to make them applicable to Christians today. This approach is called "principlism." While not perfect, it provides consistent, well-thought-out interpretations to the Old Testament laws.

In this approach, the interpreter will try to decide what the underlying principle is to the Old Testament law. Studying how Jesus did this in Matt 5:21–48 can be very helpful. Even the laws that appear to be directly tied to culturally specific concepts can be applied using this approach.

It is important to begin by understanding the historical and literary context of the verse. For example, Lev 19:28 says, "You are not to make gashes on your bodies for the dead or put tattoo marks on yourselves; I am the LORD." Some people have tried to use this verse to say that a Christian should not get a tattoo. On face value, that is what the verse appears to say. The verse has two parts. In the first part, Israel is prohibited from making gashes or cuts on their bodies "for the dead." This refers to an ancient practice, illustrated in Jer 16:6 and 48:37,[7] of cutting oneself when in mourning. As the first half of the verse refers to the prohibition against an ancient practice, so does the second half of the verse.[8]

The historical context also aids in interpreting the words about getting a tattoo. An ancient practice connected to that part of the world was getting a tattoo of a name of a god. It signified that the one being tattooed became a slave to that god.[9] It appears that this particular ancient practice is being condemned, which is different from the modern practice of tattooing.[10]

---

[7]   1 Kgs 18:28 could be another reference to this practice.

[8]   Also included in the literary context are other verses in the chapter. Lev 19:2 seems to be an introduction to the theme of the chapter: "Be holy because I, the LORD your God, am holy." Leviticus 19:18 may provide another theme to the chapter: "Love your neighbor as yourself." But the chapter also contains verses such as 27, which says, "You are not to cut off the hair at the sides of your head or mar the edge of your beard." A faithful interpreter of Scripture will be careful not to pick certain laws to apply to Christians while ignoring others, without having a good rationale.

[9]   "Tattoo," in *Encyclopaedia Judaica*, ed. Michael Berenbaum and Fred Skolnik, 2nd ed. (Detroit: Macmillan, 2007), 15:831–32. Peter Vogt, *Interpreting the Pentateuch: An Exegetical Handbook*, Handbooks for Old Testament Exegesis (Grand Rapids: Kregel, 2009), 185, mentions that it refers to "belonging to a particular group."

[10]   For a different interpretation that finds a lasting prohibition against getting a tattoo, see Vogt, *Interpreting the Pentateuch*, 185–88.

Application

Therefore, the principle that the text is pointing toward is not the contemporary practice of getting a tattoo, but the idea of associating with a false god. The principle of avoiding association with a false god could be applied in many situations, and could still be applied to contemporary tattoos. But there is not a direct connection between the two.

This does not give a wholesale allowance for Christians to get tattoos. Other principles from Scripture need to be considered. For example, the issue of stewardship: how much are you paying for the tattoo? The issue of communication: what kind of tattoo are you getting and what will that communicate to others? Some tattoos are harmful physically, and that would be a problem as well.[11] The two most important questions are probably (1) why do I want a tattoo? (2) how will my tattoo bring honor and glory to God?[12]

Laws that are typically referred to as moral laws in the Old Testament are not directly commands for Christians on the sole basis that they appear in the Old Testament. Instead, as Thomas Schreiner states, "They are normative because they express the character of God."[13]

Annotated Bibliography

BOOKS
Schreiner, Thomas R. *40 Questions about Christians and Biblical Law*. Grand Rapids: Kregel, 2010. See 89–95. This chapter helpfully navigates between those who treat the law as irrelevant and those who believe that the law is binding on Christians.

ARTICLES
Hays, J. Daniel. "Applying the Old Testament Law Today." *Bibliotheca Sacra* 158 (January–March 2001): 21–35. Hays's article is an excellent resource for grasping the significance of the Old Testament law for Christians today.

WEBSITES
Honeycutt, Will. "Should Christians Get Tattoos? 7 Points to Consider First." *Crosswalk.com*. September 9, 2014. https://www.crosswalk.com/family/singles/is-it-biblical-for-christians-to-get-tattoos.html. Honeycutt raises seven points to consider regarding getting a tattoo, far beyond interpreting a single verse in Scripture.

---

[11]   Markham Heid, "You Asked: Are Tattoos Bad for You?" *TIME*, April 5, 2017, www.time.com/4725634/tattoo-ink-dangerous.

[12]   My friend Will Honeycutt has written a great article for those considering getting a tattoo: Will Honeycutt, "Should Christians Get Tattoos? 7 Points to Consider First," *Crosswalk.com*, September 9, 2014, https://www.crosswalk.com/family/singles/is-it-biblical-for-christians-to-get-tattoos.html.

[13]   Schreiner, *40 Questions*, 94 (see chap. 12, n. 4).

CHAPTER 16

God Never Expected Israel to Keep His Law

Deuteronomy 29:4

The Legendary Teaching on Deuteronomy 29:4
and Israel's Inability to Obey God

The Old Testament narrates Israel's long history of disobedience to the Mosaic law, and Deut 29:2–4 reveals that the reason for Israel's disobedience was that God did not provide the enablement needed to secure the people's obedience. Believers in the Old Testament did their best to conform to the external standards of the law, while God's people in the new covenant experience a spiritual transformation through the working of the Holy Spirit that enables them to obey God. Believers under the old covenant could only look forward to a future time when God would do heart surgery on his people and put his Spirit within them so that they would finally have the desire and ability to obey his commands (see Deut 30:6; Isa 59:20–21; Jer 31:33–34; Ezek 36:26–27; Joel 2:28–32).

Countering the Legendary Teaching

The reason for Israel's disobedience was not the lack of divine enablement but rather the people's unbelief and refusal to follow the ways of the Lord. God provided the Mosaic law to show Israel how to live as his covenant people. Within the covenant, God demanded obedience to his commands and provided enablement to obey those commands to those individuals who had a personal relationship with him through repentance and faith. The law was a gift from God, but the problem was that many of the people within the national covenant did not personally know the Lord and thus did not have the capacity to obey the Lord.

Divine Enablement to Obey in the Book of Deuteronomy

Reading Deut 29:2–4 in isolation might suggest that Israel had not obeyed the Lord in the wilderness because he had not yet given them the capacity to obey him. We see the Lord, however, telling the people just one chapter later that obedience to the Mosaic law was "certainly not too difficult or beyond your reach" (Deut 30:11–14). The Lord had clearly revealed his commands so that his people did not have to ascend into the heavens or to cross the seas to know what he expected of them. The manner in which the Lord made his law clear and accessible is inconsistent with the idea that he then withheld the grace and enablement needed to obey his commands.

The idea that Israel was unable to obey God because of a lack of divine enablement is also at odds with the larger message of Deuteronomy. In this second giving of the law prior to Israel's entrance into the Promised Land, Moses exhorts the people to obey the Lord as the proper response to his gracious redemption. Yahweh's deliverance of Israel from Egypt provided the impetus and incentive needed for the people to obey his commands. When the Lord commanded his people to love him with all of their "heart, soul, and strength" (Deut 6:5–9) by keeping his words "in their hearts" or when he commanded them to "circumcise" their hearts so that they would obey him (Deut 10:16), he was not setting them up for failure by commanding them to do something that they were incapable of doing.

The Old Covenant: Believers and Unbelievers in a National Covenant

When reading Deut 29:2–4, one must remember that the Mosaic covenant was a national covenant that included all of Israel, believers and unbelievers alike.[1] Deuteronomy 29:2–4 specifically refers to those in Israel who had not turned to the Lord in repentance and faith. Moses is addressing people who as a nation lived in covenant with God and were the beneficiaries of national redemption out of Egypt, but belonging to this people was not the same as

---

[1]   Michael A. Grisanti, "Was Israel Unable to Respond to God? A Study of Deuteronomy 29:2–4," *Bibliotheca Sacra* 163 (2006): 176–96, esp. 190–92.

personal salvation. The widespread disobedience and rebellion of the wilderness generation reflected that most of the people of Israel had not appropriated the salvation that made possible a personal relationship with the Lord. Faith and obedience were the expected response to what God had done for Israel, but the people were "stiff-necked" and "rebellious" (Deut 9:6, 13; 10:16; 31:27). They had worshipped the golden calf at Sinai, had refused to take possession of the land after the report of the spies, had worshipped Baal at Baal-peor, and had tested the Lord with their continual unbelief and complaining. The fault for this lack of faith and obedience lay entirely with the people, who had not responded to God.[2]

Throughout the old covenant era, there was always a remnant of true believers within the nation who knew the Lord and possessed the capacity to live in obedience to his commands.[3] When the rest of the nation rebelled against the Lord, Joshua and Caleb encouraged the people to trust the Lord and to take the land. During the time of national apostasy when Ahab and Jezebel promoted the worship of Baal, the Lord promised his faithful prophet Elijah that even in his judgment he would preserve 7,000 who had not bowed to worship Baal (1 Kgs 19:18; Rom 11:4).

Those who belonged to this remnant under the old covenant were able to obey God and follow his commands. Just like believers today, they did not obey God perfectly or completely, but even when they sinned, they had access to forgiveness and atonement through the sacrifices. Those who practiced a lifestyle of obedience to God under the old covenant are often referred to as "the faithful ones" (*hasidim*, related to the word *hesed*, which conveys the idea of "covenant loyalty," 2 Chr 6:41; Pss 4:4; 18:25), and the Lord reciprocated their faithfulness by bestowing upon them the blessings of his *hesed* (Deut 7:9).

Spiritual Transformation under the Old Covenant

Paul tells us that those who are "in the flesh cannot please God" (Rom 8:8), and the same condition applied to unregenerate sinners in the old covenant era. Sinners who are born spiritually dead (Eph 2:1–3) cannot please and obey God. Thus, those Israelites who did live in obedience to God's commands experienced spiritual transformation and received divine enablement

---

2   Grisanti, "Was Israel Unable?" 189, 94.
3   Grisanti, "Was Israel Unable?" 189–90.

that facilitated their obedience.[4] We get insight into the kind of transformation that true believers experienced under the old covenant when we look at David's prayer of confession in Psalm 51. In addition to asking for cleansing and forgiveness of his sin, David petitioned the Lord to "create a clean heart" and to "renew a steadfast spirit" within him (v. 10). David's prayer reflects that God did for the Old Testament saint something on par with what God does for believers in the new covenant when he makes them "new creations" (2 Cor 5:17) and strengthens them in their hearts so that they can please and obey him (Eph 3:16; Heb 13:9). Daniel Estes explains, "By appealing to God, the psalmist implicitly acknowledges that he is unable by his own resolution to do what is right before God. He needs a new nature."[5]

When obeying God's commands, Old Testament believers were not simply conforming to an outward standard like a people who drive the speed limit while speeding in their hearts; they were being "obedient from the heart" as new covenant believers are when they obey the Lord's commands (see Rom 6:17). David loved and meditated upon the law of God (Ps 119:97, 103, 113, 163, 165), and he prayed for God's teaching and enablement so that he might be able to follow through on his desire to obey (Ps 119:29, 73, 80, 108, 117).[6]

The internal transformation that David desires and reflects in his own life happens as a result of the working of God's Spirit on the human heart and will. There is significant theological debate over how the Holy Spirit worked in the lives of believers under the old covenant. In light of statements in the New Testament that the Spirit would not be poured out until the Day of Pentecost (John 7:37–39; 14:17), some have argued that the Holy Spirit did not regenerate or indwell believers during the old covenant, while others have argued for the Spirit's indwelling of believers under the old covenant. While the primary focus of the Old Testament is upon how the Spirit empowered Israel's leaders in the execution of their appointed tasks (see Exod 31:3; 35:31; Judg 3:10; 6:34; 11:29; 14:6, 19; 1 Sam 10:6, 10; 16:13), David's requests in Psalm 51 for a clean heart and resolute spirit reflect the Spirit's influence and transformative work in the life of an individual however it might have occurred.

The Old Testament prophets also speak of the internal transformation that accompanies a right relationship with God in a similar manner. Jeremiah

---

4   Walter C. Kaiser Jr., "The Indwelling Presence of the Holy Spirit in the Old Testament," *Evangelical Quarterly* 82 (2010): 309.

5   Daniel J. Estes, "Spirit and the Psalmist in Psalm 51," in *Presence, Power, and Promise: The Role of the Spirit of God in the Old Testament*, ed. David G. Firth and Paul D. Wegner (Downers Grove, IL: IVP Academic, 2011), 128.

6   Grisanti, "Was Israel Unable?" 192–93.

speaks of God forgiving sin, placing his law within his people, and writing it on their hearts so that they might obey him (Jer 31:33–34; 32:39). This work of God would provide the remedy for the people "uncircumcised in heart" (Jer 9:25–26) and would overwrite the sin that was etched on their hearts (Jer 17:1, 9). Jeremiah promised that the Lord would bring about this transformation of Israel as a nation when he instituted the new covenant, but the prophet's command for the people of his day to "circumcise their hearts" (Jer 4:4; compare Deut 10:16) reflected that this inward change was available to them as well. In Rom 2:28–29, Paul equates circumcision of the heart with the regenerating work of the Spirit.[7]

Ezekiel 36:25–27 more explicitly connects this inward transformation God produces in his people with the working of the Holy Spirit. Ezekiel promises that the Lord would cleanse his people of their sins and then would give them a "new heart" by placing his own Spirit within them (see Ezek 11:18–19). God's work would turn the people's hearts of stone into hearts of flesh that were willing to obey him and comply with his will. Like Jeremiah, Ezekiel was speaking of the future restoration of Israel when all people belonging to the covenant would be saved and know the Lord, but this promise concerning the future did not mean that similar transformation was unavailable in the present. In Ezek 18:31–32, the Lord commands the people to "get a new heart and a new spirit" by turning to him and states that it is unnecessary for them to die in their rebellion and unbelief. Richard Averbeck explains that when Ezekiel was speaking of Israel's future transformation, "he was not suggesting that this kind of work in the hearts of people had never been seen before in anyone's life."[8] God's presence and the power of his Spirit sanctified his people and enabled them to obey him.

There is both continuity and discontinuity as we look at the working of the Holy Spirit in the Old and New Testaments. The Spirit makes sinners alive and enables them to live godly lives in both covenants, but the cross of Jesus and the coming of the new covenant era brings a fuller manifestation of the Spirit's work in the people of God. John Goldingay explains, "After the actual death of Christ, people have new concrete evidence of the length, depth, height, and breadth of the love of God, and the Spirit has more basis on which to over-

---

[7] Richard E. Averbeck, "The Holy Spirit in the Hebrew Bible and Its Connections to the New Testament," in *Who's Afraid of the Holy Spirit? An Investigation into the Ministry of the Spirit of God Today*, ed. M. James Sawyer and Daniel B. Wallace (Dallas: Biblical Studies Press, 2005), 31.

[8] Averbeck, "The Holy Spirit," 32.

whelm them with the love of God (Rom 5:5)."[9] As a result, the Spirit can now "explicitly work to the experience in us of a cross-shaped life."[10]

Application

The Old Testament teaching on the transformation of those who knew God under the old covenant dispels the misunderstanding that God left these believers to fend for themselves in their spiritual journey or that it was impossible for believers under the old covenant to obey God. Israel's long history of failure ultimately revealed the need for a Savior and a fuller, greater pouring out of the Spirit. Galatians 5:16 encourages us to "walk in the Spirit" and to draw upon his power to live in a way that is pleasing to God. Second Peter 1:3–4 also reminds us that God has given us in Christ "everything required for life and godliness." In the new covenant, as in the old, our enablement to obey comes from God as we access the power of the Spirit and apply ourselves to a life of godliness.

Annotated Bibliography

BOOKS

Averbeck, Richard E. "The Holy Spirit in the Hebrew Bible and Its Connections to the New Testament." In *Who's Afraid of the Holy Spirit? An Investigation into the Ministry of the Spirit of God Today*, edited by M. James Sawyer and Daniel B. Wallace, 15–36. (Dallas: Biblical Studies Press, 2005). Accessed August 28, 2017, at *Academia*: https://www.academia.edu/14523679/Holy_Spirit_in_the_OT_and_NT. Helpful study for demonstrating correlations between the presentations of the Holy Spirit in the Old and New Testaments.

ARTICLES

Goldingay, John. "Was the Holy Spirit Active in Old Testament Times? What Was New about the Christian Experience of God?" *Ex Auditu* 12 (1996): 14–28. Argues for continuity in the Spirit's work in the believer in the old and new covenants.

Grisanti, Michael A. "Was Israel Unable to Respond to God? A Study of Deuteronomy 29:2–4." *Bibliotheca Sacra* 163 (2006); 176–96. Discusses how the national aspect of the old covenant meant that both believers and unbelievers were part of the covenant people of God.

---

⁹   John Goldingay, "Was the Holy Spirit Active in Old Testament Times? What Was New About the Christian Experience of God?" *Ex Auditu* 12 (1996): 25.

¹⁰ Goldingay, "Was the Holy Spirit Active?," 25.

CHAPTER 17

NASA Found Joshua's Long Day

Joshua 10:12–15

The Legendary Teaching on Joshua's Long Day

Joshua 10 portrays a cosmic miracle that NASA scientists have confirmed.[1] In the 1960s, NASA scientists at the Goddard Space Center in Greenbelt, Maryland, were plotting the future positions of the sun, moon, and planets to calculate spacecraft trajectories when they confirmed the story of the long day in Josh 10:12–15. While making their calculations, the computers suddenly stopped working until one of the scientists made adjustments factoring in Joshua's missing day. The computers whirred back into action but soon jammed again because they were unable to find an entire day. The computers had only discovered a missing twenty-three hours and twenty minutes, but then the scientist recalled the story of Hezekiah and the sundial in 2 Kings 20, in which God caused the sun to go backward for ten degrees (or exactly forty minutes). The computers then worked perfectly and were able to make accurate projections because of the new data. The computers had scientifically demonstrated the veracity of the biblical account of how God had stopped the earth rotating on its axis (or slowed its rotation) so that Joshua's army could defeat a powerful enemy.

---

[1] For more detailed accounts of the origin and development of the legend of the lost day, see David Mikkelson, "NASA Discovers a 'Lost Day' in Time?" Snopes, February 25, 2000. http://www.snopes.com/religion/lostday.asp; and Bert Thompson, "Has NASA Discovered Joshua's 'Lost Day'?" *Apologetics Press*, 1999, http://apologeticspress.org/apcontent.aspx?category=11&article=1329.

Countering the Legendary Teaching

Well-meaning Christians have repeated this legendary story of the NASA computers and Joshua's long day, even though numerous sources have debunked the
myth. There is simply no way that scientists with even the most sophisticated
computers could find a lost day through astronomical calculations. Computers
are able to generate calendars from the present back to the distant past but have
no way of determining if days are missing. David Mikkelson explains that
expecting a computer to perform this task would be no different from asking someone to take a nonworking clock and determine how much time had
elapsed since the clock stopped running.

The NASA computer legend and many Sunday school lessons on this
story assume that Joshua 10 recounts a cosmic miracle, like the earth ceasing
to rotate on its axis. Skeptics have assumed a similar view when mocking the
story's credibility:

> If the earth were suddenly to stop rotating the law of inertia tells us
> that anything not securely tied down would continue to move in a
> straight line tangent to the surface of the earth at its original velocity
> of 1,000 miles an hour. If this happened there would still be bunny
> rabbits and toad frogs in orbit, not to mention cataclysmic geological
> disruptions of the earth's surface. The enormous inertial forces gen-
> erated by such a sudden halt would have destroyed everything on the
> planet if not the earth itself.[2]

A careful reading of the story suggests God's supernatural intervention
in Israel's victory but not necessarily a miracle of cosmic proportions. The
unique element of this story is not what happened with the rotation of the
earth but rather how the Lord responded to Joshua's prayer.

Proposals Concerning the Long Day

SUPERNATURAL MANIPULATION OF LIGHT
Although God as Creator would have the logistic ability to accomplish
changes to the earth's rotation without flying bunny rabbits, a cosmic miracle

---

[2]   B. R. Tilghman, *An Introduction to the Philosophy of Religion*, 108, quoted in J. Gordon
McConville and Stephen N. Williams, *Joshua*, Theological Horizons Old Testament Commentary
(Grand Rapids: Eerdmans, 2010), 159.

on this scale seems out of proportion for a localized event involving a battlefield skirmish. The Bible uses phenomenological language elsewhere in speaking of the sun rising and setting (e.g., Eccl 1:5), so perhaps here the sun "standing still" refers to a refraction of light or some other means by which God miraculously extended the daylight hours so that Israel could attain total victory over the enemy. We could envision something happening here similar to what occurred when God caused the shadow on the steps to go backward as a confirming sign of his promise to heal Hezekiah (2 Kgs 20:9–11; Isa 38:7–8).

The Sun Ceased Shining (Storm or Eclipse)

Another possibility is that the heat from the sun was diminished, either by the storm or by a solar eclipse. This respite from the heat refreshed the Israelite troops so that they could finish the battle. The verb *damam* would then mean that the sun ceased shining, rather than that it stopped moving across the sky. The cooler weather, however, would have refreshed the Amorites just as well, and the use of the verb *'amad* to depict the sun standing in the middle of the sky and delaying to set for nearly a day does not fit well with this explanation.[3] Solar eclipses also occur at the beginning of the month (new moon), not when the sun and moon are in opposition to each other (full moon) as in this passage.[4]

Joshua Received an Omen

Some have suggested that the text portrays Joshua seeking an omen involving the alignment of the sun and moon that would have been a favorable sign to the Israelites, or more likely, a portent of disaster that would have caused fear and consternation among the enemy.[5] Joshua himself need not have believed in such omens for them to be effective in weakening the resolve of the pagan armies fighting against Israel. The positioning of the sun in the east over Gibeon and the moon in the west over the Valley of Aijalon indicates the morning hours, and it is difficult to understand why Joshua would have requested additional hours of daylight if it were no later than midmorning.[6] It was considered a good omen if the full moon occurred on the fourteenth day of

---

[3]   David M. Howard Jr., *Joshua*, New American Commentary (Nashville: Broadman & Holman, 1998), 243.

[4]   John H. Walton, "Joshua 10:12–15 and Mesopotamian Celestial Omen Texts," in *Faith, Tradition, and History: Old Testament Historiography in Its Near Eastern Context*, ed. A. R. Millard, J. K. Hoffmeier, and D. W. Baker (Winona Lake, IN: Eisenbrauns, 1994), 187.

[5]   Walton, "Joshua 10:12–15," 181–90.

[6]   Walton, "Joshua 10:12–15," 182.

the month, but the sun and moon standing opposite on another day was a sign of impending disaster, including military defeat.[7] The peoples of the ancient Near East attached great significance to omens, which were regularly used to determine when to engage in battle. An omen of disaster would have caused panic among the enemy, and Joshua's ability to command the sun and moon would have demonstrated the superiority of Yahweh to the Canaanite gods.

The connection of this text to an ancient omen would help to explain the emphasis on the positioning of the sun and moon, and the verbs "wait, stand, and stop" frequently appear in Mesopotamian omens relating to celestial bodies.[8] The problem is that there is no explicit mention of an omen or the response that such an omen would have likely caused.[9] It is also not clear why verse 13 would need to emphasize that the omen remained in place until Israel had defeated its enemies when the omen would have had to appear only briefly to have its desired effect on the enemy.[10]

POETIC ACCOUNT OF GOD'S DRAMATIC INTERVENTION

In Josh 10:9–12a, we first have a prose account of Israel's defeat of the Amorite kings that includes a description of Joshua's all-night march, the slaughter of the enemy, and the Lord throwing down hailstones on the enemy, as well as a summary statement of Israel's victory. The poetic section—beginning with "Joshua spoke to the LORD" in verse 12 and extending to the end of verse 13—provides a poetic flashback depicting the same battle recounted in verses 9–11.[11] This type of combined prose/poetry account of an Israelite battle also occurs in Exodus 14–15 and Judges 4–5.

In light of the fact that verses 12b–13 are poetry, we likely have a highly figurative account of what transpired in the battle. David Howard argues that the poetry in verses 12–13 is likely recounting the same events described in the preceding prose section. The all-night march of Joshua's troops is poetically described as the moon "stopping" or "standing still" (*'amad*) (v. 13a); the lengthy battle that concluded at sunset is depicted as a day in which the sun "stopped" (*damah*) in the middle of the sky and delayed setting until the bat-

---

[7]   Walton, "Joshua 10:12–15," 183–86.

[8]   Walton, "Joshua 10:12–15," 186.

[9]   Howard, *Joshua*, 244.

[10]   Richard S. Hess, "Joshua," in *Zondervan Illustrated Bible Backgrounds Commentary*, ed. J. H. Walton (Grand Rapids: Zondervan, 2009), 2:47.

[11]   The particle *'az* + the imperfect form of the verb "to speak," likely reflects that Joshua's speech occurs prior to the conclusion of the events from the previous section. See Howard, *Joshua*, 238nn191–92.

tle had ended (v. 13b).[12] Similarly, Robert Hubbard suggests that the imagery hyperbolically underscores the magnitude of the great victory that Israel was able to accomplish in a single day.[13] Ancient military accounts often highlighted how a god or king was able to defeat his enemies in a single day.[14] In one account, a king claims to have captured seventy cities in a single day.[15]

The Old Testament employs cosmic language elsewhere to depict other battle scenes. Judges 5:20 portrays the stars as fighting with Israel when they defeated the Canaanite king Sisera, and Hab 3:11 even pictures the sun and moon as "standing still" (*'amad*) as the Lord appears as a warrior to defeat his enemies. K. Lawson Younger has noted parallels between Joshua 10 and other ancient Near Eastern battle accounts. The Hittite king Murshili and the Assyrian king Sargon were able to defeat their enemies with the assistance of hailstorms sent from the gods.[16] An inscription on a stela of Thutmose III recalls how a star (perhaps a comet) beamed on the enemy so that the Egyptians could defeat them.[17]

What Likely Happened in Joshua 10?

Sorting through the interpretive options for Joshua 10 is difficult, but the most likely explanations appear to be either the supernatural manipulation of light or a miraculous storm that the Lord sent to aid the Israelites in their battle with the Amorites. The narrator in Joshua 10 affirms a supernatural occurrence but does not provide a scientific explanation of what actually occurred. The text combines prose and poetry to provide a highly figurative account with polemical overtones. The Lord providentially sent a devastating hailstorm at just the right time to help rout the enemy. This story demonstrates God's control over the forces of nature like the story of the conquest of Jericho (Joshua 6) in which God appears to use an earthquake to bring down the walls of Jericho. The Lord was fighting for his people in order to fulfill his covenant promise that they would possess the land of Canaan. What actually occurred here is something that science can neither confirm nor disprove.

---

[12]   Howard, *Joshua*, 245.
[13]   Robert L. Hubbard, *Joshua*, New International Version Application Commentary (Grand Rapids: Zondervan, 2009), 295.
[14]   Douglas Stuart, "The Sovereign's Day of Conquest," *Bulletin of the American Schools of Oriental Research* 221 (1976): 159–64.
[15]   K. Lawson Younger, *Ancient Conquest Accounts: A Study in Ancient Near Eastern and Biblical History Writing*, Library of Hebrew Bible/OT Studies 98 (New York: Bloomsbury T&T Clark, 2009), 216.
[16]   Younger, *Ancient Conquest Accounts*, 208–10.
[17]   Younger, *Ancient Conquest Accounts*, 217–18.

Application

In highlighting what was unique about this day, the biblical narrator does not focus on the solar and lunar phenomena but rather on how the Lord responded to Joshua's prayers and delivered the people of Israel. The Lord had certainly answered prayers before, but in this instance, Joshua is the one who proposes to the Lord the particular military strategy that led to Israel's victory. In other episodes of holy war, it is the Lord himself who commands several unusual strategies employed by the Israelites.[18] The Lord in this situation essentially allowed Joshua to call the winning play. The expression used for the Lord hearing Joshua's prayer (*shama' + beqol*—"listened unto the voice of") often conveys the idea of obedience to a person and is used only a few other times with the Lord as the subject (see Gen 30:8; Num 21:3; 1 Kgs 17:22).[19] The story of Joshua's long day reminds us to approach God boldly with our requests, knowing that the Lord is able to do what seems humanly impossible and that he delights in giving surprising answers to our prayers.

Annotated Bibliography

BOOKS

Walton, John H. "Joshua 10:12–15 and Mesopotamian Celestial Omen Texts." In *Faith, Tradition, and History: Old Testament Historiography in Its Near Eastern Context,* edited by A. R. Millard, J. K. Hoffmeier, and D. W. Baker, 181–90. Winona Lake, IN: Eisenbrauns, 1994. Informative discussion in support of the idea that the movement of sun and moon in Joshua 10 reflects an ancient omen.

Younger, K. Lawson. *Ancient Conquest Accounts: A Study in Ancient Near Eastern and Biblical History Writing.* Library of Hebrew Bible/OT Studies 98. New York: Bloomsbury T&T Clark, 2009. Comparative study of biblical and ancient Near Eastern battle/conquest accounts.

COMMENTARIES

Howard, David M., Jr. *Joshua.* New American Commentary. Nashville: Broadman & Holman, 1998. Provides the best overview of the different interpretive views on this passage.

WEBSITES

Thompson, Bert. "Has NASA Discovered Joshua's 'Lost Day'?" 1999. http://apologeticspress. org/apcontent.aspx?category=11&article=1329. One of several Christian websites that affirms the supernatural nature of the story in Joshua 10 but that refutes the legend of NASA scientists finding the lost day.

---

18   Hubbard, *Joshua,* 296n57.
19   Hubbard, *Joshua,* 295.

CHAPTER 18

———

You Can Know God's Will by Putting out the Proverbial Fleece

Judges 6

The Legendary Teaching on Gideon's Fleece and Judges 6

Gideon putting out the fleece in Judg 6:36–40 to confirm God's calling of him to deliver Israel from the Midianites provides a model for Christians to follow in determining God's will for their lives. After God's call, Gideon first asked God to make the fleece wet while the ground was dry. After God provided this sign, Gideon asked for the fleece to be wet and the ground dry. The fact that God provided the signs that Gideon asked for encourages us to "put out the fleece" when we need to know God's will for important decisions such as where to live, whom to marry, or whether to take a new job. We can ask God for confirming signs or circumstances so that we can know we are making the right decision.

Countering the Legendary Teaching

"Putting out the fleece" is such a common practice that it is part of our Christianese. "If my prospective employer calls with a job offer by the end of the week, then I will know it's God's will." Or, "If I get an A on my biology exam, it will be God's confirmation that I should apply to medical school." A closer look at Judges 6–8, however, suggests that Gideon is hardly a model for how believers are to seek guidance from God. Gideon's response to God's call for him to be the deliverer of his people is one of doubt and fear that borders on outright unbelief. Daniel Block comments, "Contrary to popular

107

interpretation, this text has nothing to do with discovering or determining the will of God. The divine will is perfectly clear in his mind (v. 16). Gideon's problem is that with his limited experience with God he cannot believe that God always fulfills his word. The request for signs is not a sign of faith but of unbelief."[1]

Gideon Seeks Confirming Signs

The angel of the Lord first addresses Gideon in Judg 6:12 as a "valiant warrior," but Gideon's character and responses to God hardly match this honored designation. Gideon is the only one of the judges to whom God personally appears in a theophany, but Gideon persists in asking for confirming signs even after God has clearly indicated what he is supposed to do.[2] When the angel assures Gideon that the Lord is with him, Gideon's reaction was to question why God had allowed the Midianites to oppress his people in the first place (v. 13). Gideon's response to the Lord was cynical and presumptuous and reflected a disregard for the seriousness of Israel's unfaithfulness to the Lord.

When the Lord calls Gideon to go and deliver Israel, Gideon objects that he is unworthy for the task because of the smallness of his clan and his youth (vv. 14–15). Such objections of unworthiness are the proper response to God's calling and commonly appear in other call narratives as well.[3] Moses objects that he is slow of speech (Exod 4:10), Isaiah proclaims that he is a man of "unclean lips" (Isa 6:5), and Jeremiah protests that he is a child and does not know how to speak (Jer 1:6). Gideon's objections, however, go beyond proper humility and reflect more the kind of doubt that seeks to evade God's calling.

It is not clear how well Gideon knew the Lord at the time of his calling. Gideon's father was at best a paganized Yahwist who worshipped the Canaanite gods (v. 25), and it seems that Gideon has not had the opportunity to observe what a life of faith in the Lord entailed or to receive the kind of teaching that would help him to follow the Lord. This deficit in his life likely explains why the Lord is patient and gracious with Gideon's repeated requests for confirmation of his presence and promises.

---

[1]   Daniel I. Block, *Judges, Ruth*, New American Commentary (Nashville: Broadman & Holman, 1999), 272–73.
[2]   K. Lawson Younger, *Judges and Ruth*, New International Version Application Commentary (Grand Rapids: Zondervan, 2012), 173.
[3]   For a helpful chart comparing the narrative of Gideon's call to other OT call narratives, see Younger, *Judges and Ruth*, 174–75.

In verses 17–18, Gideon makes his first request for a confirming sign by asking the angel to wait as he prepares an offering for him. When Gideon brings the food he has prepared, fire miraculously comes from a rock and consumes the meat and bread, a visible demonstration of God's presence. Rather than the sign overcoming his unbelief and leading to faith, Gideon fearfully believes that he is about to die for seeing the angel of the Lord.

Gideon responds in fear once again when the Lord calls on him to perform his first action—to destroy his father's altar to Baal and the Asherah pole. Devotion to pagan deities was the real reason for Israel's oppression at the hand of the Midianites (vv. 7–10). Gideon obeyed God's directive but did so in the middle of the night out of fear of his family members and the men of his city, reflecting his continued reticence about the Lord's calling on his life.

Everything that happens prior to Gideon putting out the fleece in verses 36–40 demonstrates the redundancy of his request for more signs and confirmation. God has clearly communicated his directives to Gideon. There is no question that God had commanded Gideon to deliver Israel from its oppressors and promised him success. Even as Gideon requests further confirmation in the signs of the fleece, he twice acknowledges in verses 36–37 that God has clearly promised ("as you said") that he would deliver Israel.

Gideon first asks for the wool fleece placed on the threshing floor to be wet and for the ground to be dry. The fact that the fleece was wet enough to wring water out of it while the ground was dry suggests something out of the ordinary has taken place. Gideon says that he will "know" that God will use him to deliver Israel if God fulfills this sign, but Gideon does not keep his word and asks for still another sign with the fleece to assuage his doubt and unbelief. Gideon's request in verse 39 for God not to be angry with him seems to reflect his own awareness that he has begun to test God's patience. The second sign with the fleece is more supernatural in nature, as the ground is wet while the fleece lying on it is dry.

The tests concerning the fleece were not arbitrary requests but related to the Lord demonstrating his sovereign power over Baal. Canaanite mythology taught that Baal was the source of fertility and the rains needed for good crops and harvests. In one Canaanite legend, the weakness of Baal causes the dew to disappear, and Baal even has a daughter who is named "Dew."[4] The signs with the fleece were designed to show that the Lord was more powerful than the gods that the Midianite oppressors and even Gideon's family worshipped.

---

4   Chisholm, *Commentary on Judges and Ruth*, 278–79 (see chap. 6, n. 5).

The Lord had already demonstrated his power and control over Baal when Baal did not avenge the destruction of his own altar, but Gideon still needed further confirmation of the Lord's superiority.

If the signs associated with the fleece emboldened Gideon's faith, the Lord's reduction of the size of his army as he prepared to face the Midianite horde presented another challenge. The Lord reduced Israel's army down to three hundred men, and they went to battle with torches, jars, and trumpets so that Israel would know that they had defeated their enemies in the Lord's strength and not in their own. On the very night of the attack on the Midianites, the Lord offers one more confirming sign to Gideon. The Lord commands Gideon to go down to the Midianite camp secretly so that he might overhear the dream of a Midianite soldier foretelling Israel's ultimate victory in battle. This event finally convinces Gideon to trust in the Lord. The irony of the situation is that Gideon believes the promise of victory when it is conveyed in the dream of a pagan soldier about a loaf of bread rolling through his camp (Josh 7:13–14), but he does not trust this promise when it comes directly from God himself.[5] When Gideon finally acts, the Lord provides the victory over Midian that he had promised all along.

Gideon: A Model for Believers Today?

In many ways, Gideon's putting out the fleece reflects the influence of his pagan upbringing. His use of the fleece is similar to other forms of divination employed in the ancient Near East for consulting the gods or seeking knowledge about the future—practices specifically forbidden in the Mosaic law (see Deut 18:10–12). At best, his actions are a questionable means of receiving divine guidance. In Judg 6:39, Gideon requests that he be allowed "to test" (*nasah*) God just once more, but the Lord had commanded Israel not to "test" (*nasah*) him (Deut 6:16) and had punished Israel in the wilderness for doing this very thing (Exod 17:2, 7; Num 14:22).[6] Gideon was treading on dangerous ground as he put these tests before the Lord; as Block observes, "The remarkable fact is that God responds to his tests. He is more anxious to deliver Israel than to quibble with this man's semi-pagan notions of deity."[7]

When seeking to apply the principles of biblical narratives, it is important to learn the difference between the descriptive and prescriptive elements

---

5   Younger, *Judges and Ruth*, 190.
6   Block, *Judges, Ruth*, 273.
7   Block, *Judges, Ruth*, 273.

of the story. Biblical narratives often describe biblical characters acting in certain ways without prescribing that we should act in the same way. We should also not assume that the way God responded to a certain individual or acted in a specific circumstance is how God will always act or respond. Like other judges in the book of Judges, Gideon is a mixed character with both positive features and negative flaws that we should not necessarily emulate.

The unusual circumstances behind the events in Judges 6–7 further argue against viewing the putting out of the fleece as a normative practice for seeking God. Israel is steeped in idolatry, and Gideon faces an enormous task and a formidable enemy. Bruce Waltke comments, "I have heard of Christians speak of 'putting out a fleece' on whether to purchase a car, invest in a new product, and select a school. Those kinds of decisions, while certainly important to the individual believer, are not the same scale for determining the course of a nation whom God has selected for blessing."[8]

Gideon's act of putting out the fleece is not a normative practice for believers today. The confirming signs that God provided in response to Gideon's tests were unique to the calling of a leader in a time of national crisis for the people of Israel and are not a promise that God is committed to doing the same for us when we are facing decisions. Trusting in signs, tests, and confirming circumstances is a poor substitute for decisions made from a posture of trusting faith and godly wisdom.

Application

Contrary to much popular Christian teaching, the Bible never instructs believers to "find" the will of God for their lives. We are to obey God's "will" as revealed in the commands and directives of Scripture. For example, it is God's "will" for believers to abstain from sexual immorality (1 Thess 4:3) and to be thankful in all circumstances (1 Thess 5:18). As for the working out of God's "will" in terms of his providential plans for our lives (see Rom 1:10; 15:32), our responsibility is to trust prayerfully God's wise and loving direction in our lives. These plans are part of the "hidden things" that belong to the Lord (Deut 29:29). James 1:5 encourages believers to ask for wisdom as they face trials, but this wisdom involves having understanding in how to live godly in difficult circumstances rather than insider information about the future to guide and direct

---

    8   Bruce K. Waltke, *Finding the Will of God: A Pagan Notion?* (Gresham, OR: Vision House, 1995), 67–68.

our choices. God may choose to give personal guidance or to direct through providential circumstances, but nothing in Scripture suggests this type of guidance is the norm for believers who are to walk and live by faith not by sight.

Annotated Bibliography

Books

DeYoung, Kevin, and Joshua Harris. *Just Do Something: A Liberating Approach to Finding God's Will*. Chicago: Moody, 2014. Wise pastoral counsel on how believers are to obey the revealed will of God and prayerfully trust God when making decisions.

Friessen, Garry, with Robin Maxson. *Decision Making and the Will of God: A Biblical Alternative to the Traditional View*. Rev. ed. Sisters, OR: Multnomah, 2004. Excellent discussion of popular misconceptions concerning "the perfect will of God" for a believer's life.

Waltke, Bruce K. *Finding the Will of God: A Pagan Notion?* Gresham, OR: Vision House, 1995. Helpful study that challenges popular Christian conceptions of the will of God and the emphasis on signs and confirmations from God when Christians are facing important decisions.

Commentaries

Block, Daniel I. *Judges, Ruth*. New American Commentary. Nashville: Broadman & Holman, 1999. Scholarly evangelical commentary. Careful analysis of Gideon narratives with clear explanation of the fleece incident.

Younger, K. Lawson. *Judges and Ruth*. New International Version Application Commentary. Grand Rapids: Zondervan, 2002. Scholarly evangelical commentary with exposition of text and suggestions for contemporary application. Addresses the problem of Christians needing signs when discussing Gideon and the fleece.

Websites

"Is It Acceptable to 'Lay out a Fleece' to God in Prayer?" *Got Questions*. Accessed February 23, 2018. https://www.gotquestions.org/prayer-fleece.html. Helpful discussion of why "putting out fleece" is not a model for Christian prayer.

CHAPTER 19

___

God Never Wanted Israel to Have a King
1 Samuel 8–12

The Legendary Teaching on Israel Having a King (1 Samuel 8–12)

The fact that Israel was a theocracy meant that God alone was to rule over his people and that Israel was not to have a human king like other nations. Gideon refused the request of the people of Israel to be their king by reminding the people that God was their king (Judg 8:22–23). The Lord became angry with the people when they asked for a king in the days of Samuel, because such a request reflected that they had rejected him as their ruler (1 Sam 8:7; 10:19). God allowed Israel to have a king only as a concession to their sinful request. The negative assessments of kingship found in 1 Samuel 8–12 reflect why God was opposed to Israel having a king (see 1 Sam 8:6–18; 10:17–19; 12:16–22).

Countering the Legendary Teaching

The argument to be developed here is that kingship was part of God's design and plan for Israel and that the reason for God's anger when the people request a king in 1 Samuel 8 is not the request itself but rather the reasons and motives behind the request. One indication that human kingship was not in conflict with the Lord's theocratic rule over Israel was that shared divine and human kinship was part of God's design for humanity from the very beginning. God created humans in or as his image and gave them dominion over the earth and all other creatures (Gen 1:26–28). The word *image* (*tselem*) often refers to a statue, and the metaphor conveys the idea that God has placed humans as little statues of himself to implement his sovereign rule over the earth by

113

doing his work and reflecting his character.[1] In Egypt and other cultures, kings were viewed as the "image of God," but the Old Testament democratizes this concept in asserting that all humans reflect God's royal image. Kings would often place statues of themselves throughout their domain as an expression and reminder of their sovereignty, which is precisely what God did with humans as well. The role of humanity was to serve as God's vice-regents. God would ultimately use Israel's kings (through the line of David) to restore dominion to all of humanity.

Promises of a King for Israel and Rules for Kingship

God had specifically promised that kings would come from the line of Abraham and Jacob (Gen 17:6, 16; 35:11). When Jacob blessed his sons, he promised dominion to Judah and his descendants (Gen 49:10–11), anticipating the future reign of the house of David. When the pagan prophet Balaam was hired to put a curse on Israel prior to their entry into the Promised Land, he instead promised great blessing for Israel's future, including a ruler who would arise like a star (Num 24:17–19). At a very early stage in redemptive history, God revealed his plans to bless Israel with powerful rulers.

The rules of kingship set forth in Deut 17:14–20 reflect that God would allow Israel to have a king and that this arrangement was expected and anticipated when Israel entered the land. Eugene Merrill observes that "monarchy was the prevalent mode of government in the late Bronze Age throughout the eastern Mediterranean world. It is inconceivable that Israel would alone embrace some other system, even as a theocracy."[2] At the same time, the king's status in Deuteronomy is lessened by the way that God provides or instructs Israel to appoint other leaders (judges, 16:18; priests, 18:5; and prophets, 18:15), while it is the people who will say, "I will set a king over me" (17:14). This contrast in some sense makes the king "an unessential part of the picture."[3]

There was a leadership void in Israel following the death of Joshua, and the story of the failed leadership of the judges and the recurring statement of the epilogue of Judges that "there was no king in Israel" (17:6; 18:1; 19:1; 21:25) reflects that God's ultimate intention was for Israel to have a

---

[1]   See Peter J. Gentry and Stephen J. Wellum, *Kingdom through Covenant: A Biblical-Theological Understanding of the Covenants* (Wheaton, IL: Crossway, 2012), 191–202.

[2]   Merrill, *Deuteronomy*, 265 (see chap. 3, n. 2).

[3]   J. G. McConville, "Deuteronomy, Book of," in *IVP Dictionary of the Old Testament Pentateuch*, ed. T. Desmond Alexander and David W. Baker (Downers Grove, IL: InterVarsity Press, 2003), 187.

king. God acts in the book of Ruth to rectify this situation by preparing for Israel to have a king (see Ruth 4:13–22). The problem in Judges, however, is not simply the lack of monarchy but rather the lack of the Torah-focused ruler envisioned in Deut 17:14–20. Verses 18–20 stipulate that the king is to write out his own copy of the law so that he would read it and govern by it throughout his lifetime. Both leaders and people fail to follow the Lord and his commands. Monarchy alone would not solve the problem, but a king like the one envisioned in Deuteronomy 17 would be a step in the right direction.

The Problem with Israel's Requests for a King

The problem with Israel's initial requests for a king is that they reflect that Israel desired the wrong kind of king or wanted a king for all the wrong reasons. In Judg 8:22–23, the people come to Gideon and request that he and his sons be their kings because Gideon has "saved/delivered" (*yasha'*) them from the Midianites. The people fail to acknowledge that it was the Lord who had delivered them, using Gideon as his human instrument. The Lord had called Gideon to "save/deliver" (*yasha'*) Israel (Judg 6:14) and had reminded the fearful Gideon that his presence and power would enable Gideon to fulfill his commission (vv. 15–16). The source of Gideon's strength would be the Spirit of the Lord coming upon him (v. 34). The reduction of Gideon's army from thousands down to 300 men demonstrated that the Lord alone was the source of the victory (Judg 7:2, 7). The Lord was the one who had "handed over" the Midianites to Gideon (Judg 7:2, 9, 14). In requesting a king, the people had ignored the true source of their victory.

Gideon's response to the people in Judg 8:23 is often offered as proof that the Old Testament is opposed to human kingship, but Gideon instead reflects his own mixed motives and failure to properly understand how his leadership relates to the Lord's kingship. Gideon initially appears to reflect humility and respect in refusing to encroach upon the Lord's kingship, but he then turns around and acts like the despotic kings of the other nations that the Israelites were not supposed to imitate.[4] Gideon causes a problem by fashioning an ephod out of gold, an idolatrous object used for obtaining oracles (Judg 8:27; compare 1 Sam 14:3; 23:9; 30:7).[5] Gideon also accumulates multiple wives

---

[4]   See Waltke, *Old Testament Theology*, 683–84 (see chap. 6, n. 9).
[5]   Chisholm, *Commentary on Judges and Ruth*, 291–92 (see chap. 6, n. 5).

and a concubine in violation of Deuteronomy 17 (Judg 8:30–31) and has a son named Abimelech ("my father is king") (Judg 9:1). All of these actions undermine the credibility of Gideon's protest that he does not desire to be Israel's king.[6]

Gideon's more subtle royal aspirations take on pathological proportions in his son Abimelech, who slaughters his seventy brothers before becoming the first human to claim the title of king in Israel (Judges 9). Jotham's fable, depicting Abimelech as a worthless shrub, is not a polemic against kingship but rather an indictment of Abimelech's lack of character and of the men of Shechem for turning to him for leadership.[7]

The Lord's response to Israel's request for a king in 1 Sam 8:6–9 is that his people have rejected him as their king and are once again rebelling against him. Although this statement might appear to indicate that God was unequivocally opposed to the institution of kingship, the real issue is the motivation behind Israel's request. The reason for their request was that they desired to "be like all the other nations" by having a human ruler who would go out and fight their battles for them (1 Sam 8:20). David Firth explains that the request for a king was "fundamentally a new idolatry, an attempt to establish a model of government that supplants Yahweh's authority with that of the king."[8] The way in which the Lord had delivered Israel from the Philistines in 1 Samuel 7 in response to Samuel's intercession and the miraculous ways that the Lord had fought on Israel's behalf throughout their history demonstrated that the Lord was more than capable of delivering Israel from their enemies in ways that no human ruler could. But the people were more inclined to trust the human deliverer than the Lord as their source of security. Despite the Lord's negative assessment of the people's request, 1 Sam 2:10, 34–35 indicates that the Lord was already preparing to give Israel a king.[9]

In the story of Saul's appointment as Israel's first king, there are both negative (1 Sam 8:4–22; 10:17–27; 12:1–25) and positive (9:1–10:16; 11:1–15) assessments of the prospects for kingship in Israel. The text reflects the ambiguities that having a king would involve for Israel. The king would fight their battles, but he would also confiscate their lands, take their sons and daughters for his own services, and impose heavy taxes on them.[10]

---

6   Waltke, *Old Testament Theology*, 684.
7   Waltke, *Old Testament Theology*, 684–85.
8   David G. Firth, *1 & 2 Samuel*, Apollos Old Testament Commentary (Downers Grove, IL: InterVarsity Press, 2009), 116.
9   Firth, *1 & 2 Samuel*, 111.
10   For more on the tensions between kingship and the socioeconomic egalitarianism reflected in the

Similar ambiguities are present with the selection of Saul as king. The Lord accedes to the people's request and gives them a king of impressive physical stature as they have desired (1 Sam 9:2), but Saul is ultimately not the right man for the job. Saul is reticent to go to battle and is unable to deliver Israel from the Philistines. His rule would ultimately dissolve due to his paranoid fixation with his rival David.

God's Blessing of Kingship in Israel and the Hope for the Future

In spite of the negative circumstances surrounding the rise of kingship in Israel, kingship was a gift from God rather than merely a concession to Israel's stubborn sinfulness. The Lord would replace Saul, the king the people wanted, with David, the king he desired for Israel (1 Sam 13:14). The Lord would graciously enter into a covenant with David's line that established the Davidic kings as God's adopted sons and promised to establish David's throne forever (2 Sam 7:13–14). Despite the persistent unfaithfulness of the majority of David's sons, the Lord kept the lamp of the Davidic dynasty burning (see 1 Kgs 15:4; 2 Kgs 8:19). In the Psalter, the royal psalms celebrate the blessings of the Davidic king as God's anointed ruler and reflect the ongoing hope of God's ultimate fulfillment of his covenant promises to David even where there was no king on the throne (see Pss 2; 45; 72; 110; 132; 144). Though the prophets of Israel and Judah denounced the sinful behavior of the kings of their day, they looked forward to the time when the Lord would fulfill his covenant promises to David by raising up the ideal king of justice and righteousness (see Isa 9:2–7; 11:1–9; 32:1; Jer 23:5–6; 30:8–9; 33:15–16; Ezek 34:23–24; 37:24–25; Hos 3:5; Amos 9:11–12; Mic 5:2–5; Zech 9:9–10).

Application

The rule of Jesus as the Davidic Messiah will ultimately fully restore the image of God and dominion for redeemed humanity (compare Ps 8:3–8 with Heb 2:5–9; Dan 7:13–14, 26; Matt 19:28; Rev 2:26–27). The working out of salvation history reflects both the wisdom and grace of God. Even the negative story of how Israel got its first king becomes part of how God would ultimately

Mosaic law, see Wright, *Old Testament Ethics for the People of God*, 54–61, 89–99 (see chap. 12, n. 2).

restore humanity to its rightful place as his vice-regents. Jesus presently rules as the son of David at the right hand of the Father in heaven, and through Jesus, God's people will share in the dominion of God's eternal kingdom.

Annotated Bibliography

BOOKS

Waltke, Bruce K., with Charles Yu. *An Old Testament Theology: An Exegetical, Canonical, and Thematic Approach.* Grand Rapids: Zondervan, 2007. Helpful chapter ("The Gift of Kingship") summarizing the Old Testament perspective on kingship.

COMMENTARIES

Firth, David G. *1 & 2 Samuel.* Apollos Old Testament Commentary. Downers Grove, IL: InterVarsity Press, 2009. Scholarly evangelical commentary with careful analysis of Israel's request for a king in 1 Samuel 8–10.

JOURNAL ARTICLES/WEBSITES

Howard, David M., Jr. "The Case for Kingship in Deuteronomy and Former Prophets." *Westminster Theological Journal* 52 (1990): 101–15. *Biblical Studies.* Accessed August 25, 2017. https://biblicalstudies.org.uk/article_kingship_howard.html. Provides a detailed analysis of key Old Testament texts supporting the idea that kingship was God's design for ancient Israel.

Howard, David M., Jr. "The Case for Kingship in the Old Testament Narrative Books and the Psalms." *Trinity Journal* 9 (1988): 19–35. Accessed August 25, 2017. http://faculty.gordon.edu/hu/bi/ted_hildebrandt/OTeSources/19-Psalms/Text/Articles/Howard-KingshipPsalms-TJ.htm. Demonstrates divine support for kingship in Old Testament Historical Books and Psalms.

CHAPTER 20

Christians Should Never Question
the Authority of Church Leaders
1 Samuel 24–26

The Legendary Teaching on "Touch Not the Lord's Anointed"

David's refusal to "touch the Lord's anointed" when he has two opportunities to kill Saul in 1 Samuel 24 and 26 reflects his understanding of the absolute authority of those who are divinely appointed to positions of leadership. Just as David refused to take matters into his own hands when it came to removing Saul from his office as king, believers today are not to challenge or question the authority of church leaders. Challenging the teaching or actions of a spiritual leader demonstrates a refusal to submit to their authority as instructed in the New Testament (Heb 13:17). Those who challenge leaders whom God has placed in authority are guilty of rebellion against God himself, and those who dare to criticize the leaders God has placed over the church will suffer divine discipline and chastisement for their sin.

Countering the Legendary Teaching

David's resolve not to "lift his hand" against the Lord's anointed (1 Sam 24:6; 26:9, 11, 23) refers not to the questioning of Saul's authority, but rather to David's refusal to kill the king out of respect for the fact that God had chosen Saul to rule over his people Israel. The expression "Do not touch my anointed ones" (touch not the Lord's anointed) appears only in Ps 105:15 and the parallel passage in 1 Chr 16:22 and has nothing to do with submission to spiritual leaders, but refers instead to God's protection of the patriarchs from violence at the hands of foreign kings.

The term *anointed one* is never used for spiritual leaders in the New Testament, and kings as the Lord's "anointed ones" had a special authority that is not the same as the authority granted to leaders in the church today. Even though kings had a higher level of authority than that conferred on spiritual leaders in the church, they were still accountable to others for how they exercised their divinely appointed offices and roles. The use of the command "touch not the Lord's anointed" to suggest that spiritual leaders are not accountable to others ignores the original context of this command and reflects a distorted view of how leadership is to be exercised within the church.

David's Refusal to Act against "the LORD's Anointed" (1 Samuel 24, 26)

In 1 Samuel 24 and 26, David is on the run from Saul, who is seeking to kill David and eliminate him as a rival to the throne. Then the tables are turned. Even though he has the opportunity to remove the threat to his own life by killing Saul, David states that he will not "lift [stretch out] his hand" (*shalah* + *yad*) against the "LORD's anointed" (24:6; 26:9, 11, 23). On the first occasion, David and his men observe Saul slipping into a cave to relieve himself. Rather than killing the king, David cuts off the corner of the king's robe that he later shows to Saul as proof that he has no interest in taking the king's life. On the second occasion, David finds Saul and his men asleep in their camp but refuses to allow Abishai to put Saul to death.

David informs his men that he could not be found "innocent" if he lifts his hand against Saul as God's anointed one (26:9). David refuses to kill Saul because God, through Samuel, has chosen Saul as king (1 Samuel 9–10).[1] The symbolic act of anointing has confirmed the divine choice of Saul as king (1 Sam 10:1).[2] David even refuses to act against Saul in spite of the fact that Samuel has already anointed David as Saul's replacement (1 Sam 16:11–13). Later when an Amalekite soldier would take credit for killing a mortally wounded Saul, David orders the man executed specifically for the crime of lifting his hand "against the LORD's anointed" (2 Sam 1:14–16). David acted above reproach with regard to Saul and would have nothing to do with his downfall or death.[3]

---

[1]   Contrast Saul's willingness to put to death the anointed "priests of the LORD" in 1 Sam 22:13–19.
[2]   The term *anointed one* refers primarily to priests and kings in Israel, who were both anointed with oil in a ritual of inauguration into their office. For "anointed one(s)" as a title for the king in Israel/Judah, see also 1 Sam 2:35; 16:6; 2 Chr 6:42; Pss 2:2; 84:9; 132:10, 17.
[3]   See Robert B. Chisholm, *1 & 2 Samuel*, Teach the Text (Grand Rapids: Baker, 2014), 161–63, 173–75.

"Lifting one's hand against the LORD's anointed" in 1 Samuel 24 and 26 is far removed from its typical application to contemporary church life and refers instead to acts of violence or murder. Slander, gossip, and false accusations against spiritual leaders in the church are sinful acts that threaten the spiritual health and vitality of any local church, but that is a different category from this; for David to challenge Saul's authority as king or to commit violence against him would be to challenge the sovereign authority of Yahweh himself. It was the Lord's prerogative to choose Israel's kings, and the Lord would later make a covenant with David that gave divine approval for the house of David to rule permanently over Israel. Each Davidic king was adopted as the Lord's "son" and ruled as his earthly vice-regent (see 2 Sam 7:13–16; Ps 2:6–7). Their authority over the nations was a reflection of the Lord's sovereign rule (Ps 2:7–9; compare Ps 89:9–14, 20–29). Although church leaders chosen by God and gifted for their roles in the church are to be given respect and honor, their authority is not the same as the political, military, legal, and spiritual authority given to Israel's kings as the rulers over God's people. Acting to remove the king when not directed by the Lord to do so was an act of political treason that threatened to undermine the stability of Israel as a nation. The assassination of kings and heirs to the throne would often have disastrous effects in both Israel and Judah.[4]

Even with their royal authority as the Lord's anointed, kings were not above criticism, rebuke, and confrontation for their sinful conduct. David would not lift his hand against Saul, but he directly confronted Saul for how he had treated him unfairly. He also called on God to act on his behalf in bringing divine retribution against Saul (1 Sam 24:9–15). Perhaps the most difficult and dangerous aspect of a prophet's job description in ancient Israel was to denounce kings for specific acts of sin and disobedience. Prophets confronting kings is a common story line in the Hebrew Bible. The prophets in these instances were not acting on their own initiative but rather at the direction of the Lord himself. Samuel rebuked Saul for his disobedience and lack of trust in the Lord and even informed the king that the Lord had rejected him as king because of his failure to carry out the Lord's directives (1 Samuel 13, 15). Nathan confronted David for his sins of adultery and murder (2 Samuel 12). And Elijah denounced the apostasy and violence of Ahab (1 Kgs 17:1; 18:18; 21:17–24). False prophets were often on the royal payroll because they refused to confront the king's sinful behavior (1 Kgs 18:19;

---

4   Note the condemnation of the assassinations and constant regime changes that characterized the northern kingdom of Israel in Hos 7:5–7, even though many of these kings were not directly chosen by God in the same manner as Saul or David.

22:6). These examples clearly demonstrate that there were times when it was necessary to question and challenge the authority of the "Lord's anointed."

"Touch Not the Lord's Anointed"
(Psalm 105:15 and 1 Chronicles 16:22)

The only reference to "touching the Lord's anointed" is found in Ps 105:15 (and its parallel text in 1 Chr 16:22). Psalm 105 celebrates the Lord's saving acts throughout Israel's history that have demonstrated his faithfulness to his covenant promises. Just as with "lifting a hand against the Lord's anointed" in Samuel, the phrase "touch not the Lord's anointed" refers to physical violence and has nothing to do with challenging the authority of a leader.[5] Psalm 105:9–15 specifically recalls the Lord's covenant faithfulness to the patriarchs in Genesis before Israel became a nation. The Lord promised to give the land of Canaan to Abraham and his descendants, but the patriarchs themselves never possessed the land, as they wandered from place to place as aliens. Even though Abraham's family was small in number (only sixty-six people in Gen 46:26 as Jacob prepares to go down to Egypt), the Lord watched over his fledgling people. In protecting his chosen servants, the Lord ordered kings not to "touch" them or to "harm his prophets."[6] This directive seems to refer to when the Lord threatened Abimelech with death if he took Sarah into his royal harem (Gen 20:1–7; compare 12:10–20; 26:6–11).[7] The term *anointed one* elsewhere in the Old Testament specifically refers to kings and priests, but here reflects Abraham's special status before the Lord.[8] The patriarchs are even referred to as "prophets" because they communicated with God and were able to intercede on behalf of others (see Gen 20:7).[9] In its only Old Testament reference, "touch not the Lord's anointed" has nothing to do with God's people submitting to their leaders, but rather to foreign kings not using their power to harm or kill God's servants. The protection that the Lord gave Abraham was reflective of his protective concern for all the people of Israel and not just their leaders. In Zech 2:8–9, the Lord promises that he will judge

---

5   The Hebrew verb for "to touch" (*naga'*) elsewhere has this same meaning of "to strike, to harm, disturb, or to touch violently" (see Gen 26:29; Josh 9:19; 2 Sam 5:8; 14:10).

6   The only other Old Testament text associating "anointing" with prophets is 1 Kgs 19:16.

7   John Goldingay, *Psalms*, vol. 3, *Psalms 90–150*, Baker Commentary on the Old Testament Wisdom and Psalms (Grand Rapids: Baker Academic, 2008), 209.

8   Goldingay, *Psalms*, 209, suggests that the term is used metaphorically here because the patriarchs functioned as kings and priests (see Gen 12:7–8; 14:1–24).

9   Goldingay, *Psalms*, 209.

Israel's enemies because anyone who "touches/harms" (*naga'*) Israel is actually "touching" (*naga'*) the Lord's own eye.

Leadership Authority and Accountability in the Local Church

Spiritual leaders in the church are appointed by God to teach the Word of God, to oversee the life of the community, to protect the church from those who seek to harm it, and to train its members for the work of ministry (see Acts 20:28–30; Eph 4:11–16; 1 Pet 5:1–4). Paul reminds Timothy of his responsibility to "preach . . . rebuke, correct, and encourage" (2 Tim 4:2). Those appointed by God will answer to God for how they serve in their appointed roles (Heb 13:17; 1 Pet 4:5) and will even be judged by God by a more exacting standard for how they have lived out their teaching (Jas 3:1).

Because of the authority given to leaders in the church, the church body has the responsibility to respect and honor their leadership. The writer of Hebrews instructs his readers to "remember" their leaders (perhaps those who have already died), to "imitate" their faith and lifestyle, and also to "obey" their teaching and to "submit" to their authority (Heb 13:7, 17). As George Guthrie explains, this obedience and submission does not mean that church members are to "give their leaders a 'blank check' or uncritical deference in all situations," but it does mean submitting to these leaders as they faithfully teach God's Word and model a lifestyle of Christian discipleship.[10] This type of submission enables the leader to do the difficult work of ministry with joy and fulfillment.

The common misunderstanding that "touch not the LORD's anointed" refers to the unquestioned following of a spiritual leader ignores the responsibility of the church and its members to constantly assess and evaluate if the teaching of their leaders conforms to Scripture and to the standards of sound doctrine. Jesus warned his disciples of the constant threat of false prophets (Matt 7:15; 24:11, 24). Paul's recurring charge to Timothy was to counter false teaching with his preaching and his godly example (1 Tim 1:3–7, 18–20; 4:1–4; 6:2–6; 2 Tim 1:13–18; 2:14–19; 3:10–17; 4:1–4). The problem of false teachers is a prominent theme in the epistles of 2 Peter, Jude, and the letters of John, and the corruptive influence of belief systems that challenge the truth of the gospel inside and outside the church is just as real today.

---

[10]   George H. Guthrie, *Hebrews*, New International Version Application Commentary (Grand Rapids: Zondervan, 1998), 447.

The responsibility for keeping false teaching and doctrine out of the church belongs to the church body as well as its teachers and leaders. John instructs the church to "test the spirits to see if they are from God" (1 John 4:1). Church members are to have the kind of spiritual maturity and "theological radar" that enables them to identify teaching that does not conform to orthodox faith and sound doctrine.[11] The term *anointed one* is not used for church leaders in the New Testament, but 1 John 2:20, 27 does teach that all true believers have an "anointing" (*chrisma*) from the Holy Spirit that enables them to know and apply spiritual truth to their lives.[12] Church members are not to accept or follow blindly what their leaders tell them, but they are to be like the Bereans who "examined the Scriptures daily" to see if the teaching they heard was true or not (Acts 17:11).[13] Pastors and teachers with pure doctrine and sincere motives for ministry welcome this type of examination and create an open environment for church members to address questions and concerns regarding teaching, lifestyle, or leadership decisions.

Application

The misuse of "touch not the LORD's anointed" often promotes an autocratic view of ministry in which pastors or spiritual leaders seek to control and manipulate those under their care by claiming to have unquestioned authority to rule over the church. Biblical leaders model servanthood in following the example of Jesus by putting the needs of others above their own personal ambitions and agendas. The New Testament not only instructs church members to submit to their leaders, but also tells all believers to "submit" to one another out of reverence for Christ (Eph 5:18–21). All believers have a mutual responsibility to teach and serve one another (Col 3:16). The New Testament also promotes the model of a plurality of leadership in the local church so that its leaders are accountable to one another as well as to the church body as a whole (see Acts 14:23; Tit 1:5; Jas 5:14; 1 Pet 5:1). Spiritual leaders who have no accountability to others not only harm the church but also open their lives to the dangers of moral compromise and lapses of integrity. Even in ancient Israel, the king as the Lord's "anointed one" with all of

---

[11]   Gary M. Burge, *Letters of John,* New International Version Application Commentary (Grand Rapids: Zondervan, 1996), 179.

[12]   2 Cor 1:20–22 also refers to all believers as "anointed" (*chrio*) by God.

[13]   See also David A. Croteau, *Urban Legends of the New Testament: 40 Common Misconceptions* (Nashville: Broadman & Holman, 2015), 167–73, for more on this topic.

his royal power was held accountable by the prophets for how they lived and ruled in accordance with God's law.

Annotated Bibliography

COMMENTARIES
Chisholm, Robert B., Jr. *1 & 2 Samuel*. Teach the Text Commentary Series. Grand Rapids: Baker, 2013. Combines exposition of the text with suggestions and applications for teaching and preaching.
Firth, David G. *1 & 2 Samuel*. Apollos Old Testament Commentary. Downers Grove, IL: InterVarsity Press, 2009. Scholarly evangelical commentary with detailed treatments on 1 Samuel 24 and 26
Goldingay, John. *Psalms*, Vol. 3, *Psalms 90–150*. Baker Commentary on the Old Testament. Wisdom and Psalms. Grand Rapids: Baker Academic, 2008. Scholarly evangelical commentary with helpful discussion of Psalm 105.

WEBSITES
Stevens, M. Hamilton. "What Does Touch NOT My Anointed Really Mean?" *LinkedIn* (blog). December 26, 2014. https://www.linkedin.com/pulse/what-does-touch-my-anointed-really-mean-stevens-th-d-cprp. Helpful summary of issues that reflects conclusions like those found here.

CHAPTER 21

If Americans Repent, God Promises to Fix Our Nation

2 Chronicles 7:14

The Legendary Teaching on 2 Chronicles 7:14

We have a problem in our country. The politicians are corrupt, and the judicial system is filled with biased ideologues. Business leaders are overly greedy for profits at any cost. Marriages are falling apart. But there is a cure, a way to fix the problems. God himself said, "If my people who are called by my name humble themselves, and pray and seek my face and turn from their wicked ways, then I will hear from heaven and will forgive their sin and heal their land" (2 Chr 7:14 ESV). If Americans, particularly the leaders of our country, would simply humble themselves before the Lord Almighty and pray to him, if they would turn from all their sins, God will do three things. First, he will hear their prayer requests. Second, he will forgive their sins. Third, he will heal our great land. Our country will again thrive and prosper. The soil will produce bountifully. We will be victorious in our desire to see freedom spread throughout the world. Then God will fix our nation.

Countering the Legendary Teaching

These verses have a specific historical and literary context and are given to Israel, who lived under a different and, specifically, national covenant that applies to no other nation. By examining these areas, it will become clear how this verse has been misused.

Second Chronicles 3 describes Solomon building the temple on Mount Moriah in Jerusalem. It provides the details of when he built it (3:2) and the measurements (3:3–4). The many details paint a beautiful picture of this ornate building (3:5–4:22). Chapter 5 tells the story of the ark of the covenant being transferred to the temple. The ark symbolized God's presence and also refers to the covenant God made with Israel during the exodus.[1] Notice the emphasis on the Mosaic covenant: "Nothing was in the ark except the two tablets that Moses had put in it at Horeb, where the LORD had made a covenant with the Israelites when they came out of Egypt" (2 Chr 5:10). After the ark is placed in the temple, a cloud fills the temple and "the glory of the LORD filled God's temple" (5:14). Solomon gives a speech that dedicates the temple (2 Chr 6:1–11) and follows that with a prayer of dedication (6:12–42).

As a response to Solomon's prayer, God sends fire from heaven to consume the offering and sacrifices (7:1). The responses of the priests, Israelites, and Solomon himself are described, all of which honor the Lord (7:2–10). After Israel is told to return to their homes, the Lord appears to Solomon. This is the literary context leading to the verse under study.

The Immediate Context: 2 Chronicles 7:13

Second Chronicles 7:13–16 are key verses for understanding 1 and 2 Chronicles. As Martin Selman concludes: "This paragraph reveals the heart of the books of Chronicles, and is actually Chronicles' summary of the essential message of the Old Testament."[2] The Lord begins his words to Solomon by explaining that he has answered Solomon's prayers and that this newly built temple is acceptable to him (7:12; compare Deut 12:18). Verse 13 is extremely important for a proper interpretation of verse 14: "When I shut up the heavens so that there is no rain, or command the locust to devour the land, or send pestilence among my people" (7:13 ESV).

First, there is a connection to the Mosaic covenant. When the ark of the covenant was brought to the temple (2 Chronicles 5), reference was specifically made to the Ten Commandments. As part of the Mosaic covenant, Deuteronomy 28 spells out the consequences for not obeying the stipulations in the covenant. Reference to a lack of rain is made in Deut 28:23–24 (see

---

[1]   Martin J. Selman, *2 Chronicles: An Introduction and Commentary*, Tyndale Old Testament Commentaries (Downers Grove, IL: InterVarsity Press, 1994), 331–32.

[2]   Selman, *2 Chronicles*, 354.

Lev 26:19), where the "sky above you will be bronze." Eugene Merrill says that this means that the "rains would not leak through the skies."[3] Deuteronomy 28 also references the impact disobedience will have on their crops (vv. 16, 18, 30, 38–40, 42), with verse 38 explicitly referencing locusts: "You will sow much seed in the field but harvest little, because locusts will devour it." Finally, pestilence (i.e., disease) will ravage Israel if they disobey the covenant, as mentioned in verses 21–22; 27, 35, 59–61, with verse 21 stating that God "will make pestilence cling to you until he has exterminated you from the land you are entering to possess." The three calamities are referenced as consequences of disobedience to the Mosaic covenant.

In fact, Solomon referenced all three of these calamities in his prayer in 2 Chronicles 6. The lack of rain (v. 26), the locusts (v. 28), and pestilence (v. 28) are all connected to Israel's sin (vv. 27, 30). Solomon also asks that when they turn from their sin and pray to God, God would forgive them and end the calamities (vv. 28, 30).

Although these consequences are mentioned in many other places in the Old Testament in reference to Israel's sin, the placement of these three in 2 Chr 7:13, their connection to the Mosaic covenant, and the echo from Solomon's prayer all connect these calamities to the covenant Israel made with God.

Interpreting 2 Chronicles 7:14

The verse, 2 Chr 7:14, begins by limiting the scope of application: "and my people, who bear my name."[4] As Ralph Klein states, the "focus in this verse excludes the reference to the foreigner,"[5] so it is specifically referring to Israelites. Then God refers to four aspects of repentance (humbling themselves, praying, seeking God's face, and turning from their wicked ways),[6] not "four separate steps on a long road to forgiveness."[7] The verb for "humbled" (*kana*) is used several times in 2 Chronicles in significant ways. For example, in 2 Chr 12:7, the Israelites humbled themselves, and God decided not to pour out his wrath upon them. In 32:26, after the Israelites living in Jerusalem humbled them-

---

3 Merrill, *Deuteronomy*, 359 (see chap. 3, n. 2).
4 For an analysis on the structure of God's reply, see Selman, *2 Chronicles*, 353–57.
5 Ralph W. Klein, *2 Chronicles: A Commentary*, ed. Paul D. Hanson, Hermeneia (Minneapolis: Fortress, 2012), 111. Note that Selman, *2 Chronicles*, 354–55, says that his invitation can be applied to all who call on the name of the Lord.
6 See Klein, *2 Chronicles*, 111. Note that the Hebrew word for "turn," *shub*, is many times translated as repent in the Old Testament (see, e.g., 1 Kgs 8:47; 13:33; 2 Chr 6:37; Ezek 14:6; 18:30; Hos 11:5 in the CSB).
7 Selman, *2 Chronicles*, 355.

selves, God ceased being angry with them.[8] Turning away from God brings negative consequences (2 Chr 7:19–20; 36:13), but when Israel turns to God, he receives them (2 Chr 15:4; 30:6, 9).

If Israel does this, if they repent, God commits to three actions. First, he will hear from heaven, surely a response to Solomon's many requests that God listen to the prayers of his people. More specifically, Solomon has asked eight times that God, from his dwelling place in heaven, hear the Israelites (2 Chr 6:21, 23, 25, 27, 30, 33, 35, 39). Second, he will forgive their sin. This is a response to five requests made by Solomon, also in chapter 6 (vv. 21, 25, 27, 30, 39). Third, God promises to repair the damage done by the lack of rain, locusts, and pestilence by healing the land. When God removes the curses of the covenant, it reflects a restoration to covenant fellowship.[9]

Three aspects of Solomon's prayer will help in understanding this promise by God. First, in 6:25, Solomon asks that God "restore them to the land you gave them and their ancestors" when they turn to him. Second, Solomon asks God, when they turn back, to "send rain on your land" (v. 27), which would help them recover from the drought. Third, when they turn back to him (v. 29) and God forgives them (v. 30), he declares that they will honor him with their lives as "they live on the land you gave our ancestors" (v. 31). This connection to the "land" of Israel was a key aspect of the Mosaic covenant, as the nine references explicitly to the land in Deuteronomy 28 make clear, for example. This request by Solomon and promise by God appears to be fulfilled in 2 Chr 30:20: "So the Lord heard Hezekiah and healed the people."

One last indicator to demonstrate that the promises of 2 Chr 7:14 are replies to Solomon's request is the connection between 6:40 and 7:15. In 6:40, Solomon is concluding his prayer and he makes two related requests: "Now, O my God, let your eyes be open and your ears attentive to the prayer of this place" (ESV). In 7:15, God begins with the same Hebrew word used in 6:40, "now" (*'attah*): "Now my eyes will be open and my ears attentive to the prayer that is made in this place" (ESV). Notice how Solomon and God specifically referred to the prayers that were made in "this place," a reference to the newly finished temple in Jerusalem. As Josh Buice concludes:

---

[8]   See also 2 Chr 33:12; 34:27. For examples where not humbling themselves led to negative consequences, see 2 Chr 33:23; 36:12. For significant examples of praying, see 2 Chr 32:20, 24; 33:3. For significant examples connected to seeking God's face, see 2 Chr 11:16; 15:4, 15; 20:4. See Klein, *2 Chronicles*, 111–12, for these examples described and explained.

[9]   See, e.g., Lev 26:40–42.

"We must remember that Americans are **not** God's people."[10] Interpreting this passage without carefully considering the historical and literary context could lead to poor applications.

Application

Second Chronicles 7:14 is not a promise that God will fix the American government if the leaders or citizens repent. It has a specific historical context, referring to the nation of Israel. The consequences for sin in verse 13 are not necessarily consequences expected today since we are no longer functioning under the Mosaic covenant but the new covenant. Similarly, the promises made in verse 14 need to be understood in light of the change in covenant. That does not mean that there are no applications for Christians today, as this verse can appropriately be applied to the church.

Russell Moore understands the seriousness of the way this verse is misused. He says that by applying this text to America, bypassing Israel as the people of God, we could wrongly think that our citizenship as Americans "is the foundation of the 'covenant' God has made with us." Further, he states, "The problem is that we are missing Christ." We end up preaching a false gospel when we bypass Christ, because he is the only mediator between God and humanity (1 Tim 2:5).[11]

God desires for all his people to humble themselves (Jas 4:6; 1 Pet 3:8; 5:5 [citing Prov 3:34], 6). He also desires that we pray for our nation (1 Tim 2:1–4). But remember that the promise in 2 Chr 7:14 is "not a divine promise to Christians in the United States that God will fix our nation. We don't have such a guarantee in Scripture."[12]

One aspect of "healing" is the forgiveness of sins (repeatedly referenced in 2 Chronicles 6), which is paralleled in the New Testament. Verses such as Acts 2:38; 5:31; 26:18; Col 1:14; and Eph 1:7 highlight the importance of this concept.[13]

Although God is concerned with the spiritual life and health of every nation, his relationship with Israel was unique. As Christians pray and live

[10] Josh Buice, "Butchered Bible–2 Chronicles 7:14," *Delivered by Grace*, May 17, 2012, http://www.deliveredbygrace.com/butchered-bible-2-chronicles-714/.
[11] Russell Moore, "2 Chronicles 7:14 Isn't about American Politics," *RussellMoore.com*, January 14, 2016, https://www.russellmoore.com/2016/01/14/2-chronicles-714-isnt-about-american-politics/.
[12] Tim Chaffey, "Commonly Misused Bible Verses: 2 Chronicles 7:14," *Midwest Apologetics* (blog), July 5, 2011, http://midwestapologetics.org/blog/?p=462.
[13] Note also the possible parallel in Mark 2:5–11.

their lives honoring God, they will surely be salt and light in their culture, thus having a positive impact on the society in which they live (see Matt 5:13–16). Even if this happens and great revivals occur throughout our nation, that does not necessarily mean that anything in the political system will be fixed.

Annotated Bibliography

COMMENTARIES

Selman, Martin. *2 Chronicles: An Introduction and Commentary*. Tyndale Old Testament Commentaries. Downers Grove, IL: InterVarsity Press, 1994. See 352–57. Selman provides a concise and accessible interpretation of this verse, placing it in its historical and literary context.

WEBSITES

Guzik, David. "2 Chronicles 7—The Temple Dedicated." *Enduring Word*. Accessed October 16, 2018. https://enduringword.com/bible-commentary/2-chronicles-7/. Helpful summary of different commentaries on the verse.

Buice, Josh. "Butchered Bible—2 Chronicles 7:14." *Delivered by Grace* (blog). May 17, 2012. http://www.deliveredbygrace.com/butchered-bible-2-chronicles-714/. A short explanation on the misuse and proper use of this verse.

Moore, Russell. "2 Chronicles 7:14 Isn't about American Politics." *RussellMoore*. January 14, 2016. https://www.russellmoore.com/2016/01/14/2-chronicles-714-isnt-about-american-politics/. Moore explains how the misuse of this verse has serious implications on the gospel, particularly in reference to the prosperity gospel.

CHAPTER 22

Behemoth and Leviathan Are Dinosaurs
Job 40–41

The Legend of Behemoth and Leviathan in Job 40–41 as Dinosaurs

The creatures Behemoth and Leviathan described by God in Job 40–41 are types of dinosaurs. The Behemoth (Job 40:15–24) is possibly an herbivorous sauropod, the largest land-creature to ever roam the earth and perhaps even the massive and long-necked Brachiosaurus. Leviathan (Job 41:1–34) is a now-extinct sea creature, perhaps the Kronosaurus, one of the largest and deadliest reptiles to have ever existed. Though the exact time of the story of Job is unclear, Job appears to be a figure from the second millennium BC, around the time of the patriarchs in Genesis. Behemoth and Leviathan in Job 40–41 offer proof (or at least strong evidence) supporting the idea that dinosaurs survived the Noahic flood and lived on the earth at the same time as biblical figures such as Job and Abraham.

Countering the Legendary Teaching

While the identification of Behemoth and Leviathan as dinosaur-like creatures is not impossible, this interpretation of these creatures in Job 40–41 is highly implausible and is not supported by the immediate context of Job 38–41, the overall message of Job, or the portrayals of Leviathan found elsewhere in the Old Testament. There is no direct evidence outside the Bible supporting the idea that dinosaurs lived with humans after the Noahic flood. Behemoth and Leviathan are more properly identified with known creatures in the ancient Near East, most likely the hippopotamus and crocodile. Egyptian art attests to

133

the practice of hippo and crocodile hunting, and hippos lived on the coast of Syria and were hunted for their ivory.[1] This chapter will argue that Behemoth and Leviathan represent real physical creatures but that they are representative of the forces of chaos and evil that stand in opposition to God.

Behemoth and Leviathan as Hippopotamus and Crocodile

The creatures most commonly identified as Behemoth and Leviathan are the hippopotamus and the crocodile.[2] The Hebrew word *behemah* is a general word for animals, both wild and domestic. The use of the abstract plural *behemot* likely reflects the size of this creature (the beast par excellence). In addition to the dinosaur and the hippopotamus, Behemoth has also been identified as the elephant, water buffalo, and rhinoceros, but several features favor the interpretation that Behemoth is a hippopotamus. The hippopotamus is the largest of land animals known from the ancient Near East, and the adult hippo weighs approximately 8,000 pounds. The hippopotamus is herbivorous (Job 40:15), and verses 21–22 appear to describe its marshy habitat. Robert Alden comments, "During the day hippopotami spend much of the time submerged, except for their nostrils, eyes, and ears, which remain above the water in order to sense everything around them. They are good swimmers and prefer the sluggish swamps and marshes of the Nile and other African rivers."[3]

One of the problems with the identification of Behemoth as a hippopotamus and the primary evidence offered for favoring the interpretation of Behemoth as a dinosaur is the comparison of this creature's tail to a cedar tree in Job 40:17. The hippopotamus has a small, curly tail. The verse does not say that Behemoth's tail is as large as a cedar but rather that he "stiffens" or "bends" his tail like a cedar.[4] If the hippopotamus is in view, one possible solution suggested by Marvin Pope is that the "tail" in verse 17 refers to the penis of the male hippo.[5] Body appendages like the "hand" and "foot" are used euphemistically for the sexual organ at other places in the Hebrew Bible, and the description of

---

[1]   For bibliographic sources, see Izak Corneilus, "Job," in *Zondervan Illustrated Bible Background Commentary*, ed. J. H. Walton (Grand Rapids: Zondervan, 2009), 5:298nn346–47.

[2]   For an extended discussion of the identity of these creatures, see David J. A. Clines, *Job 38–42*, Word Biblical Commentary (Nashville: Thomas Nelson, 2011), 1183–1203.

[3]   Robert L. Alden, *Job*, New American Commentary (Nashville: Broadman & Holman, 1993), 397.

[4]   The meaning of the Hebrew verb *hapats* that appears only here is unclear. Interpreters who view Behemoth as an elephant understand verse 17 to be a reference to its trunk.

[5]   Marvin H. Pope, *Job*, Anchor Bible (New York: Doubleday, 1965), 323–24.

the beast's powerful belly and loins may suggest a reference to sexual potency.[6] Other features of Behemoth make the identification of this creature as a sauropod-type dinosaur extremely unlikely. There is no mention of the creature's long neck, and it is difficult to imagine a large sauropod resting under lotus plants or hiding in reedy marshes.

Several features of the Leviathan in Job 41 favor the identification of this creature as a crocodile.[7] The use of hooks to catch the crocodile (41:1–2) is attested by the ancient historian Herodotus (*Histories*, 2, 68–70).[8] The creature has powerful jaws and large teeth (41:14). The description of Leviathan's interlocking scales that cannot be penetrated (41:13–17, 23) also corresponds well to the crocodile. Like the crocodile, Leviathan's habitat is both land and water, and it leaves traces behind in the mud as it moves along (vv. 30–33).[9]

Behemoth and Leviathan: More than Physical Creatures

The naturalistic interpretation of Behemoth and Leviathan certainly fits well with the focus in God's first speech in Job 38–39 on his provision and care for various animals. There is mention of the lion, raven, mountain goat, donkey, wild ox, ostrich, horse, and hawk. Because of his suffering, Job had questioned God's management of the world and his justice in his treatment of him. God's first speech demonstrated that Job lacked both the power and wisdom to question God's providential management of his creation. The way in which God provided for his various creatures reflected his goodness and concern for the creation at large. Job appropriately responded to God's revelation by acknowledging his own insignificance and refusing to further question God's ways (Job 40:1–5).

The opening words of God's second speech to Job in 40:6–14 suggest that the argument moves forward and addresses a separate issue. Here God challenges Job to take on the role of divine judge and to deal with the proud and the wicked by sending them down to the underworld. God informs Job that oversight of the world also involves dealing with the evil that exists in

---

6   The Latin Vulgate refers to the creature's "testicles" in verse 17b, and the KJV renders the second half of the verse: "the sinews of his stones are wrapped together." Alden, *Job*, 396n91.

7   An alternative view is that Leviathan is a whale (see Ps 104:26).

8   John G. Gammie, "Behemoth and Leviathan: On the Didactic and Theological Significance of Job 40:15–41:26," in *Israelite Wisdom: Theological and Literary Essays in Honor of Samuel Terrien*, ed. John G. Gammie (New York: Union Theological Seminary, 1978), 224.

9   Gammie, "Behemoth and Leviathan." For the correspondence between Leviathan and the crocodile, see also Clines, *Job 38–42*, 1191.

the world. Job believes that God has treated him unfairly, but Job has failed to consider the powers of evil and chaos that are at work in the world. In light of how God's second speech to Job is focusing on the reality of evil, an extended description of his power over mere natural creatures (whether crocodile, hippopotamus, or even dinosaurs) seems to be a less than adequate way of asserting Yahweh's unique power to control chaos and judge the wicked.

The descriptions of Behemoth and Leviathan strongly suggest that they portray more than creatures from the natural realm, even with allowances for highly figurative language. Behemoth has bones and limbs like "bronze tubes" and "iron rods" (40:18). God alone is able to subdue him (40:19), and no man is able to capture him (40:21). Leviathan breathes out fire and smoke and boils the water with his presence (41:18–21, 31–32). No weapon can prevail against him, and "he has no equal on earth" (41:26–33).[10]

Behemoth and Leviathan are likely symbolic of some greater reality. John Walton explains, "I suspect those in antiquity would have viewed the hippopotamus and crocodile as reminiscent of Behemoth and Leviathan, and perhaps even as their spawn in some sense, but Behemoth and Leviathan are the archetypes and personify abstractions that the hippopotamus do to a much lesser degree."[11] The hippopotamus and crocodile in their size and ferocity are representative of the powers of chaos at work in the world. This understanding allows for a fuller comprehension of the greatness of God that is conveyed here. The claim that God subdues the hippopotamus or the crocodile is far less impressive than the fact that God subdues the forces of chaos and evil.[12]

In the Baal epic of Canaanite literature, Baal slays a seven-headed dragon named Lotan (the equivalent of Leviathan) as part of his defeat of the forces of chaos headed by Yam, the god of the sea. Baal establishes his kingship by subjugating the waters of chaos. In Babylonian literature, Marduk slays the sea-monster Tiamat as part of the creation process. In Job 3:8, Job calls for those who pronounce curses to "rouse Leviathan," who will remove the day of his birth. No physical creature would have the power to undo Job's birthday.[13] Job 26:12–13 also states that God "crushed Rahab" and "pierced the fleeing

[10]   John Day, *God's Conflict with the Dragon and the Sea: Echoes of a Canaanite Myth in the Old Testament* (Cambridge: Cambridge University Press, 1985), 77.

[11]   John H. Walton, *Job*, New International Version Application Commentary (Grand Rapids: Zondervan, 2012), 406–7.

[12]   Tremper Longman III, *Job*, Baker Commentary on the Old Testament Wisdom and Psalms (Grand Rapids: Baker, 2012), 451.

[13]   Eric Ortlund, "The Identity of Leviathan and the Meaning of the Book of Job," *Trinity Journal* 34 (2013): 23.

serpent" by subduing chaos at creation. Rahab, meaning "boisterous one," is, along with Leviathan, used as a name for a sea monster/dragon in the Old Testament (Ps 89:10; Isa 51:9). In Job 9, the Lord as creator is portrayed as the one who "treads on the waves of the sea" (v. 8) and who causes "Rahab's assistants" to "cringe in fear" (v. 13). We see similar associations between Leviathan and the cosmic forces of chaos in passages like Ps 74:12–14 and Isa 27:1. The prevailing use of Leviathan elsewhere in Job and in the Old Testament as a whole further demonstrates that something more than a physical creature is in view in Job 41.

The description of Behemoth as "the foremost [first] of God's works" in 40:19 suggests the primeval nature of this beast, and the image of God drawing the sword against Behemoth in the same verse also reflects the conflict with chaos. Robert Fyall notes that the mythical story of a fierce bovine creature subdued or killed by a god appears throughout the ancient Near East.[14] In Egypt, the god Seth, who was represented by a hippopotamus, was killed by the god Horus. In the Gilgamesh Epic from Mesopotamia, Gilgamesh and Enkidu kill the "bull of heaven." In the Canaanite literature, Anat, the consort of Baal, claims to have defeated various chaos monsters, including the sea-creature Arsh and Etki "the calf of El."[15] Behemoth in Job 41 thus appears to be related to an oxlike creature associated with chaos in other ancient Near Eastern literature.

In using mythological allusions to portray physical creatures as representative of the powers of chaos, the Joban author is not portraying something mythical or make-believe. Rather, this author poetically and polemically uses this imagery to demonstrate that the power of evil within God's creation is a reality. Eric Ortlund explains that the depiction of Behemoth and Leviathan speaks "within Job's cultural context in order to communicate that there is a terrible evil at loose in the world that YHWH promises to defeat—but that he has not defeated yet."[16] In the larger theology of the Bible, the dragons and sea monsters of the ancient Near East point to the reality of Satan and powerful forces of evil that are at work in the world. Job has questioned God's justice because of his unfair suffering, but perfect justice does not exist in a fallen world. Job has no understanding of the powers and forces of evil that are at work in the world that factor into why and how suffering and death

---

[14] Robert S. Fyall, *Now My Eyes Have Seen You: Images of Creation and Evil in the Book of Job*, New Studies in Biblical Theology (Downers Grove, IL: IVP Academic, 2002), 131.

[15] Fyall, *Now My Eyes Have Seen You*, 132.

[16] Ortlund, "Identity of Leviathan," 17.

occur. After the speech concerning Behemoth and Leviathan, Job recognizes the audacity of his pretentious assertions against God and repents in recognition of his human frailties (42:1–6).

Application

The book of Job reminds us that powerful forces of evil are responsible for the suffering and death that exist in our fallen world. There will never be perfect justice on this side of eternity. The book of Job encourages us to remember that God's sovereignty is unchallenged by these malevolent powers. In the larger canon of Scripture, God promises to vanquish the powers of evil and chaos (Isa 27:1; 51:9–11). The kingdom of God will prevail over the wicked empires that emerge from the chaotic sea (see Daniel 7) and the evil spiritual powers that stand behind these nations (see Isa 24:21). The motif of God's conflict with the sea carries over into the New Testament, and the sea miracles of Jesus demonstrate that his mission entails the defeat of Satan, evil, and death itself. The book of Revelation promises that God would ultimately vanquish the "fiery red dragon" (Satan) and the "beast" (Antichrist) (Rev 12–13; 19:17–20:10) and that the sea would be no more when God eliminates evil and destroys the power of death (Rev 21:1–4). Believers live in hope and confidence of God's ultimate triumph over evil even in the midst of great suffering.

Annotated Bibliography

BOOKS
Fyall, Robert S. *Now My Eyes Have Seen You: Images of Creation and Evil in the Book of Job.* New Studies in Biblical Theology. Downers Grove, IL: InterVarsity Press, 2002. Biblical theological study of Job that connects Behemoth and Leviathan in Job 40–41 with previous sections in the book.

COMMENTARIES
Walton, John H. *Job.* New International Version Application Commentary. Grand Rapids: Zondervan, 2012. Good starting point for the depiction of Behemoth and Leviathan as something more than physical creatures.

JOURNAL ARTICLES
Ortlund, Eric. "The Identity of Leviathan and the Meaning of the Book of Job." *Trinity Journal* 34 (2013): 17–30. Makes a strong argument for identifying Leviathan as representing the forces of evil and chaos.

CHAPTER 23

Psalm 22 Directly Predicts the Crucifixion of Jesus

Psalm 22:16

The Legendary Teaching on Psalm 22:16

There are more than 300 direct messianic predictive prophecies from the Old Testament that Jesus fulfills. Psalm 22 not only anticipates the future suffering of the Messiah but even predicts with surprising accuracy the crucifixion of Jesus with its reference in verse 16 to the piercing of his hands and feet. This exact predictive fulfillment, long before Roman crucifixion even existed, offers powerful confirmation that Jesus was indeed Israel's promised Messiah.

Countering the Legendary Teaching

Psalm 22 speaks prophetically of the sufferings of Christ but in the form of typology rather than a direct and specific prediction of crucifixion as the manner of Jesus's death. Psalm 22:16 does not refer to crucifixion, and there is even significant variation in the various textual witnesses for this verse, raising questions concerning the actual reading of this verse that are difficult to answer.

The Text of Psalm 22:16—What Does the Verse Actually Say?

The Hebrew of Ps 22:16 in the Masoretic Text (the standard form of the Hebrew Bible) reads quite differently from what is found in most English translations.[1] Instead of "they pierced my hands and my feet," the Hebrew

---

[1]   Verse 16 in the English text is v. 17 in the Hebrew text.

reads, "like a lion, my hands and my feet." Is this reading even coherent, and, if so, what could it possibly mean? The broken syntax caused by the absence of a verb makes this reading problematic, but this verse appears in a section that compares the psalmist's enemies to wild animals and dangerous predators (vv. 12–21). The enemies are like strong "bulls" (v. 12), roaring "lions" (v. 13), and vicious "dogs" (v. 16). The same animals are mentioned in reverse order in verses 20–21 (dogs, lions, wild ox), which heightens the perception of the psalmist being surrounded by animals that seek to tear him apart. The word for "lion" (*'ari*) is the same word used in verses 13 and 21 and fits well in this context. The Jewish Publication Society Tanakh 1917 translation reads, "like a lion, they are at my hands and feet." It is also possible that a verb like "to tear" or "pin down" has fallen out in the transmission of the text.[2] A textual note in the NET Bible suggests that the broken syntax of the line is for rhetorical effect and is designed to convey the terror of the psalmist as he is unable to even express a complete thought. The reading of the Hebrew text cannot be simply dismissed out of hand.

Other textual evidence provides an alternate reading of the verse that is followed by most of our English Bibles. The alternate reading "they pierced my hands and my feet" comes from the Septuagint, the Greek Old Testament, and is also reflected in the Syriac and Latin Vulgate versions.[3] This reading from the Septuagint is significant in that it predates the Christian era by at least a century and a half. The Hebrew standing behind this reading in the Greek Old Testament also reflects only a slight variation from what is found in the Masoretic Text, requiring the change of one consonantal letter from "like a lion" (*ka'ari*) to the verbal "they dig/bore" (*ka'aru*—from the verbal root *karah*).[4] The insertion of the consonant *aleph* (') into the spelling of the verb *karah* is problematic, but may reflect the use of this consonant to represent a vowel letter, which was common before vowels were later added to the text.[5]

---

    2   For further support of this approach to the problem, see Brent Strawn, "Psalm 22:17b: More Guessing," *Journal of Biblical Literature* 119 (2000): 439–51.

    3   The later revisions of the Septuagint by Aquila and Symmachus use different verbs but reflect a similar reading: "they bound my hands and feet."

    4   Some Hebrew manuscripts in the Masoretic tradition also reflect the reading of the verb *ka'aru* or *karu* in the place of "like a lion." For further discussion of these readings, see Allen P. Ross, *A Commentary on the Psalms*, Vol. 1:1–41, Kregel Exegetical Library (Grand Rapids: Kregel, 2011), 523n9. Some have argued that the Hebrew Psalm Scroll from Nahal Hever (which predates our Masoretic manuscripts by roughly a thousand years) supports the reading of the Septuagint, but the final letter of the word in question is too faded to determine if the text reads "they have pierced" or "like a lion."

    5   The translation of *ka'aru* or *karu* as "to pierce" is somewhat problematic in that the verb (and the corresponding Greek *horuxan*) often refers to the digging of a well. Scholars have proposed numerous

Even if "they pierced" is the correct reading, the imagery in the verse is comparing the psalmist's enemies to wild animals that puncture and pierce his hands as they tear with their teeth. There is certainly a similarity to the type of wounds that Jesus would suffer on the cross, but it is a stretch to view verse 16 as a specific prediction of the crucifixion of Jesus.

The Life Situation and Experience of the Psalmist

In Psalm 22, the psalmist is speaking in the language of lament concerning his own experiences as a righteous sufferer. The psalm is attributed to David who cries out for deliverance from vicious enemies who seek to put him to death. The background of the psalm is perhaps when Saul or Absalom tried to kill David. The use of extreme imagery and hyperbolic language is characteristic of laments and reflects here the depth of the psalmist's anguish. In the midst of this terrible ordeal, the psalmist ultimately expresses his confidence that God would deliver him from his enemies. The psalmist reflects on his own experiences here, and there is no evidence prior to the time of Jesus that Psalm 22 was read messianically.[6]

Although the psalmist is poetically speaking of his own experiences, the New Testament also appropriates the language of the psalm to speak of the suffering of Jesus. Richard Patterson states that there are fourteen direct citations of Psalm 22 in the New Testament and several more potential allusions.[7] Note the most important of these references:

1. "My God, my God, why have you abandoned me?" (v. 1; Matt 27:46; Mark 15:34).
2. "Everyone who sees me mocks me; they sneer and shake their heads" (v. 7; Matt 27:39; Mark 15:29; Luke 23:35).
3. "He relies on the LORD; let him save him; let the LORD rescue him, since he takes pleasure in him" (v. 8; Matt 27:43).

---

alternatives to the Masoretic and Septuagint readings, including: "to be pluck, cleaned" (from *'arah* prefixed by *ke*), "to pierce, bore" (from *kwr*—a verb not attested elsewhere in the OT); "to be shrunken/shriveled" (from a root of *karah* not attested in the OT); and "to be consumed/exhausted" (from *kalah*, due to the fact that *l* and *r* are often interchanged in Hebrew). For more on the various proposals, see Bruce K. Waltke and James M. Houston, *The Psalms as Christian Worship: An Historical Commentary* (Grand Rapids: Eerdmans, 2010), 493n66.

6   Ben C. Witherington III, *Psalms Old and New: Exegesis, Intertextuality, and Hermeneutics* (Minneapolis: Fortress, 2017), 72.

7   Richard Patterson, "Psalm 22: From Trial to Triumph," *Journal of the Evangelical Theological Society* 47 (2004): 227–28.

4. "They divided my garments among themselves, and they cast lots for my clothing" (v. 18; Matt 27:35; Luke 23:34; John 19:24).
5. "I will proclaim your name to my brothers and sisters; I will praise you in the assembly" (v. 22; Heb 2:12).

It is interesting that John does not cite or quote Ps 22:16 when referring to the "piercing" of Jesus on the cross, but instead quotes from Zech 12:10, "They will look at me whom they pierced" (John 19:34–37; see Rev 1:7). The piercing also refers to the wounding of Jesus's side after his death rather than his crucifixion. Perhaps the specific connection to Ps 22:16 is not mentioned because it was obvious in light of how the whole psalm is applied to Jesus, but the omission is curious if the verse is to be read as an explicit prediction of the crucifixion.

Jesus as the Ultimate Example of the Righteous Sufferer

Psalm 22 speaks prophetically of the suffering and death of Jesus but in the form of patterning and typology rather than as a direct prediction-fulfillment. The experiences of David as a righteous sufferer anticipate the suffering and death that Jesus would endure as the ultimate righteous sufferer. The remarkable reversal from lament to praise that begins in verse 22 ultimately speaks to the triumph of Jesus over sin, death, and his enemies (vv. 27–31). Ben Witherington comments, "Psalm 22 is not an allegory of the death of Jesus out of due season, it is the story of a righteous sufferer in his own age, who foreshadows some of the things that will happen to the quintessential righteous sufferer, Jesus."[8] Although the connection of Psalm 22 to Jesus emerges only in retrospect, the psalm still speaks prophetically because the Spirit as the divine author of Scripture intended this psalm to point forward to Jesus. Moo and Naselli explain, "David was not necessarily aware of his language's ultimate significance, but God so ordered David's experiences and psalm that they anticipate the suffering of 'David's greater son.'"[9]

The classification of Psalm 22 as typology rather than prediction-fulfillment is preferred because many of the details regarding how this psalm ultimately applied to Jesus were not clear until after the death of Jesus. Brent

---

[8]   Witherington, *Psalms Old and New*, 74.
[9]   Douglas J. Moo and Andrew David Naselli, "The Problem of the New Testament's Use of the Old Testament," in *The Enduring Authority of the Christian Scriptures*, ed. D. A. Carson (Grand Rapids: Eerdmans, 2016), 729.

Sandy explains that "the intent of Psalm 22 was probably not prediction," and even if the psalm was predictive in some sense, "we would not have been successful in determining in advance how it would be fulfilled." Someone reading this psalm before the cross would have been more likely to conclude that Jesus would suffer the Roman execution of being thrown to wild animals rather than crucifixion.[10]

Typological applications of other passages from the Psalms appear throughout the New Testament. The experiences of David often anticipate the experiences of Jesus as the son of David par excellence. In Psalm 41, David confesses his sin and prays for the Lord graciously to heal him from the illness he has experienced as a form of divine discipline (vv. 3–4, 10). David's enemies, however, have enjoyed his suffering and anticipate when he will be dead and gone (vv. 5–8). Even David's friend with whom he had shared bread has betrayed him (v. 9). In John 13:17–20, Jesus informs his disciples that one of them would betray him and then introduces a quotation of Ps 41:9 with the words, "the Scripture must be fulfilled." The "fulfillment" in view in John 13:18 is a patterning or correspondence between the experiences of David and Jesus. Various verses from Psalm 69 that depict the opposition the palmist experiences because of his zeal for the Lord are applied to Jesus in the New Testament (v. 4—John 15:25; v. 9—John 2:17; v. 21—John 19:28–29). Nevertheless, if one tried to read the psalm as a direct prophecy of how Jesus would die, the best guess would probably be death by poisoning (v. 21).

Rather than an apologetic that points to more than 300 specific predictive prophecies fulfilled by Jesus, an approach that might allow for more authentic conversations would be to note important prophetic patterns in the Hebrew Bible that point forward to Jesus. One of those patterns is the pattern of rejection and suffering experienced by those whom God raises up to lead and deliver his people. Stephen in his sermon found in Acts 7 traces this pattern through the Old Testament to Jesus. Isaiah 53 further speaks of a righteous servant who would by his suffering and death become a "guilt offering" on behalf of the people. The death and resurrection of Jesus enabled the apostles to understand that Jesus was the One who fulfilled this role of suffering servant by dying for the sins of others (see Acts 8:26–40).

---

[10] D. Brent Sandy, *Plowshares and Pruning Hooks: Rethinking the Language of Biblical Prophecy and Apocalyptic* (Downers Grove, IL: InterVarsity Press, 2002), 37.

Application

After his resurrection, Jesus explained from the Hebrew Scriptures to two of his confused and discouraged disciples the necessity of his suffering as prelude to his exaltation (Luke 24:25–27, 44–47). It was the teaching of Jesus that led the apostles to read passages such as Psalm 22 as pointing forward to Jesus's suffering on the cross. Even if Psalm 22 is not a precise prediction of how Jesus would die, it clearly foreshadows the suffering that Jesus would endure. The cross and subsequent exaltation of Jesus confirmed that he was indeed the expected Messiah and provides the basis of our forgiveness and right standing with a holy God.

Annotated Bibliography

COMMENTARIES
Ross, Allen P. *A Commentary on the Psalms, Vol. 1, 1–41*. Kregel Exegetical Library. Grand Rapids: Kregel, 2011. Scholarly evangelical commentary with detailed exposition of Psalm 22, including discussion of textual issues in 22:16.

BOOKS
Witherington, Ben, III. *Psalms Old and New: Exegesis, Intertextuality, and Hermeneutics*. Minneapolis: Fortress, 2017. Detailed expositions of various psalms and their usage in the New Testament.

ARTICLES
Patterson, Richard. "Psalm 22: From Trial to Triumph." *Journal of the Evangelical Theological Society* 47 (2004): 213–33. Scholarly exposition of Psalm 22.

WEBSITES
Davidson, Paul. "A Few Remarks on the Problem of Psalm 22:16." *Is That in the Bible?* (blog). September 28, 2015. https://isthatinthebible.wordpress.com/2015/09/28/a-few-remarks-on-the-problem-of-psalm-2216/. Good overview and discussion of the various textual options for 22:16.

CHAPTER 24

―

Imprecatory Psalms Are Horrible
Models for Christian Prayer

Psalm 109

The Legendary Teaching on the Imprecatory Psalms

Many Christians regularly read the Psalms devotionally and find great comfort in promises that the Lord is a caring "shepherd" (Psalm 23) and "a refuge and strength" in times of trouble (Ps 46:1). Mixed into the beautiful poetry of the Psalms, however, are a number of shocking and disturbing prayers known as the "imprecatory psalms," in which the psalmists petition God to bring curses and death upon their enemies. These vicious and vindictive prayers are reflective of the inferior ethos of the old covenant; even if they were appropriate prayers to the wrathful God of the Old Testament, they are not prayers that followers of Jesus should offer to the gracious and merciful God of the New. These prayers endorse a hatred that contradicts Jesus's instructions to love one's enemies and to pray for them (Matt 5:43–47; Luke 6:27–28) and are at odds with Paul's exhortations to "bless and do not curse" (Rom 12:14). The inclusion of the imprecatory psalms within Scripture does not remove the fact that they are "barbarous" and "a disgrace to human nature."[1]

---

[1]   C. S. Lewis wrote concerning the imprecatory psalms, "The hatred is there—festering, gloating, undisguised—and also we should be wicked if we in any way condoned or approved it, or (worse still) used it to justify similar passions in ourselves." C. S. Lewis, *Reflections on the Psalms* (London: Collins, 1961), 22.

Countering the Legendary Teaching

There are imprecatory prayers and curses against the enemies of the psalmists in at least forty different psalms, and imprecations are also prominent in the prayers of Jeremiah and Lamentations. In the more severe imprecations, the psalmist asks God to destroy not only his enemy but also his enemy's family (109:6–20), looks forward to the righteous bathing their feet in the blood of the wicked (58:10), and pronounces blessing on those who bash the skulls of infants (137:9).

Rather than expressions of venomous hatred or "curses parading as prayers," imprecations in the Old Testament are cries for God's judgment in times of extreme injustice and violent oppression.[2] The downtrodden and oppressed cry out when divine intervention is their only recourse against their powerful enemies. Erich Zenger observes that these psalms often reflect a conflict "between the powerless poor and the too-powerful rich."[3] Those who pray for the destruction of Edom and Babylon in Psalm 137 are survivors of the fall of Jerusalem who have lived through the atrocities of military siege and the trauma of deportation. Zenger notes that this psalm "is not the song of people who have the power to effect a violent change in their situation of suffering, nor is it the battle cry of terrorists."[4] In Psalm 58, the psalmist prays for God to knock out the teeth of his enemies because they are like powerful lions in their assaults on him (v. 6). Rather than taking the punishment of the wicked into his own hands, the psalmist is giving judgment over to God in recognition that vengeance belongs to him (see Deut 32:35, 41, 43; Rom 12:19). Gordon Wenham notes that nothing suggests in these prayers that the psalmist himself "will take revenge or even dictate a time table for divine retribution."[5]

Intense and Passionate Cries for Justice

In assessing the imprecations, we need to remember that the psalmists often express their prayers to God in highly figurative and hyperbolic language. Rather than reading the curses and imprecations in the Psalms in a strictly literal manner, the interpreter recognizes the psalmist to be expressing the depth

---

[2]   Gordon J. Wenham, *Psalms as Torah: Reading Biblical Song Ethically*, Studies in Theological Interpretation (Grand Rapids: Baker, 2012), 179.

[3]   Erich Zenger, *A God of Vengeance? Understanding the Psalms of Divine Wrath*, trans. Linda M. Maloney (Louisville, KY: Westminster John Knox, 1996), 12.

[4]   Zenger, *A God of Vengeance?*, 48.

[5]   Wenham, *Psalms as Torah*, 173.

of his emotion, the severity of his suffering, and the urgency of the need for divine intervention. The psalmist no more expects God to literally cause his enemy to melt away "like a slug that moves along in slime" (58:8) than he is wanting God to believe that he is swimming in a bed of tears (6:6) or eating a meal of tears and ashes (42:3; 102:9). Curse language was incorporated into various types of covenantal relationships within the ancient Near East, including the one between Yahweh and Israel (Leviticus 26; Deuteronomy 28). It is thus only natural that divine judgment of the wicked would be conceived of in these terms as well.

Although the punishments prayed for by the psalmists are often harsh and severe, these requests were informed by God's own revealed standards of justice. God had promised Abraham that he would "bless those who bless you and curse anyone who treats you with contempt" (Gen 12:3). In petitioning for the curses of divine judgment against those who had mistreated them, the psalmists were praying for God to fulfill his covenant promises.[6] The Mosaic Law had also established the principle of *lex talionis* ("eye for eye, tooth for tooth") (Deut 19:16–21) as a standard of justice and retribution, and the imprecatory prayers of the Old Testament regularly ask God to act in accordance with this standard as he redresses wrong.[7] As horrific as the imprecation calling for the death of Babylonian infants in Ps 137:9 may appear, the Babylonians had committed similar atrocities in the siege and destruction of Jerusalem.[8] The principle of *lex talionis* is not God's final ethical word or ultimate standard of righteousness, but it was one that God himself had established to regulate the punishment of crimes in ancient Israel.

The imprecatory prayers in the Old Testament are not reflective of an ethic that allowed Israel to hate its enemies. Imprecations are not the only prayers that the people of God pray in the Hebrew Bible concerning the wicked or their enemies. In Psalm 35, David prays for God to judge his enemies (vv. 4–10) because of the duplicitous way in which they had repaid evil for good by seeking David's downfall after he had prayed and grieved for them when they were gravely ill (vv. 11–16; compare Ps 109:4–5).[9] Jeremiah instructed the exiles to pray for the "peace of Babylon" (Jer 29:7) in the same way that faithful Israelites

---

6   John N. Day, "The Imprecatory Psalms and Christian Ethics," *Bibliotheca Sacra* 159 (2002): 169.
7   Day, "The Imprecatory Psalms and Christian Ethics," 168.
8   Zenger, *A God of Vengeance?*, 49–50. Zenger also suggests that the children in view in Ps 137:9 would be the royal children, and thus the verse expresses hope for the extermination of the "dynasty of terror" that has inflicted great violence on the Jewish people. The image of killing infants also conveys primarily the idea of complete and total military defeat (see Isa 13:16; Nah 3:10).
9   Wenham, *Psalms as Torah*, 171.

were to pray for the "peace of Jerusalem" (Ps 122:6). As Michael Widmer has noted, this directive from the prophet is amazingly a call to pray for those "who have killed your kin, destroyed your home, and given your land to others."[10] These Old Testament examples reflect an ethic in line with Jesus's instruction for his disciples to pray for their enemies (Matt 5:44–47; Luke 6:27–29).

The Imprecatory Psalms from a New Testament Perspective

Although the imprecatory prayers in the Old Testament remain instructive for the church today, there are elements of discontinuity, important covenantal shifts, and aspects of progressive revelation that inform the Christian application of the imprecatory psalms. Ancient Near Eastern curse language no longer carries the same cultural significance as it did in the world of the Old Testament. Israel as the people of God in the Old Testament was a national entity that was promised security in its land and military victory over its enemies as a reward for obedience to Yahweh's commands. Israel's military victories were important moments in redemptive history. In contrast, the church exists among the nations and is no longer called to advance God's kingdom purposes through war and military conquest. Jesus radically alters the concept of holy war in his willingness to die for his enemies, and disciples of Jesus follow his example in their willingness to lay down their lives rather than take lives for the advancement of the gospel.[11] Rather than a holy war against human enemies and armies, followers of Jesus are now engaged in a spiritual battle against Satan and the forces of evil (Eph 6:12–18).

Although the people of God were called to love their enemies under the old covenant, new covenant believers have an even higher ethic of love in light of how God has demonstrated his love through the cross.[12] Stephen reflects the highest imitation of Jesus when he prays for God to forgive his persecutors (Acts 7:60), just as Jesus prayed for God's forgiveness of his enemies responsible for his death (Luke 23:34). The progressive revelation of the New Testament concerning the afterlife also adds needed perspective on the working out of God's judgment of the wicked. This fuller revelation clarifies

---

[10] Michael Widmer, *Standing in the Breach: An Old Testament Theology and Spirituality of Intercessory Prayer*, Siphrut 13: Literature and Theology of the Hebrew Scriptures (Winona Lake, IN: Eisenbrauns, 2015), 439.

[11] Note, however, how Jesus returns as the divine Warrior in Rev 19:11–21 (compare Isa 63:1–6).

[12] Jesus rebukes James and John when they ask if they should pray for fire to come down from heaven against the Samaritans (Luke 9:54–55). The Samaritans are also not guilty of the violence and injustice that normally occasion the Old Testament imprecations.

that the ultimate judgment of the ungodly will occur in the final judgment, and thus believers can pray for this final reckoning as the means by which God will make right all injustices rather than praying for physical death and retribution in this life against the wicked (see 2 Thess 1:6–10).

In spite of these discontinuities, there remains a legitimate place for imprecation as a righteous response to the extreme evil and injustice that exists in our fallen world.[13] The coming of Jesus did not eradicate human wickedness, and thus these prayers give continued expression to the valid desire of Christians to see God act as a righteous judge in redressing these wrongs and bringing an end to evil.[14] Christians in the West may not resonate with these psalms as much as believers in other parts of the world who regularly encounter violent opposition and persecution. In Rev 6:10–11, Christian martyrs gathered around the throne of God continue to cry out to God for vindication and for his vengeance against those responsible for shedding their blood. Followers of Jesus in the New Testament express imprecations against those who actively pervert or oppose the gospel message (Gal 1:8–9; 5:12; 1 Cor 16:22). It would even seem that praying for the final judgment of the wicked would be one of the ways that God's people hasten the coming of God's kingdom of peace and righteousness to earth (see 2 Pet 3:12).

Application

Because of their own experience of divine grace, followers of Jesus give priority to prayers for divine grace and mercy for even the worst of their enemies. The fact that Paul was a violent persecutor of the church before his conversion reminds us that no one is beyond the reach of God's grace. When Simon attempted to purchase the power of the Holy Spirit, Peter responded to him, "May your silver be destroyed with you" (Acts 8:20), but he also called for the sorcerer to repent and pray for the forgiveness of his sins (v. 22). Although love and blessing are the primary disposition of followers of Christ, prayers for divine judgment and justice are particularly appropriate "in extreme circumstances against hardened, deceitful, violent, immoral unjust sinners."[15]

Believers should rightly feel anger, just as God does over mass shootings or

---

[13]   Some would argue that the contemporary application of the imprecatory psalms is simply the idea that believers can be honest in prayer, even if their prayers are not in line with God's desires. See Ben Witherington, *The Living Word of God: Rethinking the Theology of the Bible* (Waco, TX: Baylor University Press, 2007), 25.

[14]   Widmer, *Standing in the Breach*, 416.

[15]   Day, "Imprecatory Psalms and Christian Ethics," 168.

the beheading of Christians in the Middle East. To feel nothing or to become desensitized to such horrific evil is the worst possible response. Rather than acting on their anger in an escalating cycle of violence and retribution, the faithful trust God to defend their cause. By praying the imprecatory psalms, Christians learn to empathize with the oppressed and are reminded of their responsibility to relieve suffering in every way they possibly can.[16]

The imprecatory psalms also have value for Christians today in reminding them of God's holy hatred of sin, evil, and injustice. Christians not only petition for the judgment of the wicked but also for sin and evil to be expunged from their own hearts. After asking for God to slay the wicked in Psalm 139, David asks for God to search his heart for any sin and wickedness (vv. 23–24). God's people cannot genuinely pray for the judgment of the wicked without hating their own sinfulness and lack of righteousness.

Annotated Bibliography

BOOKS
Copan, Paul. *Is God a Moral Monster? Making Sense of the Old Testament God.* Grand Rapids: Baker, 2011. Helpful discussions of divine violence in the Old Testament and the specific problem of the imprecatory psalms.
Zenger, Erich. *A God of Vengeance: Understanding the Psalms of Divine Wrath.* Translated by Linda M. Maloney. Louisville, KY: Westminster John Knox, 1996. The definitive critical work on the imprecatory psalms.

COMMENTARIES
Ross, Allen P. *A Commentary on the Psalms.* 3 vols. Kregel Exegetical Library. Grand Rapids: Kregel, 2011–2016. Scholarly, evangelical commentary providing detailed exegesis and exposition of the Psalms.

WEBSITES
Day, John N. "The Imprecatory Psalms and Christian Ethics." *Bibliotheca Sacra* 159 (April–June 2002): 166–86. Accessed July 2, 2017. http://faculty.gordon.edu/hu/bi/ted_hildebrandt/otesources/19-psalms/text/articles/day_imprecatoryps_bs.htm. Offers a compelling case for the ongoing validity of the imprecatory prayers for Christians today.
Storms, Sam. "10 Things You Should Know about the Imprecatory Psalms." February 6, 2017. http://www.crosswalk.com/faith/bible-study/10-things-you-should-know-about-the-imprecatory-psalms.html. Offers helpful perspectives on why these prayers appear in the Psalms and how they represent righteous cries for divine justice.

---

[16] Wenham, *Psalms as Torah*, 177–78.

CHAPTER 25

Psalm 116 Teaches How God Welcomes His Saints at Death

Psalm 116:15

The Legendary Teaching on Psalm 116:15

The statement that the death of the faithful is "precious/valuable" (*yaqar*) to the Lord in Ps 116:15 speaks of God's joy at receiving his children into his presence when they die. This heavenly joy over the blessed home going of God's saints contrasts to the earthly sorrow associated with the separation of death. This verse provides an Old Testament equivalent to the promise that absence from the body for the believer means presence with the Lord (2 Cor 5:8) and that departing this life to be in God's presence is "far better" for the saint than remaining on in this life (Phil 1:21–23).

Countering the Legendary Teaching

Psalm 116 is not about the death of the believer and the anticipation of a joyous afterlife but rather a thanksgiving psalm for how the Lord had delivered the psalmist from a life-threatening danger. The psalmist celebrates his deliverance from death so that he might "walk before the LORD in the land of the living" (v. 9) and promises that he would offer praise and sacrifices in response to how the Lord had rescued him (vv. 12–14, 17–19). This experience had confirmed for him that his life and death were under God's control and protection. The psalmist was confident that because of the Lord's protection he would fully live out his days. A parallel reference in Ps 72:14 further helps to validate this understanding of valuable in the Lord's sight; speaking of the Israelite king, it states that he rescues the needy from oppression because "their lives [blood] are precious (*yaqar*) in his sight." Like the Lord, the king values and protects his people when they are in trouble.

Limited Understanding of the Afterlife in the Old Testament

When assessing the Old Testament teaching on the afterlife, it is important to keep in mind the concept of progressive revelation and the more fully informed perspective we have in light of the resurrection of Jesus and the teaching of the New Testament. The Old Testament clearly reflects an awareness that physical death is not the end of human existence. Enoch and Elijah were both translated to heaven; even though their experiences were unique, these stories reflect the possibility of existence beyond this life. Samuel appears postmortem to the shock of the medium that Saul solicited to rouse him (1 Samuel 28). The Pentateuch uses the expression "gathered to his peoples" with references to the deaths of Abraham, Ishmael, Isaac, Jacob, Moses, and Aaron (Gen 25:8, 17; 35:29; 49:33; Num 20:24; 27:13; Deut 32:50), and similar expressions are used to refer to the death of Joshua's generation (Judg 2:10) and King Josiah (2 Kgs 22:20; 2 Chr 34:28).[1] Many of the kings of Israel and Judah (and Jacob and Moses) are said to have "slept with" their "fathers," an expression that does not refer to burial (which often follows) or burial in the family tomb (which does not always occur).[2] David "slept with his fathers" (KJV) even though they were not buried in Jerusalem as he was (1 Kgs 2:10).

Despite an awareness of an afterlife, there is little revelation in the Old Testament concerning what this existence is like. The place where the dead go when they depart this life is referred to as Sheol, which is a place of darkness (Job 10:21; Ps 88:6, 12; Lam 3:6) and of inactivity and silence (Pss 94:17; 115:17).[3] In Isaiah 14, the inhabitants of the underworld have to be aroused from their sleep at the arrival of the king of Babylon (vv. 9–11), and in Ezekiel 32, those in Sheol are described as lying still (v. 21). The underworld is a place of captivity from which there is no escape (Isa 38:10; Jonah 2:6).[4] Though God has access to Sheol, those in Sheol are viewed as "separated from God" (Pss

---

[1]   Philip S. Johnston, *Shades of Sheol: Death and Afterlife in the Old Testament* (Downers Grove, IL: InterVarsity Press, 2002), 33.
[2]   Johnston, *Shades of Sheol*, 34–35.
[3]   Johnston, *Shades of Sheol*, 76.
[4]   Johnston, *Shades of Sheol*, 76.

6:5; 88:3, 10–12; Isa 38:18).[5] The Israelite view of the underworld appears to share many of the perspectives found in Mesopotamian literature. N. T. Wright explains that for those dwelling in Sheol, "there is no suggestion that they are enjoying themselves; it is a dark and gloomy world. Nothing much happens there. It is not another form of real life, an alternative world where things continue as normal."[6]

Some interpreters have equated Sheol with the grave, and Sheol is translated as "grave" in the NIV in every instance except one. This translation for Sheol works in many passages (see Ps 16:10; Isa 28:15), and the use of parallel terms such as "pit" (*bor*) (Ps 30:3, NIV), "decay" (*shahat*) (Ps 16:10, NIV), and Abbadon ("Destruction," Ps 88:11, NIV) reflect the close connection between the grave and Sheol. Nevertheless, the translation *grave* is not appropriate in those contexts that imply consciousness in Sheol. Numbers 16:30–33 and Psalm 55:15 also speak of individuals going down to Sheol alive, further reflecting that the term cannot be equated with the grave.[7] Psalm 139:8 states that the Lord is present even if the psalmist makes his bed in Sheol, a statement much more in line with Sheol being the underworld than the grave.[8] The inhabitants of Sheol are identified as "shades/spirits" (*repa'im*), reflective of their diminished existence (compare Job 26:5; Ps 88:10; Isa 14:9–10).

The KJV frequently translates "Sheol" as "hell" (e.g., Pss 16:10; 18:5; 86:13), but this translation is inaccurate in that Sheol "is not considered a place of punishment or where punishment takes place."[9] Sheol is the destiny of all individuals in the Old Testament. Based on Jesus's parable of the rich man and Lazarus (Luke 16:19–31), we can tentatively infer that Sheol was divided into two parts. The rich man is in a place of torment; Lazarus is in a place of comfort at the side of Abraham.[10] The idea of different compartments in the underworld, however, is not found in the Hebrew Bible and only emerges in Jewish intertestamental literature.[11]

In Gen 37:35, Jacob believes that his son Joseph is dead and laments, "I

---

5   John H. Walton, *Ancient Near Eastern Thought and the Old Testament: Introducing the Conceptual World of the Hebrew Bible* (Grand Rapids: Baker Academic, 2006), 321.

6   N. T. Wright, *The Resurrection of the Son of God*, Vol. 3, *Christian Origins and the Question of God* (Minneapolis: Fortress, 2003), 88.

7   Walton, *Ancient Near Eastern Thought*, 320.

8   Walton, *Ancient Near Eastern Thought*, 320.

9   Walton, *Ancient Near Eastern Thought*, 321.

10   Jesus then likely descended into Sheol/Hades (Acts 2:27, 31) so that in his ascension he might lead the souls of the righteous into the presence of God in heaven (Eph 4:8–10).

11   J. Richard Middleton, *A New Heaven and a New Earth: Reclaiming Biblical Eschatology* (Grand Rapids: Baker Academic, 2104), 231–32.

will go down to Sheol to my son, mourning" (compare Gen 42:38; 44:31). In Ps 89:48, the psalmist asks the question, "What courageous person can live and never see death? Who can save himself from the power of Sheol?" Petitioners in the Psalms express their fear that they are about to go down to Sheol unless God intervenes on their behalf (Pss 6:5; 88:3, 11), and others give thanks that God has delivered them from Sheol by sparing their lives (Pss 30:3; 86:13). Job and Hezekiah also envision going down to Sheol when they die (Job 17:13–16; Isa 38:10).[12] In Job 3:13–19, Job expresses his desire to be at rest in death, and the place he envisions going is the same as where the wicked go to be at rest—the abode of "the small and great." Job also speaks of his desire that the Lord would temporarily hide him in Sheol until his troubles are over, in contrast to what actually happens when humans die and "lie down never to rise again" (Job 14:12–13).[13]

Because of this limited eternal perspective, the Hebrew Bible emphasizes the idea that God rewards the righteous and punishes the wicked in this life. The wicked often die before their time as punishment for their sins (Pss 37:35–36; 49:13–14; 55:23), and this reality is why Sheol is most frequently identified with the wicked. Proverbs also warns that physical death causing a person to go down to Sheol is often the consequence of sinful and foolish actions (Prov 5:5; 7:27; 9:18).

The Emerging Hope of Resurrection Life in the Presence of God

The full promise of victory over death and the grave does not appear until the New Testament. Nevertheless, the first biblical promises of resurrection appear to come from the Hebrew prophets. In Isaiah 25–26, the prophet

---

[12]   The fact that the righteous and wicked share a common fate in the Old Testament argues against the use of 2 Sam 12:23 as a proof-text for the idea that infants who die go to heaven. When David states that he will one day go to his deceased son, David is merely observing that he will one day enter the underworld as his son had in death. An informed hope of a joyous reunion with deceased relatives in the afterlife at this point in salvation history is minimal at best. While there is no clear proof-text for the belief that all who die in infancy enter into the presence of the Lord, one can make a strong argument for this idea on the basis of the justice and mercy of God. For further discussion, see Michael F. Bird, *Evangelical Theology: A Biblical and Systematic Introduction* (Grand Rapids: Zondervan, 2013), 593–94.

[13]   Traditional interpretations have viewed Job 19:25–26 as reflecting an affirmation of the resurrection, but the passage is notoriously difficult to interpret, and a clear expression of resurrection hope seems out of tenor with the rest of the book. Job anticipates a legal defender (Redeemer) who will advocate on his behalf so that he will be vindicated even if this vindication occurs after death. This expectation implies an afterlife, but some interpreters have understood this vindication to occur after Job's physical ailments have ravaged his body. One has to be careful of reading ideas of resurrection and Christ's redemptive work into this text, since these ideas are revealed at a much later time. For discussion of the basic interpretive issues surrounding this passage, see Robert Alden, *Job: An Exegetical and Theological Exposition of Holy Scripture*, New American Commentary (Nashville: Broadman & Holman, 1994), 205–9.

promises that the Lord will one day "destroy the burial shroud" that covers all people and will "swallow up death forever" (25:7–8). This victory over death would entail the bodies of the righteous dead awaking from the dust and the earth bringing out "the departed spirits" (26:19).[14] Daniel 12:1–2 anticipates a resurrection of both the righteous and the wicked, with the righteous being raised to "eternal life." The most positive hope concerning the afterlife in the Psalter likely appears in the promise of Ps 49:15 that God will "redeem" the psalmist "from the power of Sheol," in contrast to the riches of the wealthy that cannot "redeem" them from death (49:7). The promise infers more than simply deliverance from physical death. As Tremper Longman explains, "The psalmist's hope here is not simply a long life (after all, the wicked rich might live long, and he knows he will die), but rather a life forever with God."[15]

Application

Psalm 116:15 reminds believers that their lives are in God's hands and under his control and protection. Our days are a gift from God, and even when and how we die are part of God's providential plan for our lives. The prophet Jeremiah faced beatings, persecution, death threats, hostile kings, the capture of Jerusalem, and a kidnapping, but he was invincible as God's servant until he finished the mission that God had given to him. The apostle Paul faced similar dangers when serving the Lord and even a conspiracy against his life in which more than forty people vowed not to eat until he was dead (Acts 23:12–22), but the Lord delivered Paul from every threat until he finished the divinely appointed course for his life.

Jesus is "the resurrection and the life" (John 11:25–26), and he has come back from the other side to announce that his followers have nothing to fear because he has overcome the grave. We are blessed to live on this side of salvation history, and we can face death with the confident assurance of resurrection life in the presence of God forever. We grieve over the death of fellow believers, but we grieve with hope. We serve the Lord even with the willingness to die for him, knowing that our labor in the Lord has an eternal reward (1 Cor 15:58). The hope of resurrection changes everything.

---

[14]   Some would see here (as in the vision of the valley of dry bones in Ezekiel 37) only a figurative reference to the national restoration of Israel rather than the promise of personal resurrection.

[15]   Tremper Longman III, *Psalms: An Introduction and Commentary*, Tyndale Old Testament Commentary (Downers Grove, IL: InterVarsity Press, 2014), 215.

Annotated Bibliography

BOOKS

Johnston, Philip S. *Shades of Sheol: Death and Afterlife in the Old Testament*. Downers Grove, IL: InterVarsity Press, 2002. The key work referenced in this chapter for those wishing to do further study on the concept of death and the afterlife in the Old Testament.

Wright, N. T. *The Resurrection of the Son of God, Vol. 3, Christian Origins and the Question of God*. Minneapolis: Fortress, 2003. Comprehensive historical and theological development of the biblical teaching on resurrection and the afterlife.

COMMENTARIES

Longman, Tremper, III. *Psalms: An Introduction and Commentary*. Tyndale Old Testament Commentary. Downers Grove, IL: InterVarsity Press, 2014. Provides an overview of each psalm with attention to literary, theological, and interpretive issues that is accessible for a wide audience.

WEBSITES

Alcorn, Randy. "Is There an Expectation of Eternal Life in the Old Testament?" August 7, 2015. https://www.biblestudytools.com/bible-study/topical-studies/is-there-an-expectation-of-eternal-life-in-the-old-testament.html. Summary of key passages dealing with the afterlife in the Old Testament.

CHAPTER 26

Proper Parenting Guarantees Godly Children
Proverbs 22:6

The Legendary Teaching on Proverbs 22:6

Proverbs 22:6 guarantees that if parents will teach and train their children to know the Lord and live godly lives, their children will never depart from their faith. The right training produces the right outcomes. Even if the child might turn away from the faith for a time, when older, the offspring will return to God. A child permanently abandoning the Christian faith is a reflection of parental neglect and failure to teach and model the correct values and beliefs.

Countering the Legendary Teaching

Proverbs 22:6 highlights the lifelong influence of parental training. Nevertheless, the legendary teaching on Prov 22:6 has heaped tons of guilt and blame on many faithful Christian parents whose children have abandoned the faith. It is important to understand that while this proverb does speak of the enduring value of parental influence, it does not offer an absolute promise or guarantee that children will follow the Lord if their parents train them in the right way. Proverbial statements reflect general principles as to how life works, but these principles do not always prove true, and since we live in a fallen world, there are exceptions to the rules.

Interpretive Issues in Proverbs 22:6

Proverbs 22:6 teaches the principle that training a child in the way of wisdom has lifelong impact. Accurate interpretation of the verse requires resolving issues concerning the meaning of: (1) the verb *to train* (*hanak*); (2) the noun *child* (*na'ar*); and (3) the phrase *in the way he should go* (KJV).

THE MEANING OF "TO TRAIN"

The verb *to train* (*hanak*) appears in three other passages in the Hebrew Bible (Deut 20:5; 1 Kgs 8:63; 2 Chr 7:5); a related noun appears seven times (Num 7:10, 11, 84, 88; 2 Chr 7:9; Neh 12:27; Ps 30:1). In each case, the word refers to the dedication of a house or a building. Allen Ross explains that this word is likely chosen to reflect that parental training "should be with a purpose," just like the dedication of a building for a specific use or function.[1] The verb and noun forms for *hanak* are never associated with instruction and discipline elsewhere in the Old Testament, and the writer had a number of key wisdom words for teaching or training that he could have used here. If parental instruction is in view, the emphasis of this particular verb then would seem to be more on the process of initiating the child in the right way of living. The CSB reflects this nuance: "Start a youth on his way; even when he grows old he will not depart from it."

THE AGE OF THE CHILD/YOUTH

The term for *youth/child* (*na'ar*) in this verse does not refer exclusively to young children. The word elsewhere refers to an unborn child (Judg 13:5–12), a newborn (1 Sam 4:21), an infant (Exod 2:6), a weaned child (1 Sam 2:21), and of young boys like Ishmael (Gen 21:12) and Isaac (Gen 22:5, 12). The term also applies to Joseph at the ages of seventeen (Gen 37:2) and thirty (Gen 41:12, 46), and is also used with reference to men who are old enough to marry (Gen 34:19), engage in warfare (2 Sam 18:5, 12), act as spies (Josh 6:22), participate in priestly service (Judg 18:3, 15), and work as servants (Gen 22:3; Num 22:22; Judg 7:10–11).[2] The six other uses of this word in Proverbs seem to refer to youthfulness in general. Proverbs 20:11 observes that character already begins to demonstrate itself in a *na'ar*. The *na'ar* in 1:4 and 7:7 is a person needing understanding. The remaining uses of *na'ar* in the book are in contexts that stress the need for discipline and correction (22:15; 23:12; 29:15, 21).

The proverb in 22:6 is not designating a specific age but merely stressing

[1]   Allen Ross, "Proverbs," in *Expositor's Bible Commentary*, rev ed., ed. Tremper Longman III and David E. Garland (Grand Rapids: Zondervan, 2009), 6:188.
[2]   See Francis Brown and S. R. Driver, *Brown-Driver-Briggs Hebrew and English Lexicon*, reprint ed. (Peabody, MA: Hendrickson, 1996), 654–55.

the importance of proper parental influence for helping the child get started in the right direction. The topics that the father addresses with his son in Proverbs, such as marital and sexual advice (5:1–16; 15:21), economic counsel (10:5; 11:1), political instruction (25:6–7; 29:12), and military advice (24:6), would seem to indicate that the book focuses more on training for an adolescent than for a young child.[3] The term *na'ar*, however, is broad enough to include the entire process.

TRAINING THE CHILD "ACCORDING TO HIS WAY"

The most disputed feature of Prov 22:6 is the meaning of the phrase that reads in Hebrew, "according to his way." Ted Hildebrandt summarizes five different views on the meaning of this phrase: (1) the moral view, (2) the vocational view, (3) the personal aptitudes view, (4) the personal demands view, and (5) the status view.[4] The view taken here and in the English translations as a whole is the moral view. The word *way* is commonly used with this meaning in Proverbs (seventy times), as the book contrasts the straight path of wisdom that leads to blessing (e.g., 2:8, 20; 3:23; 4:11; 6:23; 8:20; 9:6; 11:5) with the crooked and dark path of folly that leads to calamity and death (e.g., 1:15, 31; 2:12; 4:14, 19; 7:27; 12:15, 26; 13:15).[5] This view is also in line with the emphasis on the importance of parental training and instruction in the book of Proverbs (13:24; 19:18; 22:15; 23:13–14; 29:15, 17).

The word *way* does not have moral qualifiers or adjectives here as in other passages (Prov 2:8; 6:23; 9:6). The Hebrew phrase *according to his way* also does not have the "should" ("in the way that he *should* go") found in many English translations, but the overall goal of parental instruction in Proverbs is to enable the child to live a wise life and to enjoy the benefits of wisdom (2:1–15; 3:1–4, 13–18; 4:1–9). Proper parental training will lead the child to make the path of wisdom "his way," in the sense that it will be the only way of life that the child views as acceptable. We see a similar idea expressed in Prov 23:19, where the son is commanded to "be wise" and to set his heart "on the way." In doing so, the way of wisdom will become the direction of his life.[6]

The vocational view of "according to his way" is unlikely because vocational choice is not a major theme in Proverbs, and the son would normally

---

3   Ted Hildebrandt, "Proverbs 22:6a: Train up a Child?" *Grace Theological Journal* 9 (1988): 13.
4   Hildebrandt, "Proverbs 22:6a," 14–16.
5   John A. Kitchen, *Proverbs: A Mentor Commentary*, reprint ed. (Ross-shire, UK: Mentor, 2006), 496.
6   Michael V. Fox, *Proverbs 10–31*, Anchor Yale Bible (New Haven, CT: Yale University Press, 2009), 698.

be expected to follow his father's vocation in the ancient Near East. The personal aptitudes view argues that "according to his way" indicates that the parent is to train the child in accordance with the child's natural inclinations or in ways that are age-appropriate and intellectually attainable. This understanding offers helpful advice, but it is difficult to see how this outcome is the specific goal of parental instruction or even contingent upon how the parent teaches or trains.[7]

The personal demands view understands 22:6 as a negative warning of the dangers of parental failure to provide the right kind of training and instruction. In this view, "according to his way" refers to the evil and selfish inclinations of the child. Gordon Hugenberger explains that this verse envisions parents failing to discipline their children and simply allowing them to go their own way, causing reinforcement of the child's sinful and selfish tendencies to such a degree that they will not turn away from them even in old age.[8] Other passages in Proverbs warn of the dangers of parents failing to discipline their children (19:18; 22:15; 29:15). The major problem with this view is that the verb *hanak* suggests something purposeful and intentional and thus seems to be an unlikely way of referring to a lack of training and discipline. There are not enough contextual clues to indicate here the use of an ironic or sarcastic command.

The status view of "according to his way" offered by Hildebrandt is influenced by the fact that the *na'ar* is often a person of status who performed important military or religious roles or who served persons of influence.[9] Thus, Hildebrandt views Prov 22:6 not to refer to child-rearing but rather to the parents' initiation of a *na'ar* into his official duties as a "high-born squire" with the training and respect befitting his status.[10] The word *way* (*derek*) however does not refer to status, and there is not enough contextual detail to support this more nuanced or specialized meaning for *na'ar*.[11] As noted above, the usage of *na'ar* in Proverbs refers to young persons needing instruction and discipline, and the closest contextual references (22:15; 23:13) clearly have youth in view rather than squires.

The traditional view that Prov 22:6 refers to parental initiation/training into the way of wisdom that includes fearing the Lord as its starting point still

[7]   Daniel J. Estes, *Handbook on the Wisdom Books and Psalms* (Grand Rapids: Baker, 2005), 248.
[8]   Gordon P. Hugenberger, "Train up a Child," in *Basics of Biblical Hebrew Grammar*, ed. Gary D. Pratico and Miles V. van Pelt, 2nd ed. (Grand Rapids: Zondervan, 2007), 162–63.
[9]   Hildebrandt, "Proverbs 22:6a," 10–14.
[10]   Hildebrandt, "Proverbs 22:6a," 16.
[11]   Fox, *Proverbs 10–31*, 698.

seems the best explanation of the passage. The focus in Proverbs does appear to be more on the initiation into adulthood than the teaching of small children. Proverbs 22:6 expresses optimism in the outcome of parental instruction and anticipates that a child initiated or trained in the right way will remain on this path even in old age. The verse says nothing about a prodigal child returning to the right path after a misspent youth but rather envisions children living their entire lives in the right direction.

The Nature of Proverbial Statements: Not Promises or Guarantees

When assessing the message of Prov 22:6, it is important to remember the basic features of proverbial sayings. Proverbial sayings teach general principles about how life works, but they are not promises or absolute guarantees. Proverbs 13:25 teaches that the righteous will have enough food to satisfy their appetites, but the proverb in 13:23 observes that the poor are often deprived of food because of injustice. Proverbs 22:4 teaches that riches are one of the rewards of humility and fear of the Lord (compare 3:16; 8:18), but Prov 15:16 reminds that "little with the fear of the LORD" is better than great treasure mixed with a life of turmoil. Wealth is generally a consequence of wise living, but righteousness does not guarantee financial prosperity. Proverbs 22:6 teaches that parental influence lasts for a lifetime, but it does not guarantee that a parent's wise training will cause children to live a godly life.[12] Conversely, the wickedness of a son or daughter is not a sure indicator of parental failure.

Because of their brevity, individual proverbs offer key insights on life, but they are not comprehensive treatments of the topics they address. The English proverb "an apple a day keeps the doctor away" is a good reminder of the importance of fruits and vegetables for a healthy diet, but adding a daily apple to a high-fat diet will not produce good health. Similarly, Prov 22:6 does not give every possible outcome of parental training. The influence of a parent is only one factor in the development of a child's moral character. Other persons beside the parent will have a sharpening influence on the child's personality and character (21:17), and so the father warns his son to choose his friends and companions wisely (Prov 1:10–15; 13:20; 24:1; 28:7). Children can bring great sorrow to parents by rejecting their wise counsel (10:1; 17:25), and the smooth words of the adulterous woman may become

---

[12] Peter Gentry, "Equipping the Generations: Raising Children, the Christian Way," *Journal of Discipleship and Family Ministry* 2 (2012): 99, notes the special emphasis in Proverbs, and unique to the culture of the ancient Near East, on the teaching and instruction of the mother (1:8; 4:3; 6:20; 31:1, 26).

more alluring than the guidance of the parent (5:3; 7:10–23). Individuals, rather than their parents, bear ultimate responsibility for their choices.

Application

Proverbs 22:6 reminds us that wise and godly parenting helps children to start their life in the right direction, but it is not a promise or guarantee that wise parenting always produces godly children. Parents have a responsibility to teach and train their children in the ways of the Lord (Deut 6:4–9; Eph 6:4), but children themselves, as they grow into maturity, are ultimately responsible for their own faith commitments and moral choices. Parents have far greater influence on their children than the church or educational system ever will, and this verse offers encouragement for parents to use their influence in positive ways. This verse, however, should not be used to blame or heap guilt upon godly and caring parents when their children turn away from the Lord and choose to go their own way.

Annotated Bibliography

BOOKS
Longman, Tremper, III. *How to Read Proverbs.* How to Read Series (Downers Grove, IL: InterVarsity Press, 2009). Helpful discussions on how to read, interpret, and apply proverbial statements in the larger context of Old Testament Wisdom Literature.

COMMENTARIES
Waltke, Bruce K. *The Book of Proverbs.* 2 vols. New International Commentary on the Old Testament (Grand Rapids: Eerdmans, 2004, 2006). Scholarly, evangelical commentary for those looking for detailed exegetical analysis of the text.

WEBSITES
DeRouchie, Jason. "Train up a Child in the Way in the Way He Should Go." *Desiring God.* September 20, 2016. http://www.desiringgod.org/articles/train-up-a-child-in-the-way-he-should-go. Helpful discussion of interpretive issues found in this verse.

CHAPTER 27

Without Vision, People Perish

Proverbs 29:18

The Legendary Teaching on Proverbs 29:18

Most organizations have a difficult time knowing what to focus on, finding a direction. Many of them, and their employees, wander about without a clear purpose. The Bible provides a clear, concise explanation for this problem: "Where there is no vision, the people perish" (KJV). The solution for this problem is also clear: successful leaders must cast a clear vision. By doing this, people will know where they are headed, and they will know the purpose for their particular task in the grand scheme. This verse does not mean that they will literally die, but that they will "run wild" (CSB); they will not be able to focus. They will have no hope of reaching their dreams. One leader concluded: "I've seen it with my own eyes—without vision, people lose the vitality that makes them feel alive."[1]

Countering the Legend

In countering this legend, we are not casting aspersions upon those who advocate creating a vision for organizations. Vision casting seems to be a helpful tool to bring focus to an organization. However, the question is whether Prov 29:18 is teaching this principle.

The English word *vision* can refer to several concepts; in this context, many understand it as referring to a desired future. By explaining the end

---

[1]   Bill Hybels, *Courageous Leadership: Field-Tested Strategy for the 360° Leader* (Grand Rapids: Zondervan, 2012), 31.

goal, the vision, people in the organization can trace from the goal back to the present, figuring out the steps necessary to take. However, the Hebrew word for "vision" (*hazah*) is never used this way in the Old Testament. In fact, two old Bible translations (before the King James Version) translate this verse differently than the KJV. The Wycliffe Bible (completed ca. 1395) says: "When prophecy faileth, the people shall be destroyed." The Bishops' Bible (originally completed in 1568) says: "When the worde of God is not preached, the people perishe." Both of these translations give a hint that the translation of "vision" might be misleading.

The word translated as "perish" (*para'*) in the KJV also needs to be studied. All three senses of the Hebrew word are connected to the idea of "letting loose." The first sense refers to cutting (Lev 10:6) or unbraiding the hair (Num 5:18). The second sense refers to running wild (Exod 32:25). The third sense refers to neglecting (Prov 1:25; 8:33).[2] This verb is never translated as "perish" by any modern translation in its sixteen uses in the Old Testament.

The Meaning of Proverbs 29:18

If "vision" and "perish" are not the best translations of the Hebrew words, what do the words mean? Most modern translations do a great job of translating these words. Some Bible versions translate "vision" as "revelation" (CSB, NIV) or "prophetic vision" (ESV). The word refers to communication from God to a prophet,[3] which is clear in 1 Sam 3:1: "The boy Samuel served the LORD in Eli's presence. In those days the word of the LORD was rare and prophetic visions were not widespread." The word for "prophetic vision" is the same one used in Prov 29:18.

A similar situation exists for the word *perish*. Modern Bible versions translate it as "cast off restraint" (ESV, NIV) or "run wild" (CSB). The second sense is likely what the author was referring to, with Exod 32:25 and the Israelites being out of control as a possible background text to verse 18.

Another key to interpreting this text is understanding parallelism in

[2]   Victor P. Hamilton, "עָרַף," in *Theological Wordbook of the Old Testament*, ed. R. Laird Harris, Gleason L. Archer Jr., and Bruce K. Waltke (Chicago: Moody, 1999), 736–37.
[3]   See Duane A. Garrett, *Proverbs, Ecclesiastes, Song of Songs*, New American Commentary (Nashville: Broadman & Holman, 1993), 231; Derek Kidner, *Proverbs: An Introduction and Commentary*, Tyndale Old Testament Commentaries (Downers Grove, IL: InterVarsity Press, 1964), 168. Note that C. H. Toy, *The Book of Proverbs*, International Critical Commentary (Edinburgh: T&T Clark, 1899), 512, believes that a better translation is "guidance" since Israel seemed to run wild when prophetic vision was occurring.

Hebrew poetry. There are several different types of parallelism in Hebrew poetry, and Prov 29:18 is an example of contrast parallelism, in which the second clause typically begins with the word *but*. Sometimes each clause can be better understood when interpreted in contrast to the other, which is common in Proverbs (particularly when the wise and foolish are contrasted).

The second clause says, "but one who follows divine instruction will be happy." Listening to or following instruction is contrasted with not having revelation from God. Running wild is contrasted with being happy or "blessed" (ESV, NIV). This contrast confirms our understanding of the first half of the verse. It would make little sense for listening to instruction to be contrasted with casting a vision for an organization. Duane Garrett summarizes the meaning of this verse well: "Social harmony and restraint cannot be achieved without the exhortations of the prophets and the teaching of the law."[4]

Application

Having a clear direction in life is important. Casting vision for an organization can be helpful. But Prov 29:18 addresses neither of these issues. Instead, the author is telling us that we need the Word of God to live controlled lives filled with a joy from the knowledge that we are living in a right relationship with God. Living a life of self-control is a fruit of the Spirit (Gal 5:23). Only through the Word of God can we know that we are living holy lives. We live in a time where Scripture is abundantly available, yet many Christians do not read it. About 53 percent of Americans have not read more than half the Bible.[5] Only 45 percent of people who regularly attend church read the Bible more than once per week and 20 percent never read the Bible.[6] As Christians, we need to read the Bible so our minds can be transformed rather than be conformed to the world (Rom 12:2). Left to ourselves, we will "run wild," not living a life of blessedness or satisfaction. And the text does not say merely to "read" the Scripture, it refers to the one who "follows" (CSB) or "keeps" (ESV) it. Both the Old and New Testaments emphasize the importance of being a doer and not simply a hearer:

---

[4]   Garrett, *Proverbs, Ecclesiastes, Song of Songs*, 231.
[5]   Bob Smietana, "LifeWay Research: Americans Are Fond of the Bible, Don't Actually Read It," *LifeWay Research*, April 25, 2017, https://lifewayresearch.com/2017/04/25/lifeway-research-americans-are-fond-of-the-bible-dont-actually-read-it/.
[6]   Ed Stetzer, "The Epidemic of Bible Illiteracy in Our Churches," *Christianity Today*, July 6, 2015, https://www.christianitytoday.com/edstetzer/2015/july/epidemic-of-bible-illiteracy-in-our-churches.html.

Because if anyone is a hearer of the word and not a doer, he is like someone looking at his own face in a mirror. For he looks at himself, goes away, and immediately forgets what kind of man he was. But the one who looks intently into the perfect law of freedom and perseveres in it, and is not a forgetful hearer but a doer who works—this person will be blessed in what he does. (Jas 1:23–25)

Annotated Bibliography

COMMENTARIES

Garrett, Duane A. *Proverbs, Ecclesiastes, Song of Songs*. New American Commentary. Nashville: Broadman & Holman, 1993. See 231. Garrett provides a good contextual interpretation of the verse.

Kidner, Derek. *Proverbs: An Introduction and Commentary*. Tyndale Old Testament Commentaries. Downers Grove, IL: InterVarsity Press, 1964. See 168. Kidner appropriately interprets the verse and provides brief but adequate evidence for it.

WEBSITES

Challies, Tim. "Where There Is No Vision . . . (Proverbs 29:18)." *Challies* (blog). March 9, 2005. https://www.challies.com/articles/where-there-is-no-vision-proverbs-2918/. After providing several examples of the misuse of this verse, Challies demonstrates the differences between the KJV and modern translations. He then succinctly interprets the verse correctly.

Gaudiosi, Michael C. "Two Most Misunderstood Passages." *The Noble Berean* 5 (January 2006). At *Faithlife Sermons*, https://sermons.faithlife.com/sermons/116807-two-most-misunderstood-passages. Gaudiosi says that Prov 29:18 and Hos 4:6 are the two most misunderstood verses in the Bible. Going back and forth between the two, he explains, in an easy to understand way, how to correctly interpret each.

McCabe, Bob. "Distorting Another Good Verse: Proverbs 29:18." *Detroit Baptist Theological Seminary*. March 22, 2013. http://www.dbts.edu/2013/03/22/distorting-another-good-verse-proverbs-2918/. McCabe does a good job explaining why the typical use of this verse is wrong and how to correctly understand it.

CHAPTER 28

Proverbs 31: A Checklist for the Perfect Wife

Proverbs 31:10–31

The Legendary Teaching on Proverbs 31

Young men, listen up. What I am about to say is extremely important for you to hear. There are so many people in unsatisfying marriages, so many divorces, and maybe if we paid more attention to the wisdom of Prov 31:10–31, we could avoid some of these issues. Because what we have in Proverbs 31 is a description, given by God, of what a wise, godly woman looks like in her behavior and character. It is a text to help young men find a good wife.

Verse 10 tells us that a wife of "noble character" (NIV) is very rare. We all want wives to "bring us good, not harm" (v. 12, NIV), someone who is hard-working (vv. 13–19). A noble wife will bring respect upon you as a husband (v. 23). She will faithfully and lovingly instruct your children (vv. 26, 28). She is someone who fears God (v. 30). Men, this is your God-given checklist for a wife.

Countering the Legendary Teaching

There are truly many attributes in Proverbs 31 that would make wonderful qualities in a wife. We would not deny that. However, these verses have been used time and time again to make wives feel like they are inadequate, like they do not measure up. There are two main reasons for this.

First, a flat reading of this text portrays this as a typical day in the life of a noble wife. Verse 12 sets the stage for an antithetical reading; the author is setting up these verses as a portrayal of "all the days of her life." In verse

167

15, she is described as rising from bed while it is still night to provide food for her family; in verse 18, she is described as not letting her lamp go out at night,[1] working late into the evening. If this is taken literally, when does she sleep? The author is saying that she worked late into the night when that was necessary to accomplish her tasks, and she rose early in the morning when that was needed. Are we truly to expect that she is daily buying fields and planting vineyards (v. 16), while also daily making clothes for her family and for selling (vv. 19, 22, 24)? These are not "ongoing concurrent businesses."[2] In verse 28, her children rise up and call her blessed. This verse demonstrates that the author is not discussing a young man looking for a wife, because it is written from the perspective of the woman already having children. Therefore, she is not a young virgin or a newlywed but a "mature woman who has" lived the life described in the passage.[3] The author is picturing a woman at different points throughout her life, involved in different activities at different points.[4]

There is a second problem with reading this passage as a checklist for finding a wife. The description is primarily about a woman who contributes to family and society, not simply about marriage. The entire book of Proverbs teaches about wisdom. Themes of wisdom throughout the entire book are now being described as lived out in the ideal woman,[5] not just in marriage but in life in general. As Al Wolters concludes, "It is widely recognized that the Song of the Valiant Woman portrays its heroine as the personification of wisdom, the incarnation of what it means to be wise."[6] Although it is true that the author is addressing how the wisdom discussed throughout Proverbs would be manifested in the life of a woman, the underlying principles of wisdom throughout this poem can apply to men as well. Most of the book

---

[1]   Note that the NET Bible footnote on this verse says, "But the line could also be taken figuratively, comparing 'her light' to the prosperity of her household—her whole life—which continues night and day."
[2]   Brian L. Webster, "The Perfect Verb and the Perfect Woman in Proverbs," in *Windows to the Ancient World of the Hebrew Bible: Essays in Honor of Samuel Greengus*, ed. Bill T. Arnold, Nancy L. Erickson, and John H. Walton (Winona Lake, IN: Eisenbrauns, 2015), 271. Webster makes an argument that the description of the Proverbs 31 woman is a depiction of her throughout her life based upon an analysis of the Hebrew verbs being used in combination with the genre.
[3]   Webster, "The Perfect Verb," 271.
[4]   Webster, "The Perfect Verb," 271, concludes: "The behaviors are typical, not constant and simultaneous. We are reading about a lifetime achievement recognition, not her daily planner."
[5]   Claudia V. Camp, *Wisdom and the Feminine in the Book of Proverbs*, Bible and Literature Series (Sheffield, UK: Sheffield University Press, 1985), 92–93.
[6]   Al Wolters, "Proverbs XXXI 10–31 as Heroic Hymn: A Form-Critical Analysis," *Vetus Testamentum* 38, no. 4 (1988): 457. Note the nuance given by Michael V. Fox: "The Woman of Strength is not a figure for wisdom. While Lady Wisdom personifies wisdom, the Woman of Strength typifies it." Fox, *Proverbs 10–31*, 910–11 (see chap 26, n. 6).

of Proverbs is addressed to men, providing wise principles for living. The final section now applies these concepts to women, which therefore does not exclude the principles from being applicable to men.[7]

An interesting parallel to Proverbs 31 is Psalm 112, which begins, "Praise the LORD! Blessed is the man who fears the LORD, who greatly delights in his commandments!" (ESV). Both Prov 31:10–31 and Psalm 112[8] are acrostic poems: a type of poetry where the first letter of each line is a subsequent letter in the Hebrew alphabet. For the woman in Proverbs 31, this likely indicates the "completeness of wisdom as embodied" in her.[9] Proverbs 31 describes a woman and Psalm 112 describes a man.[10] Both are described as fearing God (Prov 31:30; Ps 112:1). In the conclusions, beauty is contrasted with fearing God (Prov 31:30), and the wicked and righteous are contrasted (Ps 112:9–10). Both are discussed in terms of their wealth (Prov 31:16, 18; Ps 112:3). The woman's children call her blessed, and his children will be blessed (Prov 31:28; Ps 112:2). Both idealized people show compassion to the poor (Prov 31:20; Ps 112:4–5, 9) and have no fear regarding the future (Prov 31:25; Ps 112:7). This comparison is helpful because the way wisdom is lived out among men and women have significant parallels.

Interpreting Proverbs 31:10–31

Most Bible translations begin by describing the wife as having "noble character" (NIV, CSB)[11] or being an "excellent wife" (ESV). The word *hayil* is also used to refer to the strength of men in battle (1 Sam 10:26; 14:48, 52; 2 Sam 13:28). Strength in Prov 31:10 could refer to "wealth, physical power, military might, practical competencies, or character . . . (and the) last two strengths are praised"[12] in Proverbs 31. A good parallel is Ruth 3:11: "Now don't be afraid, my daughter. I will do for you whatever you say, since all the people in my town

---

[7]   Proverbs 8 and 9 reference "Lady Wisdom," that is, wisdom personified as a woman. Starting in Prov 9:13, Lady Folly is discussed.

[8]   Psalm 112 has been classified by some scholars as a "wisdom psalm." See Wolters, "Heroic Hymn," 448.

[9]   Craig G. Bartholomew and Ryan P. O'Dowd, *Old Testament Wisdom Literature: A Theological Introduction* (Downers Grove, IL: InterVarsity Press, 2011), 104. Similarly, see Tremper Longman III, *Proverbs*, Baker Exegetical Commentary on the Old Testament Wisdom and Psalms (Grand Rapids: Baker, 2006), 541.

[10]   For the following comparison between Proverbs 31 and Psalm 112, see Bartholomew and O'Dowd, 104–105; and Wolters, "Heroic Hymn," 448.

[11]   The previous Holman Christian Standard Bible (HCSB) refers to her as "capable."

[12]   Fox, *Proverbs 10–31*, 891.

know that you are a woman of noble character."[13] Ruth is a great example of a woman who did not live in fear but lived in strength, specifically in reference to her character. Also, there is an emphasis on her "strength" throughout the passage. Proverbs 31:17 says, "She draws on her strength and reveals that her arms are strong," a reference mainly to her diligent work ethic. In verse 21, she is described as "not afraid." Verse 25 describes her as clothed with "strength and honor." And the same word used in verse 10 is used again in verse 29, describing her as surpassing the strength of all other women. The description of the Woman of Strength seems to push strongly against the picture of some modern, fundamentalist portrayals that women should be passive and weak. The woman in Proverbs 31 is strong in the sense that she has the abilities and character described in the passage.[14] Michael Fox concludes, "Her primary strength is in her character, because even her practical competencies are not simply technical skills but manifestations of her focus, selflessness, and determination."[15]

The opening rhetorical question is not intended to indicate that a woman of strong character is impossible to find, but is rare.[16] The comparison with rubies is intended to extend the rarity of this woman to include the concepts of value and preciousness. Because of her noble character, her husband has "full confidence" (31:11, NIV) in her. Although the Woman of Strength could be summarized in several ways, three areas seem to be emphasized in this passage: her dedication to work, her success in business, and her character (in general).

She is described repeatedly as being dedicated to her work. She "works with eager hands" (31:13, NIV) and she brings "food from far away" (v. 14). If necessary, she rises from her sleep while it is still dark to provide food for her family (v. 15). She works vigorously (v. 17), even staying up late into the night when needed (v. 18). She makes sure her family is clothed (vv. 21–22), presumably with the clothes she made (v. 19). She is not idle (v. 27). She is diligent in her work.

She is also a successful business woman. She carefully buys a field and plants a vineyard (v. 16). She is profitable in trading (v. 18) and makes a profit selling clothes she has made (v. 24). Although some readers might be surprised

---

[13]   See also Ruth 4:11. Note that Bartholomew and O'Dowd, *Old Testament Wisdom Literature,* 110, favor the translation "valiance," believing "noble character" is inadequate. It is interesting to note that the book of Ruth follows directly after Proverbs 31 in the Hebrew canon, maybe suggesting a connection between Proverbs 31 and Ruth herself.

[14]   Note that Fox, *Proverbs 10–31,* 891, pushes against the translation or interpretation of "valor" since "the qualities listed here do not include courage of the sort usually called valorous."

[15]   Fox, *Proverbs 10–31,* 891.

[16]   Note the parallels of Job 28:12 and Eccl 7:28 noted by Bartholomew and O'Dowd, *Old Testament Wisdom Literature,* 110–11.

to read about a woman from this time period functioning in this way, there is adequate evidence from the ancient Near East to understand these activities as being fairly normal. Michael Fox says, "This is not to say that they had economic or social equality, but they were not confined to childbearing and drudge work in the home."[17]

Finally, several verses praise her character in general. She is generous in taking care of the poor and needy (v. 20). She brings honor to her husband (v. 23) and receives praise from her husband and children (v. 28). Her character is described as including strength (vv. 25, 29) and dignity (v. 25). The Woman of Strength speaks wisely (v. 26) and fears God (v. 30). She is a woman who is praised for having wisdom and desirable character.

Application

This summary of the Woman of Strength has been applied to women inappropriately. First, it is unfair to hold women to the standard set in Proverbs 31 due to the reasons stated above. As Tremper Longman concludes, "The description is an ideal and should not be used as a standard by which to measure and critique women."[18] Second, men are not excluded from the exhortations to wisdom given in this section of Proverbs. The Woman of Strength is not only an ideal woman, but an ideal person: "By reminding us that the most important features of the wise man characterize the woman too, the whole book of Proverbs, despite its male orientation, is made to apply to women as well."[19] All of the principles in Prov 31:10–31 apply to both men and women,[20] remembering that this is not the portrayal of a single day, but what a wise life would look like over a lifetime. Third, if someone wants to make Prov 31:10–31 into a checklist for what to look for in a wife (which, as discussed above, is wholly inappropriate), then, to be consistent, Proverbs 1–9 would be a checklist for a woman when looking for a husband. If this concept was applied consistently, nearly everyone would remain single! Instead of taking these concepts and looking for them in others, we should

---

[17]   Fox, *Proverbs 10–31*, 901. Note the helpful work by Christine Roy Yoder, *Wisdom as a Woman of Substance: A Socioeconomic Reading of Proverbs 1–9 and 31:10–31*, Beihefte zur Zeitschrift für die alttestamentliche Wissenschaft 304 (Berlin: de Gruyter, 2000).

[18]   Longman, *Proverbs*, 540. See similar comment by Fox, *Proverbs 10–31*, 912.

[19]   Fox, *Proverbs 10–31*, 916.

[20]   Note that Proverbs 1 (v. 7) introduces us to a life of wisdom by referencing the importance of fearing God, and Proverbs 31 (v. 30) concludes by referring to fearing God. It is likely that this forms an inclusio for the whole book. See Greg W. Parsons, "Guidelines for Understanding and Proclaiming the Book of Proverbs," *Bibliotheca Sacra* 150 (April–June 1993): 154n22.

honor the Lord who inspired this book by seeking to emulate in our own lives the principles of wisdom presented in this passage and the entire book.

Annotated Bibliography

BOOKS

Bartholomew, Craig G., and Ryan P. O'Dowd. *Old Testament Wisdom Literature: A Theological Introduction.* Downers Grove, IL: InterVarsity Press, 2011. See 101–26. This chapter on Proverbs 31 presents a good overview of the passage, providing a brief history of interpretation of the passage and theological implications for today.

Camp, Claudia V. *Wisdom and the Feminine in the Book of Proverbs.* Bible and Literature Series. Sheffield, UK: University of Sheffield Press, 1985. See 90–93, 186–91. Camp provides convincing evidence that the wisdom presented throughout the book of Proverbs is being represented in Proverbs 31.

ARTICLES

Wolters, Al. "Proverbs XXXI 10–31 as Heroic Hymn: A Form-Critical Analysis." *Vetus Testamentum* 38, no. 4 (1988): 446–57. Wolters analyzes the genre of Proverbs 31 and gives a helpful comparison to the man who fears God in Psalm 112.

CHAPTER 29

"Under the Sun" in Ecclesiastes
Refers to Life without God

Ecclesiastes 1:2-3

The Legendary Teaching on "Under the Sun" in Ecclesiastes

The expression "under the sun" in Ecclesiastes is an idiom for life without God. One Christian scholar has stated that "under the sun" is in fact "a Hebraism which literally means outside of God" and refers to a life that involves "locking God out of your pursuits."[1] Because of this "under the sun" outlook, the writer of Ecclesiastes concludes that life without God is void of meaning (1:2–3). Ecclesiastes reflects the empty life that Solomon lived when he turned away from God to pursue a life of pleasure, indulgence, and personal accomplishment.

Countering the Legendary Teaching

As a wisdom treatise, Ecclesiastes has an important message for those attempting to navigate life without God. The book teaches that human wisdom and experience apart from the fear of God can never bring blessing and success.[2] Nevertheless, the term *under the sun* that appears twenty-nine times in Ecclesiastes does not itself refer to a worldview that leaves God out of the picture, nor does it reflect that Qoheleth (the "Teacher" who wrote this book) had

---

[1] Ravi Zacharias, "What Is Worthwhile under the Sun (part 1 of 2)," Ravi Zacharias International Ministries (podcast audio), July 31, 2017, https://rzim.org/just-thinking-broadcasts/what-is-worthwhile-under-the-sun-part-1-of-4/.

[2] Richard S. Hess, *The Old Testament: A Historical, Theological, and Critical Introduction* (Grand Rapids: Baker Academic, 2016), 492.

attempted to live without God. Even if Solomon is the author of Ecclesiastes, there is no suggestion that the writer of Ecclesiastes expresses repentance for an apostate lifestyle.[3] Instead, the book contains the reflections of a wisdom teacher who has engaged in a legitimate search for meaning and purpose in this life "under the sun." This search has affirmed the limitations of human wisdom for unlocking the mysteries of life, but the vanity/futility of life observed by Qoheleth does not go away when God's existence is acknowledged. There are in fact, specific theological reasons why this vanity exists.

The Meaning of "Under the Sun" in Ecclesiastes

The expression "under the sun" in Ecclesiastes does not carry the negative connotation of a secular viewpoint but, rather, denotes "life on earth-life in this world."[4] The expression itself is neutral and refers to "the realm that the author observes in which human works and deeds are performed."[5] In Eccl 4:15, the living are described as those "who move about under the sun." Speaking of the dead, Eccl 9:6 says that "there is no longer a portion for them in all that is done under the sun." Similarly, the stillborn child in 6:5 is said to "not see the sun" in contrast to the person who might live for a thousand years. The living are also described as those "who see the sun" in 7:11, and 11:7–8 contrasts the light of "seeing the sun" with the darkness of death.[6] The dead cease to be a part of this world and no longer have a share in the common experiences of human life. The expression "under the sun" simply refers to the domain in which humans live. The same is true of the variant expression "under heaven" that appears in Eccl 1:13; 2:3; and 3:1—it refers to life in the cosmos at large (compare Exod 17:14; Deut 7:24; 9:1).[7]

The expression "under the sun" is important to the message of Ecclesiastes in that it designates the sphere and scope of Qoheleth's observation as he sets out to explore how life works. In one sense, "under the sun" conveys universality; his observations are true of all human life and experience on earth. At

---

[3] For discussion of issues surrounding authorship of Ecclesiastes, see Daniel C. Fredericks and Daniel J. Estes, *Ecclesiastes and the Song of Songs*, Apollos Old Testament Commentary (Downers Grove, IL: IVP Academic, 2010), 31–36.

[4] Thomas R. Schreiner, *The King in His Beauty: A Biblical Theology of the Old and New Testaments* (Grand Rapids: Baker Academic, 2013), 304.

[5] Doug Ingram, *Ambiguity in Ecclesiastes*, Library of Hebrew Bible/Old Testament Studies 431 (New York: T&T Clark, 2006), 257.

[6] Ingram, *Ambiguity in Ecclesiastes*, 257.

[7] Garrett, *Proverbs, Ecclesiastes, Song of Songs*, 284 (see chap. 27, n. 3).

another level, "under the sun" also conveys limitations.[8] Qoheleth's observations are temporal and earthly, while God's perspectives are eternal and
heavenly. Qoheleth's quest was "undertaken from a 'horizontal' perspective."[9]
The expression "under the sun" serves to focus "the reader's attention on this
world over against the heavenly realm, which is God's domain."[10] Humans
live on earth, but God dwells in heaven (5:2), and thus humans cannot know
everything that God knows or even everything needed for a complete understanding of life and the world.

Even with its limitations, observing how life works "under the sun" is essential for the acquisition of wisdom. Thomas Schreiner explains, "Wisdom per-
ceives what ordinarily happens in life, and it attempts to discern and understand
the mysteries and injustices of human experience."[11] Much of what Qoheleth
observed "under the sun" was troubling and difficult to comprehend. Qoheleth
saw and experienced the weariness of labor (1:3) and the lack of lasting fulfillment that even great accomplishments bring (1:14; 2:11). He saw the pathetic
plight of the person who deprives self of pleasure by constantly working to earn
more wealth that never satisfies and who has no family with whom to share
that wealth (4:7–8). Qoheleth observed human wickedness (7:20; 9:3) and the
injustices that occur in the oppression of the poor and needy (3:16; 4:1). The
wicked often receive what the righteous deserve and vice versa (7:15; 8:14). The
dark and depressing tone of the book is due in large part to Qoheleth's awareness of the pervasive reality of death (3:19–21; 6:12; 9:2–6; 12:6–8).

Qoheleth's Assessment of Life as "Vanity/Futility"

Qoheleth's assessment of human existence as "futility" (*hebel*) is not the despair
or hardened cynicism of someone who has forgotten God; rather, it is a realistic
assessment of life in a fallen world that is marred by sin and death. The assessment of life as "vanity of vanities" or "absolute futility" does not convey that
life is absurd, senseless, or devoid of any meaning and purpose. This expression
need not be read in such an extreme manner.

The expression *absolute futility* serves as a frame around the book of
Ecclesiastes (1:2; 12:8), and the word "futility" (*hebel*) appears thirty-seven

---

[8]   Richard Alan Fuhr Jr., *An Analysis of the Inter-Dependency of the Prominent Motifs within the Book of Qoheleth*, Studies in Biblical Literature 151 (New York: Peter Lang, 2013), 67–68.

[9]   Fuhr, *An Analysis*, 71.

[10]   Richard P. Belcher Jr., "Ecclesiastes," in *A Biblical Theological Introduction to the Old Testament: The Gospel Promised*, ed. M. V. Van Pelt (Wheaton, IL: Crossway, 2016), 449.

[11]   Schreiner, *King in His Beauty*, 300.

times in the book. This term for "futility" or "vanity" refers elsewhere to a breath or vapor (Prov 21:6), to "worthless" idols (Jer 10:8), and to "meaningless" talk (Job 27:12). As in Ecclesiastes, the Psalms use *hebel* to describe life as fleeting and its accomplishments as quickly forgotten (Pss 39:5–6; 62:9–10).[12] Paul House explains that Qoheleth's use of this term to describe human existence reflects that he has come to the conclusion that "life does not necessarily have discernible meaning" and that "the meaning of life cannot be ascertained solely through experience and observation."[13] Adding to this futility is the transitory nature of life and how all of life passes "like a shadow" (Eccl 6:12). Even the individual who enjoys a long life knows that death is ultimately coming (11:7–8). The word *hebel* in Ecclesiastes often appears in connection with the image of "pursuing the wind" (1:14; 2:11, 17, 26; 4:4, 6; 6:9), a figure that effectively conveys the frustration that accompanies all human endeavors and the search for ultimate meaning.

Qoheleth does not assess life "under the sun" as futile because he has ignored God. The reality is that *hebel* exists in this world with or without God. As Barry Webb has noted, even faith in God "does not relieve the observed and experienced fact of *hebel*."[14] Specific connections between Ecclesiastes and the early chapters of Genesis suggest that the fall provides the theological explanation for the futility that Qoheleth has observed in the world. The disobedience of Adam and Eve in Genesis 3 is the cause of the sin and death that has reduced human existence to *hebel*. Reflecting Gen 3:19, Qoheleth observes that all humans come "from dust" (*min* + '*apar*) and then at death "return" (*shub*) "to dust" ('*el* '*apar*) (3:20; compare 12:7).[15] The statement in Eccl 7:29 that God made "humanity" ('*adam*) upright but that they have turned to "many schemes" is reminiscent of the condition of humans before (Gen 1:27) and after (Gen 6:5) Adam's disobedience.[16] The word *hebel* is actually the proper name of Adam's righteous son Abel, whose brief life and violent death prefigure what lies ahead for humanity in a fallen world.[17] In Rom 8:20–22, Paul states that God has subjected the world to "futility" through the curse that resulted from

---

[12]   Hess, *Old Testament*, 484.

[13]   Paul R. House, *Old Testament Theology* (Downers Grove, IL: InterVarsity Press, 1998), 471–72.

[14]   Barry G. Webb, *Five Festal Garments: Christian Reflections on the Song of Songs, Ruth, Lamentations, Ecclesiastes, and Esther*, New Studies in Biblical Theology (Downers Grove, IL: InterVarsity Press, 2000), 96.

[15]   Matthew Seufert, "The Presence of Genesis in Ecclesiastes," *Westminster Theological Journal* 78 (2016): 80–81.

[16]   Seufert, "The Presence," 81.

[17]   For more detailed discussion of the connections between Abel in Genesis and *hebel* in Ecclesiastes, see Russell L. Meek, "The Meaning of הבל in Qohelet: An Intertextual Suggestion," in *Words of the Wise Are like Goads: Engaging Qohelet in the 21st Century*, ed. M. Boda et al. (Winona Lake, IN: Eisenbrauns, 2013), 241–56.

the fall and that all creation awaits its ultimate deliverance. The likelihood that Paul alludes to Ecclesiastes in this passage is suggested by the fact that the word he uses for "futility" (*mataiotes*) is the same one used to translate *hebel* in the Septuagint of Ecclesiastes. As long as the curse remains in effect, the conditions of *hebel* will continue as well.

"Under the Sun" and Qoheleth's God-Consciousness

A final reason we know that "under the sun" in Ecclesiastes does not refer to life without God is that Qoheleth's message is saturated with a God-consciousness. Some have viewed the exhortation to "fear God and keep his commandments" in the epilogue of Ecclesiastes (12:13) as a corrective to Qoheleth's teaching in the rest of the book, but the call to reverence God does not appear only in the epilogue.[18] In Eccl 3:1–11, Qoheleth affirms that God is actively involved in the affairs of this world and causes the events of life to happen at the appropriate times so that humans will live in "awe/fear" of him (3:14). He calls for his readers to "fear God" (5:7) and to "remember" the Creator in the days of youth (12:1).

In accordance with the Torah, Qoheleth encourages his readers to offer God serious and reflective worship (5:1–3) and to keep the vows they have made to him (5:4–6). Ultimately, all will answer to God as judge (3:17; 12:14). Qoheleth encourages the enjoyment of food, drink, labor, and spouse, not as a hedonist, but rather out of a recognition that these good gifts come from God as a source of happiness even in the midst of life's hardships (2:24; 3:12, 22; 5:18–20; 8:15; 9:9). The Torah promised these rewards as covenantal blessings for Israel's obedience (Lev 26:3–10; Deut 28:3–14).

Although the idea that "under the sun" refers to life without God is inaccurate, this common teaching has correctly discerned the struggle in Qoheleth's search for purpose, meaning, and a faithful understanding of God. Qoheleth appears to have progressed from a search for meaning and purpose based on human wisdom, observation, and experience (1:13; 2:9) and to the understanding that humans "are not autonomous selves but creaturely, relational selves"

---

[18]   Some have argued that the narrator at the beginning and end of the book (1:1–11; 12:9–14) critiques and corrects the teachings of Qoheleth, but this view seems unlikely in light of the praise given to Qoheleth's teaching in 12:11. It also seems implausible that a writer would provide a lengthy treatise with which he disagrees, while summarizing the points that he wishes to teach in a few short verses at the end. Iain Provan, *Ecclesiastes, Song of Songs*, New International Version Application Commentary (Grand Rapids: Zondervan, 2001), 33.

and that "we are relational selves primarily in relation to God.[19] Qoheleth has turned from the consuming hedonism that involved giving himself over to personal achievement, wine, and women (2:1–11) to genuine enjoyment of the value of work, marriage, and pleasure as gifts of God.[20] In becoming skeptical of the ability of human wisdom to discern the ultimate purpose and meaning of life, Qoheleth has more fully learned of the need to fear God, to listen to God's words, and to remember his Creator. "Under the sun" in Ecclesiastes does not suggest that life without God was ever Qoheleth's intent, but his search for truth has certainly led Qoheleth to a deeper awareness of his need for God.

Application

We see evidence all around us of the reality that knowing God is what provides ultimate meaning and purpose in a world broken by sin and death. In spite of our great affluence, more than 43,000 Americans commit suicide yearly and more than 40 million suffer some form of mental illness every year.[21] While not removing the frustrations and futility that come from living in a fallen world, faith in God and knowing Christ offers hope in the place of hopelessness. Our faith enables us to enjoy the pleasures of life as blessings from God, while at the same time keeping us from expecting more from those fleeting experiences than they could ever provide.

Annotated Bibliography

BOOKS
Boda, Mark, Tremper Longman III, and Christian G. Rata, ed. *Words of the Wise Are like Goads: Engaging Qohelet in the 21st Century*. Winona Lake, IN: Eisenbrauns, 2013. Scholarly discussion of interpretive and theological issues in Ecclesiastes.

COMMENTARIES
Fredericks, Daniel C., and Daniel J. Estes. *Ecclesiastes and the Song of Songs*. Apollos Old Testament Commentary. Downers Grove, IL: InterVarsity Press, 2010. Scholarly commentary from an evangelical perspective.

JOURNAL ARTICLES
Seufert, Matthew. "The Presence of Genesis in Ecclesiastes." *Westminster Theological Journal* 78 (2016): 75–92. Recent discussion of the intertextual connections between Ecclesiastes and Genesis.

---

[19] Craig G. Bartholomew, "The Theology of Ecclesiastes," in *Words of the Wise Are like Goads: Engaging Qohelet in the 21st Century*, ed. M. Boda et al. (Winona Lake, IN: Eisenbrauns, 2013), 371.
[20] Bartholomew, "The Theology of Ecclesiastes," 372.
[21] See the studies cited by Michael Rhodes and Robby Holt, *Practicing the King's Economy: Honoring Jesus in How We Work, Earn, Spend, Save, and Give* (Grand Rapids: Baker, 2018), 40nn9–11.

WEBSITES

Walton, John H. "Who Wrote Ecclesiastes and What Does It Mean?" *Zondervan Academic* (blog). October 21, 2017. https://zondervanacademic.com/blog/who-wrote-ecclesiastes-and-what-does-it-mean/. Prominent Old Testament scholar provides helpful overview of background and message of Ecclesiastes.

___

CHAPTER 30

The Song of Songs Is a Biblical Model
for Dating and Marriage
Song of Songs 3:6–5:1

The Legendary Teaching on Song of Songs
as a Story of Courtship and Marriage

The Song of Songs is the story of a specific couple covering their relationship from the time they met to their courtship, wedding, and marriage. This love story reflects the desire and passion shared by the couple. The Song tells of how the couple resolves conflicts and how their love deepens and matures over the course of their marriage. Because of the book's association with Solomon, some interpreters have read the book as an autobiographical account of a romantic relationship in Solomon's own life, perhaps even Solomon's true love among his many wives and concubines.

Countering the Legendary Teaching

Marital love and sexual intimacy are the focus of Song of Songs, and the marriage and wedding night of the "beloved" and his Shulammite bride portrayed in 3:6–5:1 stand at the center of the book. The book, however, is not the narrative of the romance and marriage of a specific couple (or of Solomon and one of his wives). The poetic nature and structure of the book suggest a celebration of love and marriage that is more in the form of love poetry than a chronological narrative or story. We also have to be careful not to impose on this book modern ideas of dating, courtship, and engagement.

Despite the popularity of allegorical approaches from ancient times that viewed the book to be about God's love for Israel or Christ's love for the church, the Song of Songs *really is* about marital love and sexuality. The strongest argument against the allegorical interpretation is the sexual language and imagery that appears throughout the book. It is difficult to imagine that passages such as 2:5–6; 4:1–7; 5:1; or 7:7–8 describe the love of God for his people, and such imagery is not used elsewhere when comparing divine-human relations to a marriage.[1] This focus on marriage appears elsewhere in the biblical Wisdom Literature (see Prov 2:16; 5:15–20; 6:26, 32; 7:5; 30:18–19).[2] A wise person is one who is skillful in personal relationships, and marriage is the most intimate of human relationships. Wisdom Literature deals with God's creative order, and it was established from the very beginning that it was "not good" for the man to be alone (Gen 2:18–25).

A Wedding and a Love Song

In the arrangement of the Song of Songs, it appears that the wedding scene in 3:6–11 followed by the consummation of the marriage in 4:1–5:1 has a place of central importance. The bride is perfumed and then carried in procession to the wedding in an exquisitely crafted carriage. The king awaits the bride wearing a crown or garland placed on his head by his mother. In the depiction of the wedding night, the man praises the beauty of the woman and refers to her as his "bride" as he lovingly expresses his desire for her (4:8–12). The word *bride* appears only in this section of the book. The sexual union between the lovers is depicted as the man coming to a garden and enjoying its fruit. With the consummation of the relationship, the man enters the garden to gather the myrrh and spices and to consume its honey, milk, and wine until he has his fill of love.

This wedding scene is a focal point of the book, and the exclusivity of the lovers' relationship within the context of marriage is part of the wisdom perspective of the book. Variations of the statement "My love is mine and I am his" are found throughout the book (2:16; 6:3; 7:10). Such statements reflect the covenantal nature of the marriage relationship. Despite the importance

---

[1]   Duane A. Garrett, *Ecclesiastes, Song of Songs*, New American Commentary (Nashville: Broadman & Holman, 1993), 355 (see chap. 27, n. 3). One can recognize this point while still allowing for typological readings of the book in light of the larger canon. For such an approach, see Daniel L. Akin, *Exalting Jesus in Song of Songs*, Christ-Centered Exposition Commentary (Nashville: Broadman & Holman, 2015).
[2]   Miles Van Pelt, "Song of Songs," in *A Biblical-Theological Introduction to the Old Testament: The Gospel Promised*, ed. M. V. Van Pelt (Wheaton, IL: Crossway, 2016), 419.

of the events surrounding the wedding scene in 3:6–5:1, the book does not appear to have a chronological arrangement. The description of the bride as a "locked garden" in 4:12 suggests that the woman was a virgin at the time of the marriage, but several passages appearing to describe sexual intimacy between the couple appear in the first two chapters of the book.[3] Not all of the material in the first part of the book relates to their courtship prior to marriage unless these passages are recounting dreams or anticipating the wedding night and consummation of the relationship. In 1:13–14, the woman speaks of the man spending the night "between my breasts" and employs the same vineyard imagery employed in chapters 4–5 for the wedding night. She also compares her lover to an apricot tree and of him sustaining her with raisins and apricots while he embraces her in his arms (2:3–7). In 3:1–4, the woman searches for her lover until she finds him and brings him to her mother's house where they lie together in the inner chamber. Similarly, subsequent to the wedding at the end of the book, the poetry returns to when the couple met and how their love for each other grew during that time (8:1–2, 8–12).[4] Along with these non-chronological elements in the Song, Longman also calls attention to the lack of narrative voice and stage directions that would help the reader to see a storyline in a book that largely consists of dialogue.[5]

Rather than a narrative or chronological story of the couple's relationship, Song of Songs is more love poetry celebrating the couple's marriage and the intimacy of marital love. Duane Garrett states, "The best interpretation of Song of Songs is that it is what it appears to be: a love song."[6] The book conveys the emotion and passion of the marriage relationship in an impressionistic manner but does not "fill in the details" of how this couple courted, married, and grew old together "as a true narrative would."[7] If the book is more a love song (or collection of love songs) than a story, the primary focus of interpretation and teaching of the book is explaining the imagery of the book and attempting "to bring out the emotional texture of the poems."[8] The use of the cyclical pattern of desire and fulfillment and of refrains (see 2:6; 6:3; 7:11), as well as proposed

3   Gordon H. Johnston, "14 Reasons Why Song of Solomon Probably Doesn't Tell a Single Love Story," *DTS Magazine*, February 14, 2015, https://voice.dts.edu/article/song-of-solomon-love-story-or-love-stories-gordon-h-johnston/. The passages reflecting this sexual intimacy in the early sections of the book are listed in the Johnston article.
4   Johnston, "14 Reasons."
5   Tremper Longman III, *Song of Songs*, New International Commentary on the Old Testament (Grand Rapids: Eerdmans, 2001), 42.
6   Garrett, *Ecclesiastes, Song of Songs*, 365.
7   Fredericks and Estes, *Ecclesiastes and the Song of Songs*, 291 (see chap. 29, n. 3).
8   Longman, *Song of Songs*, 44.

chiastic structures for the book, reflect the kinds of nonlinear arrangement of material more characteristic of poetry than narrative.[9]

The Love of Solomon's Life?

The issue of whether the Song of Songs describes the actual relationship that the historical Solomon enjoyed with a specific woman is complicated by the issues surrounding the authorship of the book. The superscription (1:1) that attributes the book to Solomon (preposition *le* + Solomon) can be translated in several ways ("by, concerning, for, dedicated to, in honor of"), but authorship is most likely what is indicated. Nevertheless, even if Solomon is the author of the book, it is unlikely that the book conveys the story of a particular romantic relationship in the life of Solomon or that the king who had 700 wives and 300 concubines is telling his readers about the one woman he really loved. Solomon's life experiences make him a poor example of marital commitment for us to follow. Even with its focus on the two lovers, Song of Songs also contains a reference to Solomon's harem (6:8).

Attempts at reconstructing a specific relationship in Solomon's life are also highly speculative and not particularly helpful in developing the message of the book.[10] The fact that the name Solomon appears seven times in the book (1:1, 5; 3:7, 9, 11; 8:11–12) certainly reflects how this figure stands over the book, but it is an idealized Solomon rather than the historical figure that is celebrated. Both the names Solomon and the female Shulammite (6:13) come from the verbal root *sh-l-m*, which means "wholeness" or "perfection," further suggesting that the book is to be read as an extended portrayal "of ideal intimacy instead of as the historical record of the relationship between two specific individuals."[11] The book describes the kind of love relationship that Solomon could have enjoyed if he had followed God's plan and design rather than practicing love and marriage on his own terms. Solomon was the powerful ruler, glamorous

---

[9]   Johnston, "14 Reasons." Of the many proposed chiastic structures, David Dorsey has proposed one of the most clearly recognized arrangements of the book. On each side of the wedding day and night in 3:6–5:1, Dorsey has noted three matching elements—words of mutual love and desire (1:2–2:7//8:5–14); invitations from the man and woman to each other (2:8–17//7:12–8:4); and the woman's search for her lover at night (3:1–5//5:2–7:11). See David Dorsey, *The Literary Structure of the Old Testament* (Grand Rapids: Baker, 1999), 200.

[10]   Walter Kaiser makes the intriguing suggestion that the Song describes the relationship between Solomon and Abishag the Shulammite (see 1 Kgs 1:3, 15). See Walter Kaiser, "True Marital Love in Proverbs 5:15–23 and the Interpretation of Song of Songs," in *The Way of Wisdom*, ed. J. I. Packer and Sven K. Soderlund (Grand Rapids: Zondervan, 2000), 106–16.

[11]   Fredricks and Estes, *Ecclesiastes and the Song of Songs*, 274–75.

playboy, and quintessential lover, but those who enjoy the intimacy and passion of committed love are like kings and queens in their own right.[12]

Application

A chronological or narrative reading of Song of Songs is unnecessary for recognition that the book focuses on a couple enjoying a deep and abiding intimacy. The words of the woman to her husband in 8:6–10 contain some of the most powerful sentiments about marital love ever written. Love within the marriage covenant entails both "unbridled desire" and "exclusive commitment."[13] This kind of devotion enables the husband and wife to endure hardship (8:7a) and to resist temptation (8:7b) and brings wholeness to all who experience it (8:10).[14] The enduring love and intimacy of marriage is a source of great joy and deep delight for all who experience it. The frequent use of garden and vineyard imagery in Song of Songs reminds us that the enjoyment of true marital intimacy is like returning to Eden even while we live in a fallen world.

Annotated Bibliography

BOOKS
Nelson, Tommy. *The Book of Romance: What Solomon Says about Love, Sex, and Intimacy.* Nashville: Thomas Nelson, 1998. Reads the Song as a narrative or story of the couple's relationship. Though this chapter argues against this approach, the book provides great pastoral insight into dating and marriage.

COMMENTARIES
Garrett, Duane A. *Ecclesiastes, Song of Songs.* New American Commentary. Nashville: Broadman & Holman, 1993. Scholarly evangelical commentary with helpful explanation of background issues and explanation of Song of Songs as a love song and celebration of marriage.

WEBSITES
Johnston, Gordon H. "14 Reasons Why the Song of Songs Probably Doesn't Tell a Single Love Story," *DTS Magazine*, February 14, 2015. https://voice.dts.edu/article/song-of-solomon-love-story-or-love-stories-gordon-h-johnston. Excellent discussion of arguments against reading Song of Songs as a narrative/love story.

---

[12] Another story approach to the Song of Songs reads the book as a three-person drama involving a love triangle, including Solomon, a young woman in the king's harem, and her shepherd lover. Solomon pursues the young woman to marry her, but she rebuffs the king's advances and remains faithful to her one true love. This view also reads many of these details into the text. This reading also turns Solomon, the famous figure that this book is associated with, into the villain and turns much of the love poetry in the book into Solomon's attempt to seduce the young woman. For a detailed critique, see Fredericks and Estes, *Ecclesiastes and the Song of Songs*, 281–82.

[13] Hess, *Old Testament*, 510 (see chap. 29, n. 2).

[14] Van Pelt, "Song of Songs," 431.

CHAPTER 31

Isaiah 9 Contains a Prophecy against Post-9/11 America

Isaiah 9:10–11

The Legend: Isaiah 9:10–11 as a Prophecy of Judgment against America

The Old Testament prophetic books contain direct prophecies about the future of the United States. A best-selling Christian book titled *The Harbinger* by Jonathan Cahn argued that Isa 9:10–11 contains "an ancient mystery that holds the secret of America's future."[1] While the prophecy originally related to ancient Israel and the Assyrian crisis in Isaiah's day, a new message concerning the judgment of America has emerged from this text in the aftermath of the tragic events of September 11, 2001. Several American politicians, in misquoting Isa 9:10 as an expression of American confidence in rebuilding what was destroyed on 9/11, have brought a curse on the United States because of their defiant attitude toward God. The "cut stones" and "cedars" mentioned in Isa 9:10 cryptically refer to the memorials placed at the site of the fallen Twin Towers as further expression of American defiance toward God. Isaiah 9:11 speaks of God bringing judgment and military defeat on the United States for its prideful persistence in its sinful ways.[2]

---

[1] Jonathan Cahn, *The Harbinger: The Ancient Mystery That Holds the Secret of America's Future* (Lake Mary, FL: Frontline Publishers, 2011).

[2] Although Cahn presented *The Harbinger* as a work of fiction, he has subsequently been consistent in presenting the details of Isa 9:10–11 as actual prophetic signs for America, and his approach is treated and critiqued accordingly.

Countering the Legendary Teaching

The Old Testament prophets reveal no specific details about the future of the United States of America, and oracles about historical events that have occurred in the past do not contain cryptic messages about contemporary events.[3] A quick perusal of the internet reveals that one of the common errors in popular treatments of Old Testament prophecies is the attempt to see prophecies about contemporary events in prophecies that were historically fulfilled long ago. In 2013, *TIME* magazine reported that Christian interpreters viewed the current Syrian crisis as a fulfillment of Isa 17:1–3.[4] Isaiah's prophecy, however, was against the Syria of its own day because of the alliance between Syria and Israel that was formed in response to the Assyrian threat. When interpreters ignore the historical context of biblical prophecies, they can then read into those texts whatever meanings or connections to current events they desire.

The Historical Context and Message of Isaiah 9:8–21

Interpreters who find direct predictions about the United States (or other contemporary nations) in the Old Testament either ignore the historical context of the original prophecy or (as in the case of *The Harbinger*) search for hidden meanings that extend the actual historical message of the prophet. The historical context of the book of Isaiah demonstrates that 9:10–11 has nothing to do with the United States. Isaiah prophesied in the eighth century BC when Assyria posed a major threat to both Israel and Judah. The northern kingdom of Israel would fall to Assyria in 722 BC, and the Assyrian capture of more than forty cities in Judah would cause Jerusalem to be left alone "like a shelter in a vineyard" (Isa 1:8). Isaiah 7–8 records messages and events from the time of the Syro-Ephraimite War in 734–32 BC. Rather than turning to

---

[3]   The purpose of this chapter is not to provide a detailed critique of *The Harbinger*, but rather to interact with this particular work as an example of an approach that views the Old Testament prophets as prophesying about the United States and/or making specific references to contemporary events. For a more detailed critique of this work, see David James, *The Harbinger: Fact or Fiction?* (Bend, OR: The Berean Call, 2012).

[4]   See Elizabeth Dias, "Some Evangelicals See Biblical Prophecy in Syrian Crises," *TIME,* August 29, 2013, http://swampland.time.com/2013/08/29/some-evangelicals-see-biblical-prophecy-in-syrian-crises/. For an example of a Christian writer connecting current events in Egypt to the prophecies of Isaiah 19, see Bill Salus, "Is Isaiah 19 Finding Fulfillment amidst Egypt's Chaos?" Prophecy Depot Ministries, August 15, 2013, http://www.prophecydepotministries.net/2013/is-isaiah-19-finding-fulfillment-amidst-egypts-chaos/.

God, Israel had formed an alliance with its old enemy Syria in an attempt to halt the Assyrian military advance. War ensued when Judah refused to join the coalition, and Israel and Syria invaded Judah in an attempt to remove King Ahaz and replace him with a ruler supportive of their coalition. Isaiah had encouraged Ahaz to trust in the Lord, but Ahaz had instead turned to Assyria for assistance. The Syro-Ephraimite War brought heavy losses to both Israel and Judah, but neither nation had turned to God in repentance during the crisis.

Isaiah 9:8–21 is a judgment speech against the northern kingdom of Israel related to this specific historical context. Like many other predictions in the prophetic books, this prophecy relates to events that were about to transpire in the near future. The adversaries of Rezin (Assyria) would fight against Israel, Syria would turn against Israel, and the Philistines would join in on the attacks of Israel as well (vv. 11–12). The Lord would destroy Israel because the people did not turn to the Lord in their time of crisis (v. 13). This prophecy was historically fulfilled when Israel fell to the Assyrians in 722 BC.

The "cut stones" and "cedars" in Isa 9:10 have nothing to do with the building of memorials and monuments. Rather than humbling themselves before the Lord in light of the terrible disasters he had inflicted upon them, the people boasted that they would come back stronger than ever and their buildings and fortifications would be even better than before. As Brevard Childs explains, the people were defiantly announcing, "The destroyed buildings will be replaced by even more costly substitutes: dressed stones for bricks, cedars for common sycamore wood."[5]

Historical prophecies in the canon of Scripture continue to speak as the eternal word of God but not in the manner suggested by *The Harbinger* and similar approaches to biblical prophecy. The message of Isa 9:8–21 is a powerful reminder of the dangers of pride that lead to self-sufficiency and disregard for God. In developing the contemporary application of this oracle, John Oswalt focuses on the issues of pride, adulation of human leaders, and self-interest.[6] In the book of Isaiah, pride is a major reason for God's judgment of Israel, Judah, and the surrounding nations. Isaiah even prophesied that the final day of the Lord would bring an end to all human pride so that the Lord alone would be exalted at that time (2:12–22). Cahn has correctly

---

5   Brevard S. Childs, *Isaiah: A Commentary*, Old Testament Library (Louisville, KY: Westminster John Knox, 2001), 85.

6   John N. Oswalt, *Isaiah,* New International Version Application Commentary (Grand Rapids: Zondervan, 2003), 167–70.

articulated that Isa 9:10 is a warning that God judges human pride, but he has ignored the historical context of the prophecy and misapplied the details of this text in arguing that the passage offers coded "harbingers" of the coming judgment on the United States.

9/11 and Other Calamities—a Judgment on America?

Many pastors, evangelists, or theologians speak of acts of human evil, such as 9/11, or natural disasters, such as Hurricane Katrina or the Indian Ocean tsunami, as acts of divine judgment. What could be more "prophetic" than announcing that these horrible events are judgments from God? After all, Isaiah and Jeremiah warned that the Assyrian and Babylonian invasions were God's judgment against Israel and Judah. Nahum prophesied that God would destroy the city of Nineveh for its violence and bloodshed. Joel warned that the locust invasion that had destroyed Judah's crops was a "day of the LORD" catastrophe. The problem with pastors and theologians making similar statements today is that God has not specifically revealed his purpose and plans to them in the way that he did to the Old Testament prophets. The Old Testament prophets stood in the Lord's "council" as he revealed his future plans and intentions (Jer 23:22). Our pastors or the best-selling author of the latest book on biblical prophecy do not have the same privileged insight into God's future plans. It is presumptuous and dangerous for any person to speak concerning God's ways and purposes in specific events unless God has provided that kind of direct revelation.

As a model for Christians today, Jesus himself refused to speak of God's intentions in the aftermath of two newsworthy tragedies—a tower that collapsed killing eighteen people and Pilate's brutal killing of a group of Galilean worshippers (Luke 13:1–9). Jesus did not attempt to explain why God had allowed these tragedies to happen and did not view the victims of these tragedies as specific targets of divine judgment. He warned his hearers instead that these tragedies were a reminder that all of us need to be sure we are right with God and prepared for eternity when we die. When Christians make unsubstantiated claims that certain events are divine judgment, they miss the opportunity genuinely to call people to repentance and faith, often at times when they are deeply aware of their need for God. Christians have a prophetic voice when they warn of the reality of divine judgment, but that message loses much of its credibility when we substitute fanciful speculation on current events for faithful proclamation of the message of Scripture.

America as the Covenant People of God

A second problem with interpreting the prophets as speaking directly to the United States (or any other nation) is that such approaches ignore the distinctiveness of God's special covenant relationship with the people of Israel. The Lord chose Abraham to be his instrument of blessing to the whole world (Gen 12:3), and he chose the people of Israel as his "kingdom of priests" and "holy nation" that would mediate God's blessing to the other peoples of the earth (Exod 19:5–6). The Lord adopted the Davidic kings as his "sons" so that they would serve as his vice-regents and earthly representatives (2 Sam 7:13–14; Ps 2:6–7), and the Lord had often fought alongside and for Israel's armies when he sent them into battle. The Lord has no such covenantal relationship with America or any other nation today, and the people of God today is not a national or political entity.

The Lord revealed the law to Moses and had made a covenant with Israel at Sinai to bless or curse Israel based on its obedience or disobedience to those commands. These blessings and curses are elaborated in Leviticus 26 and Deuteronomy 28. A popular Christian writer and speaker from several years ago warned on the basis of Deuteronomy 28 that floods in Missouri and droughts in Texas and California were signs of God's judgment on America. These types of calamities could certainly indicate God's disfavor with any people, but we should be careful in equating how God blessed and punished Israel with his treatment of other peoples and nations. Whatever Christian influence might or might not have influenced the founding of America, the United States does not have a special covenant relationship with God and has not replaced Israel as God's chosen nation.

Application

The Old Testament prophets offer a solemn warning that the judgments of the past point to a future judgment for all peoples and nations, but the seriousness of that message is undermined when attached to sensationalized readings of biblical prophecy that ignore historical context or that impose the interpreter's subjective readings onto the text. Since the prophets prophesied about Israel and Judah as God's covenant people, the primary application of their oracles is not to individual nations but rather to the church as the people of God. The message of the prophets serve as a warning to the church that divine judgment begins with God's own people (1 Pet 4:17) and that covenantal blessings carry with them the covenantal obligations of faithfulness and obedience to God. When looking for prophetic oracles that more directly apply to nations such as the United States, we should turn to the prophets' messages against the foreign nations surrounding Israel. The Lord judges nations today for the same reasons that he judged these nations in the past—pride, idolatry, injustice, violence, and military atrocities. Like nations today, these nations were not part of God's special covenant with Israel but were held to the standards of the Noahic covenant that God established with all humanity as a means of restraining violence and bloodshed (compare Gen 9:1–11; Isa 24:1–5).[7]

Annotated Bibliography

BOOKS

James, David. *The Harbinger: Fact or Fiction?* Bend, OR: The Berean Call, 2012. Provides an extended critique of *The Harbinger* and the historical, hermeneutical, and theological problems with the book's application of the message of Isaiah.

COMMENTARIES

Oswalt, John N. *Isaiah.* New International Version Application Commentary. Grand Rapids: Zondervan, 2003. Evangelical commentary with exposition of the text and a reflection on how to properly make contemporary application of prophetic texts.

WEBSITES

Eckman, Jim. "The Harbinger: Right Message, Harmful Exegesis." *Issues in Perspective.* February 23, 2013. https://graceuniversity.edu/iip/2013/02/13-02-23-1/. Critique of *The Harbinger* and the faulty hermeneutics underlying this book.

---

[7] For helpful discussion of the Noahic covenant and its theological implications, see Jeffrey J. Niehaus, *Biblical Theology,* Vol. 1, *The Common Grace Covenants* (Wooster, OH: Weaver Books, 2014), 185–221.

CHAPTER 32

Isaiah 14 Portrays the Fall of Satan
Isaiah 14:12–15

The Legendary Teaching on Isaiah 14:12–15 and the Fall of Satan

Isaiah 14:12–15 describes the fall of Satan and the entrance of sin and evil into God's creation. Satan, who is introduced by his name "Lucifer" ("Shining One"), was one of God's most exalted angels until he led a rebellion against God and was thrown out of heaven. Lucifer was motivated by his excessive pride and desire to be "like the Most High," attempting even to place his throne beside God's. This rebellion occurred prior to the fall of Adam and Eve in Genesis 3, and this passage explains the origin of the Serpent, that is, Satan, in the garden of Eden.[1]

Introduction and Countering the Legend

For many English Bible readers, the name Lucifer in the KJV in Isa 14:12 settles the issue as to whether the fall of Satan is in view in this text. The name Lucifer, however, is not present in the original Hebrew text and entered into the translation of the KJV through the influence of the Latin Vulgate (and the Greek Septuagint less directly).[2] The Hebrew text here reads *halel ben shahar* ("morning star, son of the dawn"). The Vulgate translated the word *halel* ("morning star" or "shining one") with the Latin, *lucifer*, which means "light

---

[1] For a brief history of this interpretation, dating back to the second century AD, see Ronald Youngblood, "The Fall of Lucifer (in More Ways than One)," in *The Way of Wisdom: Essays in Honor of Bruce K. Waltke*, ed. J. I. Packer and Sven K. Soderlund (Grand Rapids: Zondervan, 2000), 169–71.
[2] Youngblood, "The Fall of Lucifer," 173.

bearer." In the place of "Lucifer, son of the morning" found in the KJV and NKJV, other English translations read "shining morning star" (CSB), "Day Star, son of Dawn" (ESV), "star of the morning, son of the dawn" (NASB), and "morning star, son of the dawn" (NIV). Some of the translations read this title as a proper name; others do not. The name "Lucifer" also does not appear elsewhere in the Bible as a name for Satan.[3] Rather than the fall of Satan, Isa 14:12–15 prophesies the downfall and death of the king of Babylon.

The Context of Isaiah 13–14

The context of Isaiah 13–14 focuses on the fall of Babylon and the death of the king of Babylon. Isaiah prophesied that Judah would later be taken into captivity in Babylon (39:6–7), and this prophecy likely focuses on the fall of the Neo-Babylonian Empire in 538 BC that would allow the Jews to return to their homeland (14:1–3). Isaiah anticipates a future "day of the Lord," when Yahweh would judge all the nations of the earth (13:6–11) and Israel would once again become a great nation (14:2). A taunt against the Babylonian king extends from verses 4 to 14. The exact identity of the ruler (Nebuchadnezzar or perhaps a composite of all the Neo-Babylonian kings) is not as important as is the fact that a human king is clearly the object of this taunt song. This song mocks the Babylonian king as he goes down to Sheol, and the deceased kings of the earth are amazed that this powerful ruler has joined their ranks. The king takes his place in Sheol where maggots and worms will eat his decaying corpse (14:11), and his body will be disposed of without proper burial (14:18–20). The descent into Sheol in this passage involves the death of a human being, not the banishment of Satan. A reference to Satan as the power behind the king's throne in 14:12–15 is a possibility, but such a reference would certainly interrupt the flow of thought present in chapters 13–14.

Lucifer or Morning Star?

If a human king is in view, what is the significance of this reference to the shining morning star in 14:12? It appears that Isaiah is comparing the king of Babylon to the morning star, Venus. As the morning star, Venus appears brightly in the sky before dawn but is eclipsed by the glory of the sun when it fully appears in the light of the morning. In the same way, the king of Babylon

---

3   Youngblood, "The Fall of Lucifer," 170–71.

arrogantly viewed himself as being equal with God, but his godlike greatness would be exposed as a fraud when he was brought down to the grave. He would fall as quickly from his height of power as the morning star disappears from the sky at the appearance of the light of dawn.

The Lofty Language in Isaiah 14:12–15

The arrogance and pretentious pride of this figure referred to as "morning star, son of the dawn" is evidenced in his five "I will" statements:

"I will ascend to the heavens" (v. 13)

"I will set up my throne above the stars of God" (v. 13)

"I will sit on the mount of the gods' assembly" (v. 13)

"I will ascend above the highest clouds" (v. 14)

"I will make myself like the Most High" (v. 14)

It might be argued that it is impossible for a human ruler to make such boasts and that the lofty language points more to a supernatural being like Satan. It appears, however, that Isaiah has purposely used this hyperbolic language to portray the excessive nature of the king's pride. This king proposes to take his place among the angels of heaven and to make himself an equal with God. The reality behind this figurative language is that the kings of Babylon and Assyria often viewed themselves as godlike in power and authority.

The exalted language in Isa 14:12–15 may contain mythological allusions used for literary effect, and the terminology that the prophet employs specifically suggests a Canaanite background.[4] The figures "Dawn" and "Dusk" were astral deities in Canaanite mythology, and verse 13 makes reference to the "stars of El (God)." El was the high god in the Canaanite pantheon. The place where the gods assemble in verse 13 is located "in the remotest parts of the North (*zaphon*)," and Zaphon or Mount Casius is identified as the meeting place of

---

[4]   Gary V. Smith, *Isaiah 1–39*, New American Commentary (Nashville: Broadman & Holman, 2007), 315, compares the biblical writer's use of mythological imagery to someone using a fictional story or movie "to illustrate a point by making analogical remarks without quoting from it directly or committing themselves to the truthfulness of the story."

the Canaanite gods in Ugaritic literature. The title "Most High" (Elyon) is also an epithet for Baal in the Canaanite texts. The exact mythological story that inspires Isaiah's imagery here is not certain, but, in one story from Canaanite religion, a minor god named Athtar ascends the throne of Baal after Baal has been put to death in his conflict with Mot.[5] When Athtar ascends the throne, his feet do not reach the footstool of the throne, and Athtar realizes that he is inadequate to take Baal's place.[6] Isaiah 14:12–15 shares with several mythological stories a common motif of doom coming to a usurper who attempts to go beyond his proper place.

These mythological stories that were disseminated widely in Isaiah's day were the more likely source for the imagery in 14:12–15 rather than the fall of Satan, which is not specifically recounted anywhere else in the Old Testament. It would have been especially appropriate for the prophet Isaiah to use one of these pagan myths to condemn the excessive arrogance of a pagan king.

The Devil and the Details

It is unlikely that Isa 14:12–15 is describing the fall of Satan from heaven. The same can be said for Ezek 28:11–19, another passage traditionally viewed as portraying Satan's rebellion against God. Ezekiel 28 also anticipates the fall and death of a human ruler—the king of Tyre. We again encounter exalted language in these verses that appears to portray a figure who is more than human, but the opening call for a "lament for the king of Tyre" indicates the focus here is on a human ruler. In verse 2, the king of Tyre boasts, "I am a god; I sit in the seat of gods in the heart of the sea," but the prophet warns that this king would die a violent death (vv. 8–10).[7]

The Old Testament does not explain Satan's origins or provide an account of his fall from heaven. The serpent appears in Genesis 3 without any details of where he came from or even a precise identification of who or what this figure represents. The serpent may have been a member of the animal kingdom

---

5   For further discussion of the possible mythological background of this imagery, see Youngblood, "The Fall of Lucifer," 173–74; Smith, *Isaiah 1–39*, 314–16; David W. Baker, "Isaiah," in *Zondervan Illustrated Bible Background Commentary*, ed. John H. Walton (Grand Rapids: Zondervan, 2009), 4:72–73; and John N. Oswalt, *The Book of Isaiah Chapters 1–39*, New International Commentary on the Old Testament (Grand Rapids: Eerdmans, 1986), 320–22.

6   James B. Pritchard, ed., *Ancient Near Eastern Texts Relating to the Old Testament with Supplement*, *Princeton Studies on the Near East*, 3rd ed. (Princeton, NJ: Princeton University, 1969), 129–42.

7   For further discussion of the interpretive issues surrounding this passage, see Daniel I. Block, *The Book of Ezekiel, Chapters 25–48*, New International Commentary on the Old Testament (Grand Rapids: Eerdmans, 1998), 99–123. Block makes a convincing argument for the idea that the king of Tyre is compared to Adam in the garden of Eden rather than to Satan.

or, more likely, a spiritual being of some sort, but we know of the explicit connection of the serpent and Satan only from later New Testament revelation (see Rev 12:9). The fall of Satan was likely not in the minds of the prophets in Isaiah 14 and Ezekiel 28. In fact, the Old Testament, while aware of a heavenly rebellion against God and of evil spiritual beings, offers no revelation on Satan as the singular head of the heavenly beings in rebellion against God. The limited uses of the term *Satan* with reference to a heavenly being in the Old Testament employ the term as a title rather than a proper name for the prince of demons.[8]

We have two specific references to the fall of Satan in the New Testament. In Luke 10:17–19, Jesus pictures Satan falling from heaven "like lightning." This text, however, is referring to an event that occurs in connection with Jesus sending out his apostles and not to Satan's original fall from heaven. Revelation 12:1–6 portrays the dragon sweeping away a third of the stars of the sky, suggesting a heavenly rebellion but not specifying when this revolt took place. This "dragon" is equated with "the ancient serpent" from Genesis 3 and Satan in Rev 12:9.

While it seems unlikely that Isaiah explicitly referenced the fall of Satan in chapter 14, it does appear that one can see a connection between the proud king of Babylon and Satan as the power behind the throne when this passage is read in light of the larger canon of Scripture. The king's sin of pride is also the sin that caused the condemnation of the Devil (1 Tim 3:6). Throughout Scripture, Babylon also represents the domain of evil and opposition to God (see Genesis 11; Revelation 18). The prophesied downfall of the king of Babylon in Isaiah 14 points to the ultimate defeat of all the forces of evil who oppose God and his people. This king's descent into Sheol foreshadows the ultimate casting of Satan, the beast, and his false prophet into hell at the end of God's final conflict with the forces of evil in the last days (Revelation 17–20).

---

[8] The term *Satan* in Job 1–2 and Zechariah 3 has the definite article (*hassatan*) and means "the adversary." In Job 1–2, "the Satan" appears among the "sons of God" to raise questions concerning Job's piety and the motivation behind his devotion to God. In Zechariah 3, "the Satan" questions Zechariah's fitness to serve as high priest. Old Testament scholars debate as to whether this figure may have had a legitimate role as God's prosecuting attorney on the divine council, but his hostility toward God and his people in both Job 1–2 and Zechariah 3 suggests that he no longer exercises this role in a manner that serves the Lord's purposes. Regardless, we again see a clear connection to Satan as "the accuser of the brethren" only from later revelation in Rev 12:9. We read in 1 Chronicles 21 that "Satan" incited David to number the troops of Israel, but the term *satan* in the OT refers primarily to human adversaries and is likely the meaning here as well. The story of Balaam even contains a reference to the angel of the Lord as Balaam's *satan* ("adversary") (Num 22:22).

Application

The desire to be "like God" is the source of all sin (Gen 3:5), and this desire for equality with God causes us to live independently of God's commands in his Word or to believe that we know better than God how to direct the course of our lives. Having the desire for godlike status poisons our relationships and causes us to impose our will and expectations on friends, family, and even other members of the body of Christ. The ultimate source of this toxic pride is none other than Satan himself, and we are never more like the Devil and less like Jesus than when we are driven by pride and selfish ambition. Those who have a right view of themselves in relationship to God will also have the right view of themselves in relationship to others. True humility leads to submission to God and service for others.

Annotated Bibliography

COMMENTARIES
Smith, Gary V. *Isaiah 1–39*. New American Commentary. Nashville: Broadman & Holman, 2007. Scholarly evangelical commentary that provides careful and detailed explanation of Isa 14:12–15.

ARTICLES
Youngblood, Ronald F. "Fallen Star: The Evolution of Lucifer." *Bible Review* (December 1998), 22–31, 47. Accessible explanation of issues and the contextual focus on the king of Babylon in Isaiah 14 (see the footnotes for a more detailed essay by the same author).

WEBSITES
Laney, J. Carl. "Does Isaiah 14 Reveal Anything about Satan's Fall?" *Transformed*. November 17, 2014. https://www.westernseminary.edu/transformedblog/2014/11/17/does-isaiah-14-reveal-anything-about-satans-fall/. Concise argument of why Isaiah 14 refers to the fall of the king of Babylon rather than Satan.

CHAPTER 33

God Created Evil

Isaiah 45:7

The Legendary Teaching on Isaiah 45:7

Isaiah 45:7 teaches that God is the cause of moral evil in our world. The KJV of Isa 45:7 reads: "I form the light and create darkness: I make peace, and create evil, I the LORD do all these things." On his blog "Daylight Atheism," Adam Lee refers to Isa 45:7 as one of "the most shocking" passages in the Bible, because it reminds us that "evil exists because God created it."[1] Theologians attempting to resolve the dilemma of how and why evil exists in a world under the control of an all-loving, omnipotent, and omniscient deity "can pack it in and go home now," because this text (and others like it) inform us that evil comes directly from God.[2] Christians mistakenly believe that God is pure and holy when their own Scriptures teach the opposite.

Countering the Legendary Teaching

A rather simple matter of translation corrects the mistaken idea that Isa 45:7 views God as the source and creator of evil in the world. The majority of modern translations do not follow the KJV in translating the Hebrew word *ra'ah* in verse 7 as "evil" but instead offer the translation as "calamity" (ESV, NASB, NET, NKJV) or "disaster" (CSB, NIV). The point of the passage then

---

[1]   Adam Lee, "Little-Known Bible Verses V: God Creates Evil," *Patheos, Daylight Atheism* (blog), January 21, 2007, http://www.patheos.com/blogs/daylightatheism/2007/01/little-known-bible-verses-v-god-creates-evil/.

[2]   Lee, "Little-Known Bible Verses V."

is that God brings or causes "disaster" when he acts in judgment. The blog mentioned above accuses the modern translations of attempting to soften the actual teaching of Isa 45:7, but the fact that the Hebrew word *ra'ah* can refer both to moral "evil" and "disaster/calamity" is recognized in all Hebrew lexicons and easily demonstrated from the biblical text.[3] John Oswalt notes that the range of meaning for the Hebrew word *ra'ah* is similar to that of the English word "bad" in that it can refer to moral evil, misfortune, or that which does not conform to a real or imagined standard.[4]

The Old Testament prophets often made word plays based on the semantic range of *ra'ah*. On more than one occasion, the Lord commands the people through the prophet Jeremiah to turn from their "evil" (*ra'ah*) way so that he might relent from bringing upon them the "disaster" (*ra'ah*) he had planned for them (e.g., Jer 26:3; 36:3, 7). The word play effectively communicated how the Lord's punishments would fit their crimes and justly correspond to the people's actions. The same idea is found in Jonah 3:10, which states that when God saw that the Ninevites had turned from their "evil" (*ra'ah*) ways, he did not bring upon them the "disaster" (*ra'ah*) he had threatened to bring against their city.

The translation of *ra'ah* as "calamity" or "disaster" in Isa 45:7 also makes sense in light of the message of the entire oracle found in 45:1–7. In verses 1–4, the Lord promises to raise up the pagan ruler Cyrus, the future king of Persia, and enable him to subdue nations as a means of gaining Israel's release from exile in Babylon. The Lord would remove every obstacle that stood in the way of Cyrus and would give to him the treasures of the peoples he conquered. Cyrus conquered Babylon in 539 BC and issued a decree allowing the Jews to return to their homeland in 538 BC. The Lord would accomplish his purposes through Cyrus because God is the one true God over all of history (v. 5). Yahweh's ability to announce his plans in advance and then to carry them out would demonstrate his sovereignty and incomparability to all peoples (vv. 6–7). Verse 7 concludes the oracle with a powerful assertion of the Lord's control over both nature and history. He is the One who created the light and darkness, and, as the creator, he is also the One who uses both "success" (*shalom*) and "disaster" (*ra'ah*) in the working out of his plans within history.

The fact that *ra'ah* carries the meaning of "disaster" or "calamity" is further

---

[3]   See the entries on *ra'ah* in Brown and Driver, *Brown-Driver-Briggs Hebrew and English Lexicon*, 949 (categories 2 and 3) (see chap. 26, n. 2); and Koehler and Baumgartner, *Hebrew and Aramaic Lexicon*, 2:1262–64 (categories 4 and 5) (see chap. 1, n. 3).

[4]   John Oswalt, *The Book of Isaiah, Chapters 40–66*, New International Commentary on the Old Testament (Grand Rapids: Eerdmans, 1998), 204–5.

reflected by how it is contrasted here to *shalom*, which means "peace, health, or well-being." As Ben Witherington explains, the text is not saying that God created good and evil, but rather that "he brings both blessing and curse, even on his own people."[5] The Lord had brought "disaster" on his people in the judgment of exile, but he would also bring the *shalom* of restoration and return. Israel's *shalom* would also mean "disaster" for Babylon. This understanding of Isa 45:7 also accords with the clear teaching of James 1:13–17 that God is not the author of evil.

Rather than attributing the origin of moral evil to God, Isa 45:7 offers a strong affirmation of God's sovereignty. Gary Smith comments, "Everything that happens in the world is connected to God's activity, whether it appears to be good or bad. It all works together to fulfill God's purposes, even if people do not understand or accept these things as the work of God."[6] God is sovereign over all things but not in a mechanistic way that removes human ethical choices and responsibility. Even when the Lord "raises" or "stirs up" kings and armies to carry out his divine judgments (see Isa 9:11; Jer 51:1), these entities act because of their own evil desires rather than divine compulsion and are fully culpable for their crimes (see Isa 10:5–14; Jer 50:29; 51:7, 33–39). In Zech 1:15, the Lord states that he is "fiercely angry" at the nations that had gone too far in executing punishment on his own people with whom he was only "a little angry." The fact that God holds these nations responsible for their actions reflects that they acted on their own accord and that they exceeded God's intentions. Terence Fretheim comments, "The exercise of divine wrath against their excessiveness shows that the nations were not puppets in the hand of God. They retained their power to make decisions and execute policies that flew in the face of the will of God."[7]

Proverbs 16:4: Has God Created Wicked People to Destroy Them?

The fact that the Hebrew word *ra'ah* can be translated both as "evil" and "disaster" is not only the key to a proper understanding of Isa 45:7, but also

---

5   Ben Witherington, "Mistranslated and Misquoted Verses—Isaiah 45:7," *Patheos, The Bible and Culture* (blog), February 20, 2016, http://www.patheos.com/blogs/bibleandculture/2016/02/20/mistranslated-and-misquoted-verses-isaiah-45-7/.

6   Gary V. Smith, *Isaiah 40–66*, New American Commentary (Nashville: Broadman & Holman, 2009), 258.

7   Terence E. Fretheim, "'I Was Only a Little Angry': Divine Violence in the Prophets," in *What Kind of God? Collected Essays of Terence E. Fretheim*, Siphrut 14, ed. M. J. Chan and B. A. Strawn (Winona Lake, IN: Eisenbrauns, 2015), 173–74.

helps to clarify the meaning of Prov 16:4, another passage dealing with God's sovereignty over humans and the world he has created. The verse reads, "The Lord has prepared everything for his purpose—even the wicked for the day of disaster (*ra'ah*)." The verse does not mean that God causes wicked people to do evil things, and it is not teaching that God creates the wicked to accomplish his purposes or that he predestines them to do evil so that he might glorify himself by their destruction, as some have claimed.[8] The verse does not explain why God creates wicked people but rather states that God governs his world by making sure that deeds and consequences correspond.[9] The verb *to do* (*pa'al*) means "to work out, bring about, accomplish," and most English translations reflect the idea of God working out everything "for its purpose" or "for his purpose." The word *purpose* (*ma'aneh*) actually means "answer" (compare "answer [*ma'aneh*] of the tongue" in v. 1). Thus the phrase "for its answer" refers to how God causes consequences to correspond to actions as their appropriate "answer" or counterpart. In the execution of divine justice, the punishment fits the crime. God operates his world so that the wicked will ultimately experience their "day of disaster" as punishment for their deeds.[10] Even when judgment is delayed, this ultimate time or reckoning is inevitable and unavoidable. No one is exempt from judgment or accountability to God.

This interpretation of Prov 16:4 fits with the larger message of Proverbs, that the path of wisdom and righteousness leads to life and blessing, while the path of folly and wickedness leads to cursing and death. This understanding also fits with the contextual focus in Prov 16:1–7 on how God administers justice to the righteous and the wicked. The Lord "weighs motives" to determine a person's true nature (v. 2). He will not allow the arrogant to go unpunished (v. 5), and he causes others to be at peace with a righteous man (v. 7).

Application

God's people can trust that even when evil appears to be winning the day, the Lord remains in control and directs the course of history. If God used the Assyrians, Babylonians, and Persians to accomplish his purposes in the ancient world, we can rest assured that God remains sovereign over the cha-

---

8   John Calvin writes on this verse: "Solomon also teaches us that not only was the destruction of the ungodly foreknown, but the ungodly themselves have been created for the specific purpose of perishing." *Calvin's New Testament Commentaries: The Epistles of Paul the Apostle to the Romans and the Thessalonians*, trans. Ross Mackenzie (Grand Rapids: Eerdmans, 1960, 1995), 207–8.

9   Ross, "Proverbs," in *Expositor's Bible Commentary*, 6:144 (see chap. 26, n. 1).

10   Ross, "Proverbs," 6:144.

otic world that we live in today. Injustice, violence, terrorism, and even the threat of nuclear war will not prevent God from bringing history to its desired end when he rules over all in the new heavens and new earth. God's sovereignty is such that he uses even the evil plans and actions of sinful humans to accomplish his purposes without in any way being the cause or source of that evil. God is not only all powerful; he is also perfectly good and holy with no taint of evil in his character. Believers can trust that the One in charge of human history is "too pure" to even look at evil (Hab 1:13).

Annotated Bibliography

COMMENTARIES

Oswalt, John N. *The Book of Isaiah, Chapters 40–66.* New International Commentary on the Old Testament. Grand Rapids: Eerdmans, 1998. Scholarly evangelical commentary with clear explanation of meaning of Isa 45:7 and why this verse does not teach that God is the creator of moral evil.

WEBSITES

Witherington, Ben. "Mistranslated and Misquoted Verses—Isaiah 45:7." *Patheos, The Bible and Culture* (blog). February 20, 2016. http://www.patheos.com/blogs/bibleandculture/2016/02/20/mistranslated-and-misquoted-verses-isaiah-45-7/. Evangelical New Testament scholar provides brief explanation refuting idea that Isa 45:7 presents God as the creator of evil.

CHAPTER 34

―――

God's Word Will Never Return Void
When We Preach and Evangelize

Isaiah 55:11

The Legendary Teaching on Isaiah 55:11

Isaiah 55:11 promises that faithfully teaching and sharing God's Word with others will always produce fruit in people's lives, even if we do not see immediate results. If our sermon did not seem to connect with the audience or be particularly effective, God's Word still "will not return empty." When our evangelistic efforts seem to produce no converts, we can trust that God's Word is inwardly working in people's lives and will ultimately bring someone to Christ. If we are faithful in sharing God's Word, God will always use it in some way to change the people who have heard our message. Isaiah 55:11 also assures that whatever we desire will come to pass if we claim the promise that God's Word will not return void.

Correcting the Legendary Teaching

The focus in Isa 55:11 is not on how God's Word works in people's lives or how God fulfills our desires, but instead offers a powerful affirmation of the certainty of the specific promises of God's Word. God always accomplishes what he has promised to do. The reliability of God's Word is why our message has power when we share it or proclaim it to others. This interpretation of Isa 55:11 best fits with the overall appeal of the prophet's call for faith and repentance in 55:1–13 and helps provide a fitting conclusion to the larger message of Isaiah 40–55, focusing on Israel's return and restoration from exile.

There are, however, many other passages that speak of how God's Word inwardly works in individuals, and we know that God's Word is powerful enough to overcome the inadequacies of the preacher or the teacher. Paul reminds us that God works through the "foolishness" of preaching (1 Cor 1:18–25). Hebrews 4:12 teaches us that God's Word is like a piercing sword that is able to penetrate deeply into people's hearts and minds. Paul reminds us that our task when proclaiming God's Word is often to plant or water seeds that will later bear fruit in people's lives (1 Cor 3:5–9). James 1:21 also states that the Word of God is the seed that produces faith leading to salvation.

Isaiah 55:1–13: A Call to Trust Based on the Certainty of God's Promises

The message in Isa 55:1–13 that concludes chapters 40–55 invites Israel to receive God's offer of forgiveness and salvation. The Lord would take the initiative to redeem his people from exile and give the Servant as the sacrifice for their sins, but the people would have to respond to what God was doing on their behalf. They might not fully understand how the Lord would bring about their restoration, but they could trust him to fulfill his promises. The banquet of blessings was prepared, but the people had to choose to come to the table and freely eat and drink of the blessings that the Lord would provide for them (vv. 1–5). They needed to seek the Lord and turn from their sinful ways to receive forgiveness of their sins, recognizing that their thoughts and ways were not the same as the Lord's (vv. 6–9). The promise concerning the reliability of God's word in verses 10–11 serves to motivate the people's response, because the word of God guaranteed that he would forgive their sins and bless them if they truly turned to him.[1] God's word is as effective in accomplishing what it has promised as the rain and snow in nourishing the earth so that it is able to produce seed and crops for food. Shalom M. Paul explains the imagery in this way: "The Lord's word is compared to precipitation, which soaks the earth and makes it bloom. Just as rain and snow do not return to the sky until they quench the earth's thirst . . . so too the Lord's promise to redeem Israel shall come to pass."[2] Those who responded in faith would know the "joy" and "peace" of the abundant blessings that God had in store for his people in the place of the sorrow and suffering of exile (vv. 12–13).

---

[1]   Oswalt, *Book of Isaiah, Chapters 40–66*, 445 (see chap. 33, n. 4).
[2]   Shalom M. Paul, *Isaiah 40–66: A Commentary*, Eerdmans Exegetical Commentary (Grand Rapids: Eerdmans, 2012), 442.

The expression "return empty" (*shub* + *reqam*) appears in another context that helps to illustrate its usage in Isa 55:11. In 2 Sam 1:22, David laments the death of Saul and recalls his valor as a warrior by stating that Saul's sword "did not return empty." In other words, Saul's sword was effective in battle and in accomplishing its purpose of defeating the enemy. God's promises concerning Israel's restoration and return from exile have the same efficacy, and they will not fail. A contrasting image is found in Jer 14:3, when the nobles of Judah send their servants out to find water in a time of drought, but these servants "return empty" (*shub reqam*).[3] The Lord's promises never fail in this manner.

Instead of the faith called for in Isa 55:1–13, Israel has responded to God's promises of restoration and salvation with doubt and uncertainty.[4] In light of the suffering that Israel endured in the exile and the enormity of the promises the Lord was making, such a response was understandable. In Isa 40:27, the people of Israel complain, "My way is hidden from the LORD, and my claim is ignored by my God." The people also lamented, "The LORD has abandoned me; the Lord has forgotten me" (49:14). When they would observe the Lord's Servant sent to save them, the people would question how the "arm of the LORD" could be revealed through such a fragile and despised figure (53:1). The prophet employed a number of strategies to overcome the people's unbelief and assure them that God would fulfill his promises. Isaiah reminded the people that the Lord was the Creator, who had brought the universe into existence like a master craftsman sitting at his workbench (40:12–14), and that the nations, including the powerful Babylonian Empire, were nothing more than "a drop in a bucket" to the Lord (40:15). The prophet continually highlights the Lord's work as creator throughout Isaiah 40–55 as a way of reminding Israel of the Lord's unlimited and incomparable power (40:26; 42:5; 45:12, 18; 51:13).

Isaiah assured the people that the Lord would save them because of his special relationship with Israel. The Lord would protect Israel like a shepherd watching over his flock and would even carry the weak among his people like lambs as he brought them home (40:11). The Lord had chosen Israel as his "servant" people and would hold them by the right hand and protect them from all danger (41:8–13; 43:1–2). The Lord was more mindful of Israel and compassionate to them than a nursing mother to her infant child. He could not forget his people because he had inscribed the name of Zion on his hands

---

3   Paul, *Isaiah 40–66*, 444.
4   For development of this theme in Isaiah 40–55, see Rikki E. Watts, "Consolation or Confrontation: Isaiah 40–55 and the Delay of the New Exodus," *Tyndale Bulletin* 41 (1990): 31–53.

as a constant reminder of them (49:16). The Lord had temporarily divorced Israel/Jerusalem as his wife, but he would remarry her with great joy and celebration, and the barren woman of Jerusalem would have more children than she could have ever imagined (54:1–8; compare 62:4–5). The exiles were wrong to think that the Lord had rejected his people.

The ultimate answer to Israel's unbelief was the certainty of the Lord's promises. Statements concerning the efficacy of God's Word in Isa 40:8 and 55:10–11 provide fitting book ends for this section of the book of Isaiah.[5] In Isa 40:8, the prophet reminds the people of the permanency of God's Word in contrast to humans, who are like the quickly fading grass and flower. David Baker explains, "Unlike fickle humans, it is important that words spoken by the divine are unchanging."[6] No human opposition would alter or overcome God's Word. The Neo-Babylonian Empire came to an end fewer than fifty years after its armies captured and destroyed Jerusalem. Even the most powerful humans come and go, but God's Word would "remain forever."

The Lord's Control of History and His Unchanging Purposes

Babylon's defeat of Judah would obviously lead many of the Jewish exiles to conclude that the Babylonian god Marduk was greater than Yahweh and that Marduk was directing the course of history. Isaiah's message offers a strong corrective to such thinking. Yahweh is the one true God, and the gods of the nations represented by their idols are nothing. Yahweh's ability to announce the future before it happens demonstrates his superiority to these false gods and also reflects his sovereign control over the events of history (Isa 40:21; 41:4, 21–29; 42:12–13; 44:24–28).

The book of Isaiah expresses certainty concerning the reliability of the Lord's promises because it views his sovereignty over history in a manner that goes far beyond what was envisioned by the Mesopotamians concerning their gods. Since Yahweh alone controls history, his purposes and plans cannot be thwarted. In Isa 46:10, the Lord asserts, "I declare the end from the beginning and from long ago what is not yet done, saying: my plan will take place, and I will do all my will." Isaiah presents the Lord as "the commander of destinies."[7] The Mesopotamian gods like Marduk did not have intrinsic

---

5   Childs, *Isaiah*, 437–38 (see chap. 31, n. 5).
6   Baker, "Isaiah," in *Zondervan Illustrated Bible Background Commentary*, 4:132 (see chap. 32, n. 5).
7   Andrew T. Abernethy, *The Book of Isaiah and God's Kingdom: A Thematic Approach*, New Studies in Biblical Theology (Downers Grove, IL: InterVarsity Press, 2016), 78–80.

knowledge of the future or the ability to control future events in the way that Yahweh did.[8] For these gods, this control came from the Tablets of Destiny, which established the rank and authority of the gods. These tablets often changed hands among the gods; according to the Babylonian myth *Enuma Elish*, Marduk had secured these tablets at the time of creation when he had defeated Tiamat and Kingu.[9] Isaiah overturns this theology by asserting that Yahweh's decrees and plans direct the course of history. As the exiles observed the events prophesied in Isaiah taking place, they would come to recognize that Yahweh had fulfilled his plans in the working out of history. When the people wondered if their desperate situation in exile would ever change, they were to trust in the certainty of God's promises as the answer to their doubts and fears. When tempted to think that Marduk or the gods of the nations controlled their destiny, they were to observe how the Lord was directing the course of history to fulfill his plans and purposes.

Application

Contrary to popular belief, Isa 55:11 is not promising the effectiveness of every sermon or evangelistic encounter, but the verse is reminding us of the power of God's Word to accomplish everything it has promised. This verse reminds us of the effectiveness of the prophetic word and the certainty of his promises. Our power in preaching, teaching, and evangelism comes from basing our message on the faithful and reliable Word of God. We can call others to faith and encourage our own trust in God with the reminder that every promise in God's Word is true and will come to pass because God possesses the wisdom and power to make his purposes stand for all time.

Annotated Bibliography

COMMENTARIES

Oswalt, John N. *The Book of Isaiah, Chapters 40–66*. New International Commentary on the Old Testament. Grand Rapids: Eerdmans, 1986. Standard evangelical exegetical commentary with a detailed discussion of the message of Isaiah 40–55.

Paul, Shalom. *Isaiah 40–66: A Commentary*. Eerdmans Exegetical Commentary. Grand Rapids: Eerdmans, 2012. Scholarly reference commentary with a helpful explanation of this text and the significance of the phrase *returning empty/void*.

---

[8]   Baker, "Isaiah," 157.

[9]   See Baker, "Isaiah," 157, and Abernethy, *Book of Isaiah*, 78–80, for the references from *Enuma Elish*. The Mesopotamian myth of Anzu also recounts the attempt of the lesser god Anzu to steal the Tablets of Destiny.

WEBSITES

Akers, Matt. "Some Misinterpretations of Isaiah 55:1." *Such a Time as This* (blog). February 15, 2011. http://mattakers.blogspot.com/2011/02/some-misinterpretations-of-isaiah-5511. html. A brief post providing examples of how Isa 55:11 has been misinterpreted.

McCormack, Jeff. "God's Word Shall Not Return Void . . .—Out of Context Scripture." *Exploring for Truth* (blog). March 19, 2009. http://exploringfortruth.blogspot. com/2009/03/gods-word-shall-not-return-void.html#.WbbvyLKGNdh. A helpful post placing this text in its context.

CHAPTER 35

God Has Promised You a Bright and Prosperous Future

Jeremiah 29:11

The Legendary Teaching on Jeremiah 29:11

The Lord's promise in Jer 29:11, "I know the plans I have for you . . . plans for your well-being, not for disaster, to give you a future and a hope," is for all believers. If you know the Lord and have enough faith, God will bless you and help you to be successful. If you are starting a new venture, whether it is getting married, going to college, kicking off a new career, or planting a church, God has plans to help you prosper. Jeremiah promises that the Lord wants to turn your negative circumstances into positive ones so that you can thrive and enjoy the life he has planned for you.

Countering the Legendary Teaching

Bible Gateway reported that between the years 2012 and 2015, Jer 29:11 was the second-most searched Bible verse on its site (behind only John 3:16).[1] Believe it or not, an obscure passage from the Old Testament prophets was more popular than even Phil 4:13, Rom 8:28, and Ps 23:4. Many Christians would identify this passage as their life verse. It is frequently inscribed on jewelry or shared on Facebook or Twitter, because, as Ben Irwin observes, it sounds very much like a Christian motivation poster: "Woke up on the wrong side

---

[1] For the 2015 report, see Andy Rau, "The Top Ten Bible Verses of 2015 and More: Bible Gateway's Year in Review Is Here," December 28, 2015, https://www.biblegateway.com/blog/2015/12/the-top-ten-bible-verses-of-2015-and-more-bible-gateways-year-in-review-is-here/.

of the bed? Don't worry. God has a plan for your day. Facing a rough patch at work? Take a breath. Your future is bright. Money's a bit tight? Relax. God's going to prosper you."[2] Before we retweet Jer 29:11 one more time or decide to get tattooed with this verse, however, we might want to take a closer look at what is easily one of the most misused passages in all of the Bible. The verse does not promise personal prosperity or guarantee that all the circumstances in your life will have a positive outcome, but, when we understand the real message of this text, it assures us of something even better.

Jeremiah 29:11 Is for a Specific Group of People

Reading individual verses in isolation from their larger context or taking promises meant for only a specific group of people and applying them to all believers in all ages frequently leads to misuse of the Bible. When Ray Lewis was celebrating the Super Bowl XLVII victory of his Baltimore Ravens, he jubilantly quoted Isa 54:17 in front of the television cameras in the winners' locker room: "No weapon formed against you shall prosper" (NKJV). Lewis claimed God had led his team to victory, but the problem is that Isaiah 54 was written for the Jewish exiles in Babylon, not the Baltimore Ravens. When we read the larger context of Jeremiah 29, we see that these exiles are the specific recipients of the promise of verse 11. Jeremiah 29:1–28 reports the contents of a letter that Jeremiah wrote to the Jewish exiles, who had been taken away as prisoners by the Babylonians, some of them in 605 BC and more of them in 597 BC. As with the New Testament Epistles, we are reading somebody else's mail. The exiles were now living hundreds of miles from their homeland in a pagan land with pagan gods and customs. They were no longer able to worship Yahweh, enjoy his presence, or offer sacrifices at the temple in Jerusalem. The Babylonian army was a powerful military machine that controlled the Middle East. From a purely human perspective, it seemed as if there was little or no hope for Israel's future.

The Lord's promise to fulfill his plans to prosper his people and give them a hope was not addressed to individuals, guaranteeing that he would accomplish his plan for their individual lives and help each of them to achieve their personal hopes and dreams. The second-person pronouns that appear in verse 11 are all plural rather than singular, so this verse offers a collective assurance to the exiles as a group that the Lord would fulfill his promise and

---

[2]   Ben Irwin, "Five Bible Verses You Need to Stop Misusing," April 3, 2014, https://www.thepoachedegg.net/2014/04/five-bible-verses-you-need-to-stop-misusing.html.

bring them back to their homeland when the time of the exile was over (v. 10). The Lord's plans included Israel's restoration as a people, and the most amazing thing of all was that his work of restoration and renewal for Israel would begin with the exiles in Babylon.

In Jeremiah 24, the prophet says that the people living in the land were the rotten figs that needed to be thrown away and that the exiles were the good figs that God would bless. They were not good figs because of their own righteousness and faithfulness to God; they were good figs because God promised to bless and restore them. The people living in the land were in for more war and more judgment. The Babylonian army was coming back; in 586 BC, they would destroy the city of Jerusalem and burn down the temple. Many of those people who thought they were favored by God would be killed in battle or taken away as exiles themselves.

Lamentations 2:8 reveals that the Lord had an entirely different "plan" for the people who remained in the land, as opposed to the positive "plans" he had for the exiles: "The LORD determined to destroy the wall of Daughter Zion. He stretched out a measuring line and did not restrain himself from destroying." The verb for "determined" is the same Hebrew root word (*hashab*) as the noun for "plans" in Jer 29:11: "I know the plans I have for you . . . plans for your well-being."[3] When another group of Jews fled to Egypt after the fall of Jerusalem in 586 BC, Yahweh announced that his plans for them were to destroy them and to leave few survivors among them because they refused to turn away from their worship of false gods (Jer 44:26–30). Yahweh's promise of blessing and a prosperous future was only for the exiles in Babylon.

Some Bad News Along with the Good

To get the full picture of Jer 29:11, we also need to see that the prophet was communicating some bad news to the exiles along with the hopeful promise for their future. In verse 10, we read that their time in Babylon was going to last for seventy long years. Jeremiah's message offered hope in a hopeless situation, but seventy years was still hard to hear. Seventy years represented a lifetime. Back in verses 4–7, the prophet instructed the exiles to build houses, plant crops, take wives, and raise families in Babylon, which indicated they were going to be there for a long time.

What the exiles had really wanted to hear is reflected in the promises of

---

[3]   J. Daniel Hays, *Jeremiah and Lamentations*, Teach the Text Commentary (Grand Rapids: Baker, 2016), 337.

false prophets like Hananiah—that the exile would last only for a short while (Jer 28:1–4). Jeremiah was going through the streets of Jerusalem wearing an animal yoke on his neck, symbolizing Judah's subjugation and bondage to Babylon. Hananiah confronted Jeremiah, smashed the wooden yoke he was wearing on the ground, and then promised that within two years Yahweh would bring home King Jehoiachin and all the other exiles taken to Babylon. The people obviously responded more favorably to this positive message, but the problem was that Hananiah's message was nothing more than a figment of his imagination (23:16–17). Hananiah was one of many prophets in Judah who opposed Jeremiah by promising "peace, peace, when there is no peace" (6:14; 8:11). Jeremiah's message that the exile would be long-lasting was the true word from Yahweh, and the first return of the exiles from Babylon would not occur until 538 BC.

When read in its context, Jer 29:11 is clearly not a promise of personal prosperity or an assurance that everyone who knows the Lord has the prospect of a bright and rosy future without difficulty or hardship in front of them. The people who were the recipients of the promise in 29:10–11 were already living under the harsh conditions of exile as a result of divine discipline for their sins, and most of them would remain in that situation for the rest of their lives. The words *well-being* (CSB), *welfare* (NASB, JPS), *to prosper you* (NIV, NET), and *peace* (KJV, NKJV) translate the Hebrew *shalom*, which refers to a wholeness and peace much broader than financial blessing or prosperity.

Application

Even if we are reading someone else's mail, Jeremiah 29 remains the word of God for us. Before we get to the promise of verse 11, the chapter as a whole is a solemn reminder that God takes sin and disobedience in the lives of his children very seriously. God disciplined Israel and Judah because they turned away from him and chased after false gods, and Heb 12:5–9 reminds us that God disciplines and corrects us as his children as well. God disciplines us because he loves us too much to allow us to chase after things that are going to harm us or keep us from the abundant life that we can have in Christ. God may bring painful consequences for the bad choices we make to turn us away from sin and back to him. Even in his discipline, God shows grace and compassion to his people. His work of restoration would begin with the exiles in Babylon—the very people he had sent out of the land as punishment for their sins. Psalm 30:5 reminds us that God's anger is but for a moment, but his favor lasts for a lifetime.

If we reduce Jer 29:11 to a proof-text for the health and wealth gospel, we cheapen its message. God's *shalom* is much more than financial wealth and even physical well-being. The Lord promised the people of Israel that he would bless them and prosper them with long life and good harvests in the Promised Land, but their real *shalom* came from their relationship with him. The real riches we have in Christ are spiritual blessings, not financial ones (Eph 1:3, 18; 3:16). For Christians today, Jer 29:11 teaches us the principle that God is able and faithful to fulfill his purposes and plans for his people. God's good purpose for the exiles was to restore them and bring them home, and he brought down the powerful Neo-Babylonian Empire to accomplish his plans for them. God does not promise to protect us from all harm and hardship, but he does promise to fulfill his good purpose for us as believers to conform us to the image of his Son Jesus (Rom 8:28–30). Just as with the exiles in Babylon, God uses even trials and hardships for our good and to accomplish his purpose and plans in our lives.

Annotated Bibliography

BOOKS
Schultz, Richard L. *Out of Context: How to Avoid Misinterpreting the Bible*. Grand Rapids: Baker, 2012. Schultz has a helpful discussion of Jer 29:11. See 81–83.

COMMENTARIES
Huey, F. B. *Jeremiah, Lamentations: An Exegetical and Theological Exposition of Holy Scripture*. New American Commentary. Nashville: Broadman & Holman, 1993. Scholarly evangelical commentary but accessible for the general reader.

WEBSITES
Lamb, David. "The Plans God Has for Me? (Jeremiah 29:11) (3 parts, blog). December 17 and 22, 2011, January 4, 2012. https://davidtlamb.com/2011/12/17/the-plans-god-has-for-me-jeremiah-29-part-1/. Helpful series of posts on the meaning, message, and application of Jer 29:11.
Yates, Gary. "How Should We Interpret 'I Give You a Hope and a Future' (Jeremiah 29:11)?" December 21, 2013. https://www.godtube.com/watch/?v=WW7GGWNX. Short video presentation on the context and meaning of this text.

CHAPTER 36

———

The City of Babylon Must Be
Rebuilt to Fulfill Prophecy

Jeremiah 50–51

The Legendary Teaching on the Rebuilding of Babylon
(Isaiah 13–14 and Jeremiah 50–51)

The prophecies of Isaiah and Jeremiah concerning the destruction of Babylon were never completely fulfilled and thus refer to a future judgment of this city. Therefore, for the prophecies to be fulfilled, Babylon must be rebuilt. The depiction of the fall of "Babylon the Great" in Revelation 17–18 also refers to the actual city of Babylon and attaches eschatological significance to the nation and people that occupy this particular geographical location. The political turmoil in Iraq (the country that occupies the same geographical area as ancient Babylon) over the past thirty years is perhaps prelude to the eschatological day of the Lord and the second coming of Christ.

Countering the Legendary Teaching

There is nothing in Scripture that demands or clearly predicts a role for the geographical location of ancient Babylon in end-times events. A proper understanding of prophetic language indicates that the prophecies of Isaiah and Jeremiah concerning Babylon were fulfilled in history. "Babylon the Great" in Revelation 17–18 does not refer to the specific city of Babylon or the geographical environs of ancient Babylon but rather to worldwide opposition to God and his people that is epitomized by Babylon in Scripture.

The Downfall of Babylon in Isaiah and Jeremiah

When speaking of the downfall of Babylon, the prophets Isaiah and Jeremiah referred to judgments that have already occurred in history. Both prophets portray the coming destruction of Babylon as thorough and complete. In Isaiah 13–14, Isaiah prophesies that Babylon would be overthrown like "Sodom and Gomorrah" (13:19) and would never again be inhabited (13:20–22). Babylon would become nothing more than desolate swampland as the result of God's judgment (14:21–23).

There are two possible historical contexts for the judgment against Babylon prophesied in Isaiah 13–14. The first option is that this prophecy refers to the destruction of Babylon by the Assyrian king Sennacherib in 689 BC after repeated attempts by the Babylonian king Merodach-baladan to throw off Assyrian rule. One could argue for this setting in light of the larger context of Isaiah 13–23, which consists of a series of oracles against foreign nations in the context of the Assyrian crisis facing Israel and Judah in the eighth/seventh-century BC.[1] One purpose of the oracles was to discourage Judah from entering into military alliances with these nations against Assyria.[2] Oracles against Babylon and Egypt (Isa 18:1–21:10) are prominent in this section of the book because they were the two nations that Judah was most likely to turn to for military assistance (see Isa 30:1–5; 31:1–3; 39:1–8). Isaiah 23:13 explicitly attributes the coming downfall of the Chaldeans to the Assyrians. Military alliances were not the answer because the nations conspiring against Assyria were doomed themselves.

Other evidence in Isaiah 13–14 suggests the greater likelihood of the second option that these prophecies refer to the fall of the Neo-Babylonian Empire to Cyrus and the Persians in 539 BC. First, Isaiah makes reference to the stirring up of the Medes (13:17), who were allies of Cyrus when he defeated the Babylonians. Second, the defeat of Babylon is connected to the restoration and return of Israel that would occur during the reign of Cyrus (14:1–2). Third, the description of the king of Babylon in Isaiah 14 as a powerful ruler who had conquered other nations fits better with the rulers of the Neo-Babylonian Empire than Merodach-baladan from Isaiah's day.[3] Even if Assyria's defeat of Babylon in 689 BC was the focus of this original prophecy in Isaiah 13–14, it appears that the prophecy was later reapplied to the more

---

[1]   Homer Heater Jr., "Do the Prophets Teach That Babylonia Will Be Rebuilt in the Eschaton?" *Journal of the Evangelical Theological Society* 41 (1998): 25–31.
[2]   Heater, "Do the Prophets Teach?," 27.
[3]   See Robert B. Chisholm Jr., *Handbook on the Prophets* (Grand Rapids: Baker, 2002), 49–53.

decisive defeat of Babylon in 539 BC. The Lord's promise to deliver Israel from Babylon is the major focus of Isaiah 40–55. The Lord would raise up Cyrus (Isa 44:28–45:1) to conquer Babylon so that his people could return from exile.

Jeremiah's prophecies against Babylon also focus on the judgment of the Neo-Babylonian Empire that would facilitate the return of the Jews from exile. The Lord had chosen Nebuchadnezzar as a "servant" (Jer 25:9; 27:6) and had granted him authority over the nations (Jer 27:5–8, 13) to execute God's judgment on the sinful nation of Judah. Babylon's dominion, however, was temporary, and Jeremiah announced that Babylon would drink the cup of God's wrath after causing Judah and the other nations to drink from it (Jer 25:1–13). As in Isaiah, the oracles announcing the downfall of Babylon in Jeremiah 50–51 prophesy of a complete and total destruction of the city. In its defeat, Babylon would become a desolate wasteland (50:3; 51:25–26, 42–43). The city would never again be inhabited (50:40) and would become an object of horror and derision (50:11–13; 51:41). The specific mention of the Medes (who were allies of the Persians) in 51:11, 28 connects this to the fall of the Neo-Babylonian Empire in 539 BC.[4] This prophesied destruction of Babylon would also enable the Jews to return to their homeland (see Jer 50:4–5, 28–29; 51:5–7, 49–52).

After Nebuchadnezzar, the Neo-Babylonian Empire went into sharp decline, and Cyrus's armies captured Babylon in October 539 BC. The Babylonians were twice unsuccessful in revolts against Persia in 522 and 482 BC. Alexander the Great conquered Babylon in 331 BC but was unable to carry through on plans for a reconstruction of the city. By the early second century AD, the city of Babylon was in ruins.[5] The ruins of Babylon are located in the suburbs of modern-day Baghdad. Babylon never returned to its former glory, and the prophecies of Isaiah and Jeremiah concerning the fall of Babylon were historically fulfilled.

Rebuilding of Babylon and Future Judgment?

Some interpreters persist in seeing a future aspect to the prophecies of Isaiah and Jeremiah for two primary reasons. First, Isaiah connects the fall of Babylon

---

4   C. Marvin Pate and J. Daniel Hays, *Iraq: Babylon of the End-Times?*, (Grand Rapids: Baker, 2003), 49–51.
5   William R. Osborne, "Babylon," in *The Lexham Bible Dictionary*, ed. J. D. Barry et al. (Bellingham, WA: Lexham Press, 2016).

to the coming "day of the LORD" (13:6, 9, 13). In the New Testament, the "day of the LORD" refers to the eschatological judgments surrounding the second coming of Christ. For the Old Testament prophets, however, the "day of the LORD" has a broader referent and speaks of judgments that occurred in history during the times of the prophets as well as the final judgment of the last days.[6] The judgment of Babylon when Cyrus conquered the city was one of those dramatic "days" of the Lord when God intervened to defeat a powerful enemy and to deliver his people. The use of the "day of the LORD" to describe the downfall of Babylon in Isaiah 13 does not necessitate viewing this event as eschatological.

Many see a future rebuilding and destruction of Babylon for a second reason. Cyrus's capture of the city does not seem to correspond to the prophecies of Isaiah and Jeremiah that the city would be completely destroyed and left without inhabitants, never to be rebuilt. Cyrus captured Babylon without a battle, and Babylon remained an active city for several centuries. These prophecies of total destruction, however, reflect stereotypical judgment language.[7] This judgment language resembles the curse imagery found in ancient Near Eastern treaties and covenants, which employ horrific images and threats to depict the fate of those guilty of breaking the terms of the treaties.[8] The Aramaic Sefire Treaty (from the eighth century BC) contains this threat against covenant violators: "Just as a calf is cut in two, may he be cut in two, and may his nobles be cut in two. Just as a harlot is stripped naked, may his wives be stripped naked, and the wives of his offspring, and the wives of his nobles."[9] The graphic language is for dramatic effect, but no one expected the judgment to occur in precisely the manner described.

These same kinds of curses underlie the Mosaic covenant, and Moses warns of the terrible curses that the Lord would bring against the people if they disobeyed his commandments (Lev 26:14–39; Deut 28:15–68). The prophets as messengers of the covenant warned the people that God was bringing these covenant curses upon them for their unfaithfulness. They also spoke of God's judgment in hyperbolic ways as a means of getting the people's attention and motivating them to repent. Brent Sandy explains that "no one knows in advance which of the specific kinds of judgment mentioned in the curses God will use, or whether he will use methods not even mentioned."[10]

---

[6] Pate and Hays, *Iraq: Babylon of the End-Times?* 51.
[7] Heater, "Do the Prophets Teach?" 32–36.
[8] D. Brent Sandy, *Plowshares and Pruning Hooks: Rethinking the Language of Biblical Prophecy and Apocalyptic* (Downers Grove, IL: InterVarsity Press, 2002), 83–90.
[9] Quoted in Sandy, *Plowshares and Pruning Hooks*, 83. Taken from Joseph A. Fitzmyer, *The Aramaic Inscriptions of Sefire*.
[10] Sandy, *Plowshares and Pruning Hooks*, 90.

Isaiah and Jeremiah employed stereotypical destruction language to pre-
dict the downfall of Babylon, and these prophecies did need not be fulfilled
in exact detail. The prophets in fact employed the same kind of destruction
language against Israel, Judah, and Jerusalem (see Jer 9:11; 36:29). To insist
on a literal fulfillment of the warning that Judah would become an everlasting
ruin (Jer 25:9) would preclude the possibility of the future restoration that
was central to the prophet's message (Jeremiah 30–33). The fall of the Neo-
Babylonian Empire in 539 BC fulfilled the prophecies of Isaiah and Jeremiah
concerning Babylon without need of a future rebuilding of the city.

The New Testament and the Fall of "Babylon the Great"

In the New Testament, Revelation 14–18 depicts the fall of "Babylon the
Great" prior to the second coming of Christ (14:8; 16:19; 17–18) and even
quotes from the prophecies of Isaiah and Jeremiah when referring to these
judgments (18:1–8; compare Isa 21:9; 47:7–8; Jer 51:13, 45). Even with a
futurist reading of Revelation 17–18, there are strong reasons for not taking
this verse to teach that the Antichrist will have his headquarters in downtown
Baghdad. In line with the apocalyptic nature of Revelation, Babylon likely
refers not to the literal city but serves as "the symbolic city of the world that
represents oppression, captivity, and exile."[11] Babylon is not so much a specific city but more a worldwide system of evil opposed to God and his people
(compare 14:8; 16:19). The Roman Empire was the particular embodiment
of Babylon in the historical context of Revelation.[12] The church lived under
the domination of the social, political, and religious structures of Rome in
the same way that Israel had lived out its captivity under Babylon.[13] Just
as Babylon had destroyed the first temple, Rome had destroyed the second
temple in AD 70.[14] Jewish sources often referred to Rome as "Babylon," and
Peter likely does the same in 1 Pet 5:13.[15] In this typology of evil, Babylon
prefigures Rome in the same way that Rome prefigures the worldwide power
that would oppose God prior to the second coming of Jesus. Babylon's opposition to the kingdom of God thus spans the whole of Scripture from Genesis

---

[11]　James L. Resseguie, *The Revelation of John: A Narrative Commentary* (Grand Rapids: Baker
Academic, 2009), 198.

[12]　For more on this connection, see Pate and Hays, *Iraq: Babylon of the End-Times?*, 95–112.

[13]　G. K. Beale, *The Book of Revelation*, New International Greek Testament Commentary (Grand
Rapids: Eerdmans, 1999), 755.

[14]　Beale, *The Book of Revelation*, 755.

[15]　Beale, *The Book of Revelation*, 755.

to Revelation, but Revelation assures that God's judgment and the second coming of Jesus would bring a decisive end to this opposition.

Application

The judgment of Babylon in Scripture offers both promise and warning. The promised destruction of Babylon offers hope for God's people of final deliverance from oppression and persecution. Believers can rejoice as they look forward to sharing in the ultimate triumph of God's kingdom. The downfall of ancient Babylon also serves as a warning that God continues to judge nations for their hubris, violence, and injustice. Humanity, with its kingdoms, armies, religious systems, and economic resources aligned against God, will not prevail, and all of us must assess if our hearts belong to God's kingdom or the kingdoms of this world. The fall of "Babylon the Great" reminds us to be careful of where we give our ultimate allegiances.

Annotated Bibliography

BOOKS
Pate, C. Marvin, and J. Daniel Hays. *Iraq: Babylon of the End-Times?* Grand Rapids: Baker, 2003. Chapter 4 of this work contains an excellent discussion concerning the future destruction of Babylon and the place of the nation of Iraq in biblical prophecy.
Sandy, D. Brent. *Plowshares and Pruning Hooks: Rethinking the Language of Biblical Prophecy and Apocalyptic.* Downers Grove, IL: IVP Academic, 2002. Helpful discussion of the genre of prophecy and its use of stereotypical judgment language.

COMMENTARIES
Beale, G. K. *The Book of Revelation.* New International Greek Testament Commentary. Grand Rapids: Eerdmans, 1999. Scholarly exegetical commentary provides an excellent explanation of the symbolic nature of the references to "Babylon the Great" in Revelation.

ARTICLES
Heater, Homer, Jr. "Do the Prophets Teach That Babylonia Will Be Rebuilt in the Eschaton?" *Journal of the Evangelical Theological Society* 41 (1998): 23–43. Argues against the necessity of a future rebuilding of Babylon in light of historical fulfillments and the prophets' use of stereotypical language.

———

CHAPTER 37

God Intended "Ezekiel Bread" to Be a Health Food

Ezekiel 4:9

The Legendary Understanding of "Ezekiel Bread" as a Health Food

An American food company has an entire line of Ezekiel 4:9 bread products. Their sprouted 100-percent whole grain bread products and cereals are based on the recipe God gave to Ezekiel as part of a series of prophetic sign acts and consists of four types of cereal grains (wheat, millet, barley, and fitches) and two types of legumes (soybeans and lentils). The company website states that these products "are crafted in the likeness of the Holy Scripture verse Ezekiel 4:9 to ensure unrivaled honest nutrition and pure, delicious flavors." [1] One nutritional website states that "Ezekiel bread is as healthy as bread gets" and that "it is much richer in healthy nutrients and fiber" than other breads. [2]

Countering the Legendary Teaching

The claims made above about grain combinations might very well be true. I am not an expert in nutrition. But in light of the circumstances surrounding the special bread that God commanded Ezekiel to prepare and eat, the prophet Ezekiel would no doubt be quite surprised to find customers today selecting "Ezekiel 4:9 bread" in a supermarket filled with other choices. Ezekiel was part of the Jewish deportation to Babylon in 597 BC, and the Lord called

---

[1]   "Ezekiel 4:9 Bread. And Better!" https://www.foodforlife.com/about_us/ezekiel-49. See also Lee Breslouer, "The Weird Story behind Ezekiel 4:9 and the Bread It Inspired," October 11, 2018. https://www.huffpost.com/entry/ezekiel-4-9-bread-name_n_5bb67559e4b01470d04fda8f

[2]   Kris Gunnars, "Why Ezekiel Bread is the Healthiest Bread You Can Eat," May 22, 2018. https://www.healthline.com/nutrition/ezekiel-bread.

Ezekiel to be a prophet to the exiles in Babylon in 593 BC. The first years of Ezekiel's ministry involved warning the exiles that more judgment was in store for Judah that would culminate in the destruction of Jerusalem. Ezekiel 4–5 describes an unusual series of four prophetic sign acts that Ezekiel would perform as a way of visually and dramatically communicating what lay in store for Jerusalem. An enemy army would besiege the city, and the residents of the city would experience famine, deportation, and death. For the Jews living in Babylon, the sign acts conveyed that their exile would not end anytime soon. The making and eating of "Ezekiel bread," including the repulsive manner in which it was baked, was to dramatize the conditions of famine and impurity that the people of Jerusalem would endure as a result of siege and exile.

The Nature and Purpose of Prophetic Sign Acts

Sign acts, which involved a prophet dramatically acting out his message, are found in various prophetic books. Isaiah preached naked and barefoot for three years to dramatize the coming fall of Cush and Egypt (Isa 20:1–3). Jeremiah compared the spiritual condition of the people to his buried underwear, which he dug up as a visual aid (Jer 13:1–11), and he smashed a clay jar in front of the leaders of Judah as a warning of impending judgment (19:1–14). Sign acts made the prophet's message more memorable than words alone and often created curiosity concerning what the prophet had to say. The prophet acting out his message also impressed upon his audience the seriousness of his message. Jeremiah and Ezekiel frequently employed sign acts because of the hostility to their message of judgment and exile. The Lord had warned Ezekiel that he would preach to "a rebellious house" (Ezek 2:5) and to a people who were "hardheaded and hardhearted" (3:7). The people treated Ezekiel's message as a form of entertainment (33:30–33), but his sign acts were much more than theatrics. They were urgent warnings of judgment.

Unforgettable Warnings of Judgment

In depicting the coming judgment, Ezekiel was first to draw a sketch of Jerusalem on a clay brick and then to act out the siege of the city (Ezek 4:1–3). The prophet was even to construct models of towers, siege ramps, and troops as part of this elaborate depiction of the assault on Jerusalem. Ezekiel was further to represent the Lord in this sign act by placing an iron griddle between himself and the model of the city to represent how the Lord had separated himself from the people because of their sinfulness.

Ezekiel's second sign act was to lay on his left side facing the siege model for 390 days and to lay upon himself the sins of Israel (4:4–6). The siege would occur because of Israel's persistent sin, and the number 390 roughly corresponds to the time from the building of Solomon's temple to the fall of Jerusalem (970–586 BC, 384 years).[3] By lying on his side, Ezekiel was "bearing the iniquity" of the people. "Bearing iniquity" (*nasa'* + *'avon*) was the expression of the priestly role of offering sacrifices and making atonement for the sins of the people (Exod 28:43: Lev 10:17; 16:22; Num 18:1, 23), but now this expression reflected that Ezekiel would share in the people's suffering. Ezekiel performs his priestly duty in bearing the people's sin, but the guilt of their sin now demands the punishment of exile rather than the offering of a sacrifice.[4]

After lying on his left side for more than a year, Ezekiel was to lie on his right side for forty days, representing the forty years the people of Judah would spend in exile as punishment for their sins. Jeremiah warned that the Babylonian exile would last for seventy years (Jer 25:11–12; 29:10), and the numbers "40" and "70" are both round figures for a generation or a lifetime (compare Num 14:33–35).[5]

The third sign act involved the bread that Ezekiel was to eat while lying on his side for the duration of the first and second sign acts. The bread, which he was to eat at a set time each day, portrayed the diet of the residents of Jerusalem while the city was under siege and also conveyed the uncleanness under which the exiles would live in a foreign land (4:9–17). Ezekiel's bread consisted of a strange concoction of ingredients—wheat, barley, beans, lentils, millet, and spelt. Bread was normally made from either barley or wheat. Beans and lentils were not normally mixed with grains, and this mixture resulted in a coarse and inferior grade of flour. This recipe for the bread was not a health food to assure that he got his daily allotment of fiber, but rather reflected the subsistent conditions that the people of Jerusalem would experience when the city was under siege. Daniel Block explains that

---

[3]   The term "house of Israel" in 4:4 refers to the whole people of Israel and not just to the northern kingdom of Israel. The same expression is used for the exiles or the survivors of the impending fall of Jerusalem in 4:3, 13 and 5:4. See Daniel I. Block, *The Book of Ezekiel Chapters 1–24*, New International Commentary on the Old Testament (Grand Rapids: Zondervan, 1997), 176.

[4]   Kelvin G. Friebel, *Jeremiah's and Ezekiel's Sign Acts: Their Meaning and Function as Nonverbal Rhetorical Communication*, Journal for the Study of the Old Testament Supplement 283 (Sheffield, UK: Sheffield Academic Press, 1999), 220–21.

[5]   Block, *Ezekiel Chapters 1–24*, 179–80.

the ingredients reflected that the people would be "scraping the bottom of the barrel" to get enough flour and vegetable meal to make even a single loaf of bread.[6] This bread was not something that the prophet would find tasty. The Talmud (B. 'Erub. 81a) recounts an experiment in the third century AD when these ingredients were combined to make a bread so disgusting that not even a dog would eat it.[7]

The amount of this bread Ezekiel was to consume on a daily basis also reflected the realities of famine and starvation that the people of Jerusalem would experience under siege. Ezekiel was to measure out enough of his crude flour so that he had eight ounces of bread each day (4:10). Along with this meager amount of food, the prophet was allowed to drink a sixth of a gallon (lit. "*hin*") of water (two-thirds of a quart) each day. Food and water were scarce in times of siege. During the siege of Samaria narrated in 2 Kings 6, food was in such short supply that a donkey's head was selling for thirty-four ounces of silver and a cup of dove dung for two ounces (2 Kgs 6:25). Water supplies were meager during times of siege, because the water sources were normally located outside of the city walls. Food shortages would eventually reduce the inhabitants of Jerusalem to cannibalizing their own children (Ezek 5:10), in fulfillment of the covenant curses that Moses had threatened against the people before they entered the land (Lev 26:29).

The part of the sign act directing how Ezekiel was to bake the bread (4:12–15) carried a warning of the defilement that would accompany Judah's exile. The Lord instructed Ezekiel to bake his bread over human excrement, which would render the food unclean (compare Deut 23:12–14). When Ezekiel, as a priest, is unwilling to defile himself in this way, God allows him to bake the bread using animal dung instead. Animal dung was a common fuel, but the preposition for baking "on" (*be*) the dung instead of "over" (*'al*) it perhaps suggests that the dough was placed directly in the embers of the dung as it baked.[8] The cooking conditions suggested the continual uncleanness of those who would live in foreign exile, and the repulsive stench of the burning dung would have made this point even more vividly to Ezekiel's audience. Friebel explains, "Since any land except that of Israel was considered unclean, any food grown and eaten in a foreign country was *ipso facto* unclean, rendering the eaters ceremonially unclean."[9]

---

6   Block, *Ezekiel Chapters 1–24*, 184.
7   Block, *Ezekiel Chapters 1–24*, 184n109.
8   Friebel, *Jeremiah's and Ezekiel's Sign Acts*, 248.
9   Friebel, *Jeremiah's and Ezekiel's Sign Acts*, 248.

Ezekiel's final sign act in the series (5:1–4) was perhaps the most bizarre. Ezekiel shaved his head and beard and then measured out the hair on a scale. Shaving of the head was often a sign of humiliation for defeated and exiled peoples (2 Sam 10:4; Isa 7:20; Jer 2:16). To depict the varying fates of the residents of Jerusalem who would experience the impending siege, he burned a third of the hair, cut up another third of the hair with a sword, and then scattered a third of the hair into the wind. Those who did not die at the hands of the enemy army would be scattered into exile. Ezekiel folded a tiny portion of his hair into the folds of his robe to represent the small minority of the people that the Lord would protect and deliver as a preserved remnant, and even a portion of that hair was also thrown into the fire.[10]

Application

The instructions, commands, and principles of the Bible are what we need for life and godliness as followers of Jesus. The incidental details about various kinds of food often have significance in particular passages but are not provided for our nutritional and dietary benefit, whether it is Ezekiel bread (and how it was baked), Daniel's vegetarianism, or even John's "tasty" diet of locusts and honey. Following Jesus does not entail eating the same first-century AD Mediterranean diet that he ate while living here on earth.

Ezekiel bread is an obscure detail from the Old Testament, but it serves as a reminder of the seriousness of the warnings of divine judgment found in the Bible. Sin ultimately leads to death, and those who refuse to repent of their sin and believe the gospel face eternal judgment and separation from God. Even as God's people, we have to guard against the casual and calloused attitude toward divine discipline that characterized Ezekiel's hearers. Hebrews 12:6 reminds us, "The Lord disciplines the one he loves and punishes every son he receives." That discipline becomes increasingly severe when we ignore God's correction and refuse to address our attitudes and actions that need to change.

---

[10]   Ezekiel also dramatically acts out the coming exile in 12:1–20 by putting together a small pack of belongings, digging a hole in the wall of his house, and taking the bags out into the night, with his face covered in shame and grief. The prophet also trembled as he ate the provisions he took with him to depict the fear and anxiety of the exiles.

Annotated Bibliography

BOOKS

Friebel, Kelvin G. *Jeremiah's and Ezekiel's Sign Acts: Their Meaning and Function as Nonverbal Rhetorical Communication*. Journal for the Study of the Old Testament Supplement 283. Sheffield, UK: Sheffield Academic Press, 1999. Detailed discussion of prophetic sign acts, with special attention to the literary and rhetorical features of these passages.

COMMENTARIES

Block, Daniel I. *The Book of Ezekiel Chapters 1–24*. New International Commentary on the Old Testament. Grand Rapids: Zondervan, 1997. This two-volume commentary is the most thorough evangelical commentary on Ezekiel.

Duguid, Iain M. *Ezekiel*. New International Version Application Commentary. Grand Rapids: Zondervan, 1999. Evangelical commentary focuses on both an exposition of the text and ways to apply it to contemporary audiences.

CHAPTER 38

———

Gog of Magog Refers to the Leader of Russia
Ezekiel 38–39

The Legendary Teaching on Gog of Magog in Ezekiel 38–39

The ruler Gog, of Magog, who will spearhead the coalition of seven nations in the end-times assault on the land of Israel portrayed in Ezekiel 38–39, is the leader of Russia. This ruler is described in Ezek 38:3 as the "prince of Rosh, Meshech, and Tubal" (NASB) (or Russia, Moscow, and Tubolsk). Despite the massive strength of this coalition, God will intervene with an earthquake and a storm to deliver Israel and to destroy the invading armies.

Countering the Legendary Teaching

In 1999, I (Gary) had the opportunity to travel to Moscow and teach a course on the Old Testament prophets at a Bible school. You can probably guess the first question asked when we got to Ezekiel 38. "Why do American preachers and evangelists always tell us that Gog of Magog is the ruler of Russia?" Despite the popularity of this view, there is no substantive textual evidence for linking Russia with the events in Ezekiel 38–39, and this approach reflects misguided speculation on how biblical prophecy relates to contemporary events.

The identification of Gog of Magog with the ruler of Russia originated in the nineteenth century in connection with the Crimean War and was popularized in the twentieth century in the *Scofield Reference Bible* and other popular sources (e.g., Hal Lindsey's *The Late Great Planet Earth*) dealing with biblical prophecy in the context of the Cold War. A more recent take is that Russia's allies in the final assault on Israel will be a confederation of Islamic nations united in their hatred of Israel. Vladimir Putin's saber-rattling leadership and attempts to restore Russia as a military and nuclear power have led to renewed anticipation that the events portrayed in Ezekiel 38–39 are imminent. In a blog post from 2016, Lindsey offers this quotation from a representative with the National Institute for Public Policy as a warning of the return of the Cold War: "Russia is getting ready for a big war which they assume will go nuclear, with them launching the first attacks." The representative further suggests that the Syrian civil war would provide the impetus for the Russian assault on Israel.[1]

Iain Duguid has documented how Christians through the centuries have attempted to identify Gog of Magog and his armies with specific nations or figures.[2] Gog of Magog has been identified with the Goths (fourth century), Arabs invading the Holy Land (seventh century), and the Mongol hordes (thirteenth century). In the seventeenth century, Gog was identified with the Turks, the Roman emperor, and even the pope. The purpose of the vision in Ezekiel 38, however, is not to satisfy our curiosity in identifying the major players in the events depicted. Ezekiel prophesied during the time of the Babylonian exile when an invading army had devastated the land of Judah; the vision of Gog of Magog promises a future reversal of the terrible defeat of the present, a time when God would swiftly destroy the nations that invaded the land of his people.

A Connection between Gog and Russia?

The identity of Gog of Magog is unclear, but the name Gog is most commonly associated with the seventh-century BC king of Lydia named Gyges in Asia Minor (modern Turkey). This king is mentioned in the inscriptions of Ashurbanipal (668–631 BC) of Assyria and also by the Greek historian Herodotus.[3] The name Magog is often read as a contraction of the Akkadian *mat Gugi* ("land of Gog") that is also associated with Lydia.[4] Precisely how this ancient ruler might relate to Ezekiel's vision is unclear. Gyges never presented a threat to Judah, and the seventh-century dates for his reign indicate that he was no longer alive when Ezekiel received this vision (unless Gog was

---

[1]   Hal Lindsey, "Return of the Cold War," *Hal Lindsey Report*, August 17, 2016, https://www.hallindsey.com/ww-8-17-2016/.

[2]   Iain M. Duguid, *Ezekiel*, New International Version Application Commentary (Grand Rapids: Zondervan, 1999), 456.

[3]   Daniel Bodi, "Ezekiel," in *Zondervan Illustrated Bible Background Commentary*, ed. J. H. Walton (Grand Rapids: Zondervan, 2009), 4:484.

[4]   Bodi, "Ezekiel," 4:484.

a dynastic name).[5] Most likely, Gog/Gyges represents a powerful and myste-rious king from a distant land who prefigures the future military commander who would lead an assault on Israel.[6] Ezekiel's vision in its ancient context was the equivalent of someone claiming today that a Napoleon or Hitler-like figure would attack Israel.[7] The name provides no help in identifying this figure with a contemporary nation or people.

The name Gog may also suggest something supernatural or demonic about the northern horde that would invade Israel. Michael Heiser explains, "Gog would have been perceived as either a figure empowered by supernatu-ral evil or an evil quasi-divine figure from the supernatural world bent on the destruction of God's people."[8] The use of "Gog and Magog" to identify the nations that lead the final revolt against God in Rev 20:7–10 lends credibility to this view.[9] The apocalyptic and supernatural aspects attached to the name Gog is further reason for not attempting to associate this ruler with a specific contemporary nation.

Gog is described as the "chief prince of Meshech and Tubal" (Ezek 38:2–3). The title *chief prince* in Hebrew consists of two nouns—*nesi'* + *ro'sh* in which the second term functions appositionally by more carefully specifying the meaning of the first term. The word *nesi'* is a common word for "prince/ruler" in Ezekiel, and the second term, *ro'sh* ("chief, first, head"), indicates his supremacy in that he is "the leader among princes and over several tribal/national groups."[10] The translators of the Septuagint, however, read *ro'sh* as a proper name and trans-lated the title into Greek as "the prince/ruler of Ros." The NKJV and NASB follow this rendering of *nesi' ro'sh*, referring to Gog as the "prince of Rosh." This reading is possible, but one would expect the conjunction "and" before the place name Meshech if Rosh were also a proper noun and the name for a nation or people.[11] Even if Rosh is a place name, there is nothing from the time of Ezekiel that would specifically indicate a connection with the later nation or people of Russia. Daniel Block notes that the neo-Assyrian annals refer to

[5]   Daniel I. Block, *The Book of Ezekiel Chapters 25–48*, New International Commentary on the Old Testament (Grand Rapids: Eerdmans, 1998), 433.
[6]   Block, "Ezekiel," 435.
[7]   Gary Shogren, "Gog of Magog Is Dead . . . and I Have Seen His Grave," *Open Our Eyes, Lord* (blog), January 13, 2013, https://openoureyeslord.com/2013/01/13/gog-of-magog-is-dead-and-i-have-seen-his-grave/.
[8]   Michael S. Heiser, *The Unseen Realm: Recovering the Supernatural Worldview of the Bible* (Bellingham, WA: Lexham, 2015), 365.
[9]   Heiser, *The Unseen Realm*, 365. The Qumran War Scroll (1QM 11:16–17) also identifies Gog as the final enemy of God.
[10]   Block, *Book of Ezekiel Chapters 25–48*, 435.
[11]   Block, *Book of Ezekiel Chapters 25–48*, 435.

a Rashu/Reshu/Arashi, but this name designates an area to the east between Babylon and Elam, not the land of present-day Russia.[12] The name "Russia" for the land we know today did not appear until the Middle Ages, when it was brought into the region of Kiev by the Vikings.[13] It is anachronistic to read the later name Russia back into the ancient text of Ezekiel, and it is poor methodology to connect the Hebrew *rosh* with the place name Russia from another language simply because the two words sound alike.

There is also no substantive reason for connecting Meshech and Tubal in Ezek 38:2 with the Russian cities Moscow and Tubolsk. Meshech and Tubal are attested in Neo-Assyrian sources and are likely provinces of Asia Minor associated with the Scythians. Both Gog/Magog and Meshech/Tubal are connected with territories that would include modern Iran, Turkey, and the southern provinces of Russia.[14] Meshech and Tubal were known nations in Ezekiel's day (Ezek 27:13; 32:26; compare Gen 10:2; Ps 120:5; Isa 66:19).

A final argument for the Gog-Russia identification is that the hordes led by Gog will attack Israel from "the remotest parts of the north" (Ezek 38:15). Russia is to the far north of the land of Israel, but "foe from the north" in the Old Testament Prophets is a stock expression for various foreign invaders, since most armies followed the path of the Fertile Crescent and would attack Israel from the north.[15] When Isaiah and Jeremiah warn of an approaching foe from "the north" (see Isa 14:31; Jer 1:14–15; 4:6; 6:1, 22), they are primarily referring to the Assyrian and Babylonian armies that would come from Mesopotamia. The reference to a northern invader in Ezekiel 38–39 provides no direct connection to Russia.

Gog's Allies and the Final Assault of the Nations on Israel

The allies of Gog are identified by specific names in Ezek 38:3–6, and some interpreters have assumed that the nations named in the vision specifically represent the nations and peoples that live in those same geographical areas today. For example, the name Gomer is often connected to Germany. Block has noted some important features of the list of Gog's allies that would argue against this approach. There are seven allies of Gog, the same number addressed in the

---

12   Block, *Book of Ezekiel Chapters 25–48*, 435.
13   Pate and Hays, *Iraq: Babylon of the End-Times?* 69 (see chap. 36, n. 4).
14   Lamar E. Cooper, *Ezekiel*, New American Commentary (Nashville: Broadman & Holman, 1994), 331.
15   Pate and Hays, *Iraq: Babylon of the End-Times?*, 68–69.

oracles against the nations found in Ezekiel 25–32 and the same number of nations that join Egypt in Sheol in Ezek 32:17–32. The use of the number seven, as elsewhere in the Hebrew Bible, symbolizes totality and completeness, suggesting that nations from all over the world are involved in this attack on Israel rather than merely seven specific nations.[16]

These seven allies of Gog also come from all four points of the compass—Meshech, Tubal, Gomer, and Beth-Togarmah from the north; Cush from the south; Paras from the east; and Put from the west. The seven nations are representative of a worldwide assault on God and his people.[17] Duguid writes, "The point of Ezekiel 38–39 is not that at some distant point in future history these particular nations will oppose Israel, while others (America? Britain?) will rally to her aid. Rather, these seven nations from the ends of the earth, from all four points of the compass, represent symbolically a supreme attempt by the united forces of evil to crush the peace of God's people."[18]

Understanding Ezekiel 38–39 to portray the nations collectively invading Israel rather than designating specific nations that are part of this coalition also aligns with the motif of the final assault of the nations on Israel as found in several Old Testament prophetic books (see Joel 3:1–16; Mic 5:5–9; Zeph 3:8–9; Zech 12:1–9; 14:1–15). The Lord's judgment in this final battle will extend to "all nations" (Joel 3:2) and will result in the recognition of the Lord as "King over the whole earth" (Zech 14:9). Survivors from the nations will then stream to Zion to worship the Lord (Isa 2:2–4; Zech 14:16). The eschatological battles depicted in Rev 16:12–16 and 19:11–21 also portray the nations as united in their opposition to God. The only reference to the battle against Gog of Magog in the New Testament appears in Rev 20:7–10 and places the battle at the end of the millennial age portrayed in 20:1–6. What we see here again is the nations from "the four corners of the earth" joining forces to do battle with the Lord and his people. If we read Ezekiel 38–39 merely to refer to seven isolated nations, we miss the warning of worldwide opposition to God depicted in these texts.

Application

Biblical prophecy is not designed to give us a detailed road map of eschatological events but rather to provide a broad view of future events with assur-

---

[16] Block, *Book of Ezekiel Chapters 25–48*, 441.
[17] Block, *Book of Ezekiel Chapters 25–48*, 441.
[18] Duguid, *Ezekiel*, 453.

ances that God will ultimately prevail over all opposition. The final rebellion against God will occur in the eschatological day of the Lord, at which time God will judge the nations and destroy the wicked. Prophecy does not always satisfy our curiosity or give us insider information into contemporary events, but the prophetic message of the Bible does assure God's people that they are on the winning side and gives them strength to endure as they face opposition and persecution in a world that is united in its rebellion against God.

Annotated Bibliography

BOOKS

Pate, C. Marvin, and J. Daniel Hays. *Iraq: Babylon of the End-Times?* Grand Rapids: Baker, 2003. Discussion of how to read biblical prophecy in light of contemporary events with a helpful chapter on Ezekiel 38–39.

COMMENTARIES

Block, Daniel I. *The Book of Ezekiel Chapters 25–48*. New International Commentary on the Old Testament. Grand Rapids: Eerdmans, 1998. The most thorough evangelical commentary on Ezekiel with detailed exegesis of Gog of Magog prophecy.

Duguid, Iain M. *Ezekiel*. New International Version Application Commentary. Grand Rapids: Zondervan, 1999. Evangelical commentary with a detailed explanation of text and helpful summary of how Christians through the centuries have identified Gog.

WEBSITES

Shogren, Gary. "Gog of Magog Is Dead . . . and I Have Seen His Grave." *Open Our Eyes, Lord* (blog). January 13, 2013. https://openoureyeslord.com/2013/01/13/gog-of-magog-is-dead-and-i-have-seen-his-grave/. Gives an overview of popular treatments of Ezekiel 38–39.

—

CHAPTER 39

Jonah's Preaching Produced
the Greatest Revival Ever

Jonah 3

The Legendary Teaching on the Great Revival in Jonah 3

By sheer numbers, Jonah's preaching mission to Nineveh ranks as the greatest revival of all time. An entire city turned to God in repentance and faith. One writer has stated, "It was Nineveh that yielded 600,000 souls for the glory of God. It was and still is the largest harvest God has effected to date. In addition, we know that this was a genuine repentance and coming to faith, because first, the Bible said so, and second, the Lord stayed His hand in destroying the city (Jonah 3:5, 10)."[1]

Countering the Legendary Teaching

God spared the city of Nineveh from the judgment he had threatened to bring against the city because the Ninevites took Jonah's warnings seriously and repented of their sinful ways. They turned from their violence and pleaded for divine mercy with prayer and fasting. There is nothing in the book of Jonah, however, to suggest that the Ninevites turned from their pagan gods and exercised saving faith in Yahweh as the one true God. The focus of Jonah is not on the conversion of the Ninevites, but rather on the greatness of God's mercy. The Lord recognized and responded to even the less-than-perfect

---

[1] The number 600,000 comes from the reference in Jonah 4:11 to the 120,000 adults living in Nineveh. See Elizabeth Prata, "What Was the Greatest Revival Ever?" *The End Time* (blog), June 9, 2017, http://the-end-time.blogspot.com/2017/06/what-was-greatest-revival-ever.html.

repentance of the Ninevites. If the Lord was willing to spare a pagan city that was much deserving of judgment, then he would have shown even greater grace to the people of Israel and Judah had they listened to their prophets and turned from their sinful ways.

A Remarkable Response to a Bad Sermon

The Ninevites' response to the warnings of divine judgment was especially remarkable in light of Jonah's rather deficient sermon. Jonah had resisted God's command to go to Nineveh by fleeing on a ship and had even attempted to elicit the help of the sailors on the ship in his assisted suicide. The prophet had only consented to go to Nineveh after being swallowed by a great fish, and his terse five-word sermon (in Hebrew) reflected a rather half-hearted attempt to preach God's word to the Ninevites (Jonah 3:4). Jonah's sermon warned of judgment in forty days but omitted some rather important details. Jonah made no mention of the God who would bring this judgment, the reason for the judgment, the specific form of the city's impending calamity, or how the people might avert this judgment.[2] Jonah's anger over the sparing of the city (4:1–2) suggests that the prophet's feeble attempt at proclaiming divine judgment was due to the fact that he knew God's disposition to relent from sending disaster and did not want to see divine mercy extended to the hated Assyrians.

Even though Jonah gave the Ninevites every reason to ignore or dismiss him, the people of the city believed the message and took seriously its warnings of coming judgment. The response of the Ninevites stands out for other reasons as well. Despite having no previous history with Jonah or his God, the people respond immediately to the prophet's message with belief and repentance. The statement in Jonah 3:6 that "word reached the king of Nineveh" suggests that the message spread throughout the city even before Jonah could complete his preaching mission or perhaps even as Jonah was sulking over the positive response to his sermon. The Ninevites repented so quickly that they were even ahead of their king's official edict. Their repentance involved fasting from both food and drink, the most extreme form of fasting in the Old Testament.[3] The people also covered themselves in sackcloth, sat in ashes, cried out to God in

---

[2]   Kevin J. Youngblood, *Jonah: God's Severe Mercy,* Hearing the Message of Scripture (Grand Rapids: Zondervan, 2013), 103.

[3]   Mark Boda, *A Severe Mercy: Sin and Its Remedy in the Hebrew Bible*, Siphrut 1 (Winona Lake, IN: Eisenbrauns, 2009), 316.

prayer, and turned away from their sinful and violent acts.[4] The Ninevites included even their animals in the fasting and made them wear sackcloth as well. The inclusion of the Assyrian king among the repentant is also surprising in light of the many hostile responses to the prophets from the kings of Israel and Judah (1 Kgs 13:1–5; 18:17–19; 19:1–22; 22:13–28; 2 Kgs 1; Jer 26:20–23; 36–38). Perhaps the most shocking and scandalous part of the story of Jonah is that the pagan Ninevites had responded better to the preaching of one bad prophet than the people of Israel and Judah had responded to all of the faithful prophets that God had sent to them.

The Story of Jonah and the Richness of God's Mercy

Even more impressive than the Ninevites' response to God was how God himself responded to the Ninevites. Even though God's anger at the degree of Nineveh's wickedness had reached a point where judgment was imminent, he still quickly relented from sending the threatened judgment when the Ninevites repented. Jeremiah 18:8 expresses the promise that God would "relent" (*nacham*) from sending the "disaster" (*ra'ah*) he planned for a particular nation whenever that nation would "turn" (*shuv*) from its "evil" (*ra'ah*) ways, which is precisely what happens in the aftermath of Jonah's preaching to the Ninevites.[5] When God saw that the Ninevites had indeed "turned" (*shuv*) from their "evil" (*ra'ah*), he relented from the "disaster" (*ra'ah*) he had planned for them (Jonah 3:10). The willingness of God to turn from judgment reflects his merciful nature; the fact that God is willing to extend such grace to the Ninevites reflects even more so the depths of divine mercy. Later readers of the book would understand that God was acting to preserve the very people that would destroy the northern kingdom of Israel.

The Assyrians were noted for their cruelty and violence and built an empire based on threats of horrific torture to those who resisted their rule.[6] Jonah in many ways appears childish and petulant in his actions and attitudes, but he raised a legitimate issue when questioning how a just God could show mercy to such a wicked people (4:1–2). Nevertheless, God's sparing of Nineveh is one of the numerous instances in Scripture where his mercy trumps his justice. The Lord had extended this same type of mercy on many

---

[4]   Boda, *A Severe Mercy*, 316.

[5]   Youngblood, *Jonah*, 142.

[6]   For historical perspective, see Erika Bleibtreu, "Grisly Assyrian Record of Torture and Death," *Biblical Archaeology Review* 17, no. 1 (1991): 1–11.

occasions to Israel, but Jonah is scandalized that God would show similar mercy to the pagan Ninevites. When explaining why he had first refused to come to Nineveh, Jonah said that he knew of God's gracious and compassionate nature (4:2). Jonah's description of God references the revelation that the Lord had given of himself in Exod 34:6–7, when he had spared the Israelites following their worship of the golden calf. This portrayal of God becomes perhaps Israel's central confession about Yahweh's character (e.g., 2 Chr 30:9; Neh 9:17; Pss 86:15; 103:8; 111:4; 145:8; Dan 9:4; Joel 2:13; Nah 1:3, among others), but Jonah is unique in how this confession of God's character is applied to his dealings with the nations.[7] The Lord demonstrates the same grace to the nations that he has shown to his covenant people Israel.

The Ninevites: Repentance but Not Conversion

Though the Ninevites' repentance was unprecedented in many ways even among the people of Israel, their response falls short of a genuine revival and a conversion to faith in the one true God. Jonah 3:5 states that the people of Nineveh "believed in God" (the verb *'aman* + the preposition *be*). For English readers, this expression may seem to indicate saving faith. However, the Hebrew idiom does not necessarily convey the same idea. The preposition "in" (*be*) here simply marks the verb's direct object, and so the expression should be translated "believed God" (as in the CSB and many English translations).[8] Rather than the idea that the people of Nineveh trusted in God for their salvation, Jonah 3:5 is simply conveying that they believed the message from God communicated by Jonah that judgment was coming and responded accordingly.[9] In Num 20:12, the Lord tells Moses, after he struck the rock to bring water from it instead of speaking to it, that he would not enter the Promised Land because he had not "believed" (*'aman* + *be*) the Lord. The verse is obviously not stating that Moses was lacking a faith commitment to the Lord but rather points to the fact that Moses had disobeyed because he had not believed or trusted that God would do what he had said.[10] The expression *'aman* + *be* is used in some contexts to refer to a human believing or not believing something told to them by another human (see 1 Sam 27:12; Job 4:18; Jer 12:6; Mic 7:5). The expression does

---

7   Boda, *Severe Mercy*, 307.

8   John H. Walton, "The Object Lesson of Jonah 4:5–7," *Bulletin for Biblical Research* 2 (1997): 53.

9   Billy K. Smith and Frank Page, *Amos, Obadiah, Jonah,* New American Commentary (Nashville: Broadman & Holman, 1995), 261.

10   Walton, "Object Lesson," 53–54.

refer in some instances to faith commitments that go beyond what is said of the Ninevites in Jonah 3:5, but it is the larger context of these passages rather than the expression itself which indicates this fuller dimension of faith (see Gen 15:6; Exod 14:31; Ps 78:22).[11]

Nothing in the context of Jonah 3:5 suggests a deep faith commitment to the Lord on the part of the Ninevites. As Smith and Page have noted, there is no indication "that the Ninevites turned from their other gods or that they even knew the name of the Lord (Yahweh)."[12] John Walton also explains that Nineveh's repentance was less than complete: "Nineveh's reform is described in terms of turning from their wicked ways, coupled with the ritual acts of fasting and donning sackcloth. Ritual response and ethical tidying up are precisely what one would expect from pagan Assyrians—and, from every indication, they are still just that, despite the fact that they have taken a step in the right direction."[13] If looking for an example of genuine conversion in the book of Jonah, the pagan sailors whom Jonah encounters in chapter 1 are more likely candidates than the Ninevites.[14] Jesus states in Matt 12:41 that the Ninevites will rise up to condemn the generation of his day for its refusal to repent and believe in him. This statement does not prove that the Ninevites were truly converted but merely reflects their "relative responsiveness" when compared to Jesus's generation in Israel.[15] The fact that the Ninevites responded to a prophet like Jonah made Israel's rejection of Jesus even worse.

The point of Jonah is not that a great conversion took place in Nineveh, but rather that God is merciful even to those who are exceptionally wicked when there is sometimes even the smallest measure of repentance. The repentance of the Ninevites in many ways is like that of a child who is sorry for getting caught with his hand in the cookie jar, but the Lord relents from judgment anyway. We have no way of knowing how long the ethical reforms of the Ninevites may have lasted, but we do know that the city eventually returned to its evil ways, necessitating Nahum's oracles of judgment against the city and the fall of the city to the Medes and Babylonians in 612 BC.

---

[11]   Walton, "Object Lesson," 54. Even in Gen 15:6, the expression "believe in" (*'aman* + *be*) conveys that Abraham believed or trusted the message that God gave to him (see Ps 106:12, 24).

[12]   Smith and Page, *Amos, Obadiah, Jonah*, 261.

[13]   Walton, "Object Lesson," 54.

[14]   In contrast to the Ninevites, the sailors acknowledge Yahweh as the source of their deliverance and offer sacrifices and make vows to him in accordance with what one would expect of faithful Israelites (1:14–17). For more on the differences between the sailors and the Ninevites in their response to God, see Daniel C. Timmer, *A Gracious and Compassionate God: Mission, Salvation, and Spirituality in the Book of Jonah*, New Studies in Biblical Theology (Downers Grove, IL: InterVarsity Press, 2004), 72–74, 100–104.

[15]   Craig S. Keener, *A Commentary on the Gospel of Matthew* (Grand Rapids: Eerdmans, 1999), 368.

Application

The book of Jonah reminds us of the wideness of God's mercy. The Lord has "no pleasure in the death of the wicked" (Ezek 33:11). The Lord spared the Ninevites from destruction even when their repentance was less than perfect. The story of Jonah reminds us of our own need for divine grace and encourages us to remember that forgiveness is available when we turn from our sinful ways. The Ninevites were spared from judgment but then returned to their sinful ways; those who are truly converted receive not only God's forgiveness but also the grace to endure and thrive in their new life in Christ.

Annotated Bibliography

BOOKS

Timmer, Daniel C. *A Gracious and Compassionate God: Mission, Salvation, and Spirituality in the Book of Jonah*. New Studies in Biblical Theology. Downers Grove, IL: InterVarsity Press, 2011. Biblical theological study of the book of Jonah with focus on the revelation of God's character in the book and the nature of the Ninevites' response to God.

COMMENTARIES

Youngblood, Kevin J. *Jonah: God's Severe Mercy*, Hearing the Message of Scripture. Grand Rapids: Zondervan, 2013. Concise evangelical commentary that offers helpful literary and theological insights into the book of Jonah.

ARTICLES

Walton, John H. "The Object Lesson of Jonah 4:5–7 and the Purpose of the Book of Jonah." *Bulletin for Biblical Research* 2 (1992): 47–57. Helps to clarify the nature of the Ninevites' response to Jonah's preaching and how this response fits with the book's overall emphasis on the mercy of God and response to the prophetic word.

CHAPTER 40

Christians Must Bring Their Whole Tithe into the Local Church

Malachi 3:8–10

The Legendary Teaching on Malachi 3

Many Christians believe that they have the option to choose how much money to give to charity; many also believe they can choose whichever organization they desire to receive their gifts. However, a few verses in Malachi 3 clearly demonstrate that both of these statements are incorrect:

> "Will a man rob God? Yet you are robbing me!"
> "How do we rob you?" you ask.
> "By not making the payments of the tenth and the contributions. You are suffering under a curse, yet you—the whole nation—are still robbing me. Bring the full tenth into the storehouse so that there may be food in my house. Test me in this way," says the LORD of Armies. "See if I will not open the floodgates of heaven and pour out a blessing for you without measure." (vv. 8–10)

God, through the prophet Malachi, provides the amount that every follower of God must give: 10 percent. When we do not give 10 percent—our tithe—we are in disobedience and robbing God. The full tenth—all the tithe—must be given "into the storehouse" or the local church. Therefore, all followers of God are required to give 10 percent of their income to their local church. If they want to give above and beyond their tithe, then they can choose the amount and the organization.

But what if someone cannot afford to tithe? These verses also provide a promise that some have overlooked! God says to "test him," which is very uncommon in the Bible. The Lord promises to bless those who tithe obediently. If you commit to tithe to our church, and three months from now you discover you are worse off financially than when you began, then we will reimburse you all your tithe money. However, in the decades that I have made that offer, not one person ever came asking for their tithe money back.

Countering the Legendary Teaching

There are three concepts presupposed that support the legendary teaching above: (1) the tithe in the Old Testament was 10 percent of income; (2) the storehouse in Malachi 3 refers to the local church; and (3) the prosperity promised applies in the new covenant as well as the old covenant. All three of these concepts must be tested against Scripture to see if they are correct. Do not misunderstand the purpose of this chapter. Christians should give generously, sacrificially, and regularly to their local congregations. However, should Malachi 3 be used to support a specific amount and destination for Christian giving?

The first concept, that the tithe in the Old Testament was 10 percent of income, has already been addressed above in chapter 14, "The Tithe in Ancient Israel Was 10 Percent of Income." The Old Testament had several tithes that Israelites were commanded to give, including the Levitical Tithe, the Festival Tithe, and the Charity Tithe. The yearly average was closer to 23-1/3 percent, not 10 percent. They also gave their tithe only from the crops that grew on the land and animals that were fed from the land, not their overall income.

Does the Storehouse in Malachi 3 Refer to the Local Church?

Tithes in the Old Testament were to be brought to certain locations. The Levitical Tithe was to be given to the tribe of Levi, probably after it was brought to Jerusalem (Num 18:24). The Festival Tithe was brought to Jerusalem and used for the three yearly celebrations (Deut 14:23). The Charity Tithe was supposed to be stored at the city gates (Deut 14:28). Since the tithe in Malachi 3 appears to be stored up rather than used in celebrations, the reference is most likely to the Levitical Tithe.[1]

The problem in Mal 3:8 is that the people of Israel were not bringing

---

[1] Some scholars have argued that Malachi 3 is addressing the priests, but Mal 3:6 shifts from addressing priests to all of Israel. If it had been addressed to the priests, it was discussing the Priestly Tithe of Num 18:26.

the required tithe or contributions/offerings that were mandated in the Old Testament law. Although a common interpretation takes the reference to "contributions" or offerings in Mal 3:8 as optional, they too were required as described in the Old Testament law. The tithes and offerings were used to support the temple staff. But what is the "storehouse" referencing?

The storehouse was not the temple itself. It also was not a reference to local communities of believers. It was an actual building used to store what the Levites received when tithes and offerings were brought to Jerusalem. It housed crops and livestock. The storehouse is not referenced in the Mosaic law. Where does it come from?

Second Chronicles 31:10–12 contains the first reference to the storehouse in the Old Testament. It was built near the temple to store food and animals. It basically functioned like a barn. That is why correlating the storehouse to the local church is so problematic.

Is the Prosperity Promised to Faithful Tithers Directly Applicable to Christians Today?

It is unusual (though not unheard of) to test God. But in Malachi 3, God invites the Israelites to test him. Two aspects of this invitation to test need to be explored: (1) this invitation is given to a group of people (the Israelites) who were under the old covenant; and (2) this invitation to test God is modified by the phrase "in this" (v. 10, NASB).

Commands given to Israel in the Old Testament do not necessarily directly apply to Christians. There are many laws given to Israel when they were under the old covenant that do not directly apply to Christians today. Some scholars prefer to divide the law into three categories: civil, ceremonial, and moral. When a law fits into the category of "moral," then a direct application to Christians works well. As discussed in chapter 15, "The Old Testament Law Is Divided into Three Parts," this is not the best way to deal with the law. One of the problems with applying to Christians the command given to Israel in Malachi 3, as well as applying the promised prosperity, is that Israel was under a covenant different than Christians are today. The blessings and curses of Deuteronomy 28 were in full effect when God spoke those words in Malachi 3. However, as the new covenant passages make clear in the Old Testament (see, e.g., Ezek 36:22–28; Jer 31:31–34), and as Heb 8:6–8 demonstrates when discussing Jeremiah 31, Christians are not under the old covenant. Although there is a high degree of consistency between the covenants, since the same

God made them—a God who never changes—there are also some differences. Therefore, applying the blessings or the curses of Malachi to new covenant believers is inappropriate.[2]

God did not say to test him in an absolute way, but to test him "in this" (NIV, NASB). While that phrase could be understood as referring to the "way" to test God (CSB) or in this "matter" (NET), it more likely confines the testing of God to the current, specific situation that was under discussion. There is no good reason to understand this testing to be applicable in all periods at all times.

Some people have interpreted the "prosperity" promised in Malachi 3 in a very loose fashion. When God says that he will open the windows of heaven, he is simply promising rain. He is not referring to it "raining $100 bills," but to actual, water-fall rain. He also promised to keep the devourer from ruining their crops. The "devourer" is a reference to locusts (or other insects) that would eat their crops. Finally, he said that he would stop their vines from casting their fruit and instead they would have abundant crops. These are agrarian-based blessings offered to a society that was *mostly* agrarian. However, Israel was not *purely* agrarian. There were many industries in Israel that did not involve agriculture, such as fishing and building.

Conclusion

Malachi 3 was a word from the Lord to the nation of Israel. God confronted them for their failure to obey the old covenant laws they had promised to keep. In line with Deuteronomy 28, he reminded them of the curses that follow disobedience. Therefore, requiring tithing to the local church based off Malachi 3 is problematic. Hans Brandenburg's verdict is judicious: "The question of whether the command to tithe is applicable also for the new covenant era cannot be decided here."[3] Declaring that the blessings and curses of Malachi 3 apply to new covenant believers today does not sufficiently consider the change in covenants. New covenant believers must maintain faithfulness in the new covenant context.

---

[2]   In the context of the old covenant, it is important to realize that the restoration of blessings is a reference to restored covenant relationship. For this restoration to take place during the old covenant, the tithe(s) must be given. Once the relationship between God and his people is restored, then the Abrahamic promises can be fulfilled.

[3]   Hans Brandenburg, *Die Kleinen Propheten II: Haggai, Sacharja, Maleachi (mit Esra und Nehemia)* (Basel: Brunnen, 1963), 153 (my translation).

Application

This passage does have a message for Christians. Malachi 3 contains a strong reminder that the motivation for giving is extremely important. This motivation should come from a high regard for God's honor (see Mal 2:2). God looks at the heart of the giver, not just the gift. There are many ways a Christian can be motivated to give. For example, if a Christian gives to be seen by other Christians as generous (see Matt 6:2), that is problematic. But when Christian giving is driven by a reflection upon the grace and love God has demonstrated, the gift shows a high regard for God's honor.

Annotated Bibliography

BOOKS

Croteau, David A. *You Mean I Don't Have to Tithe? A Deconstruction of Tithing and a Reconstruction of Post-Tithe Giving.* Eugene, OR: Pickwick, 2010. See 121–26. This section of the book places Malachi 3 into its historical and literary context, showing that this passage should not be used to mandate Christians to give 10 percent of their income to the local church.

WEBSITES

GotQuestions Staff. "Does the Teaching on Tithing in Malachi 3:9–10 Apply to Us Today?" *GotQuestions.* Accessed on October 6, 2018. https://www.gotquestions.org/Malachi-tithing.html. Brief discussion on Malachi 3 (and tithing in general) coming to similar conclusions as this chapter.

Epilogue

A few years ago, I (Gary) finally decided that I needed help—from a local golf pro. There are four or five basic flaws in a bad golf swing, and I somehow managed to have all of them. Similarly, there are a few recurring hermeneutical flaws in the forty legends we have covered in this book.

The prevailing flaw in many of these legends is a failure to assess properly the historical and cultural backgrounds of the texts in question. The relationship between Ishmael and Isaac is not a metaphor for the present conflict between Jews and Arabs. Correctly interpreting the symbolism of the tabernacle or the purpose of clean and unclean food laws requires an understanding of the ancient Near Eastern concepts of sacred space and ritual purity. Isaiah prophesied concerning the nations of Israel and Judah, not the United States. Jeremiah's promises of "prosperity" were for a specific group of Jewish exiles, and Ezekiel's bread dramatized famine and starvation rather than a healthy diet.

Sometimes, the problem is that the "legends" import English meanings into Hebrew terms. Hebrew words such as *helper*, *vision*, and *evil* have nuances and uses in the Old Testament that are different from their English counterparts. Interaction with the Hebrew lexicons often clears up these kinds of misunderstandings.

Some of the "legends" covered in this book are the result of confusion concerning how to interpret and apply the various genres of the Old Testament. Narratives depict how biblical characters acted in the past, but their actions are not necessarily prescriptive of how believers should conduct themselves today. Old Testament narratives may describe supernatural events with highly figurative language. Proverbial statements offer observations of how life normally works but are not promises or absolute guarantees. The poetry of the Song of Songs celebrates marital love but does not necessarily tell the story of the courtship of a specific couple. Prophecies are often essentially fulfilled but not necessarily in exact detail, and prophetic visions of the future generally are not specific enough to line up with current events on the nightly news. Prophecies may also envision the future through types and patterns rather than direct and specific predictions.

Other "legends" arise from a failure to account for the progress of revelation in the Scriptures. Old Testament writers did not have the fuller understanding of New Testament writers on subjects like the Trinity, life after death, or the suffering of the future Messiah. We can certainly read the Old Testament in light of the fuller canonical perspective of the New Testament, but we need to begin by interpreting the Old Testament on its own terms. Imposing New Testament meanings on Old Testament texts causes us to lose the distinctive voice and message of the Hebrew Scriptures.

Many of the "legends" reflect flawed perspectives on the complex issues surrounding the continuities and discontinuities between the Old and New Testaments. On the one hand, some interpretive approaches place too much emphasis on discontinuities when arguing that individuals were saved by keeping the Mosaic law in the Old Testament or that Israel lacked the capacity genuinely to obey God under the old covenant. Some believe that the Ten Commandments are not for Christians today or that the laws in Leviticus have nothing to do with a Christian sexual ethic. On the other hand, some interpretive approaches go to the opposite extreme in their emphasis on continuities between the Testaments. They see the national blessings extended to Israel under the old covenant continuing to apply to new covenant believers today.

How should you respond if you hear an "urban legend" in the pulpit next Sunday morning at your church or in your neighborhood Bible study sometime in the near future (besides having an ample supply of *Urban Legends of the Old Testament*—and *Urban Legends of the New Testament*—to pass out to others)? The goal of this study is to enrich your own study of God's Word and to help groups that are digging into these passages as they study in community. We would not recommend using this resource to rebuke your pastor or to set your Bible study leader straight. We have made every attempt to approach these issues with grace and humor, because they are interesting and fun issues to explore. For the most part, these "legends" are not addressing issues of heresy or even matters that should impact our fellowship with other believers. Our desire is to create more interest in the Old Testament and not greater division between Christians. Some of the "legends" covered in the book border on the odd and the extreme, but we have attempted to use those chapters to highlight important theological and interpretive issues of God's Word and better equip you to share what you have learned with others. Our prayer is that this book will enrich your study.

Name Index

Scripture Index

9:13 *189*
10:5–14 *201*
11:1–9 *117*
13–23 *218*
13–14 *194, 217, 218*
13:6–11 *194*
13:17 *218*
13:19 *218*
13:20–22 *218*
14 *197*
14:1–3 *194*
14:1–2 *218*
14:2 *194*
14:9–11 *152*
14:9–10 *153*
14:11 *194*
14:12–15 *193, 194, 195, 196*
14:12 *193, 194*
14:13 *195*
14:14 *195*
14:18–20 *194*
14:21–23 *218*
14:31 *232*
17:1–3 *188*
18:1–21:10 *218*
20:1–3 *224*
21:9 *221*
23:13 *218*
24:1–5 *192*
24:10 *2*
24:21 *138*
25–26 *154*
25:7–8 *155*
26:19 *155*
27:1 *137, 138*
28:15 *153*
29:21 *2*
30:1–5 *218*
31:1–3 *218*
32:1 *117*
32:14 *26*
33:15 *71*
34 *2*
34:11 *2*
38:7–8 *103*
38:10 *152, 154*
39:1–8 *218*
39:6–7 *194*
40–55 *205, 206, 207, 219*
40:8 *208*

40:11 *207*
40:12–14 *207*
40:15 *207*
40:21 *208*
40:26 *207*
40:27 *207*
41:4 *208*
41:8–13 *207*
41:21–29 *208*
41:29 *2*
42:5 *207*
42:12–13 *208*
43:1–2 *207*
44:9 *2*
44:24–28 *208*
44:28–45:1 *219*
45:1–7 *200*
45:1–4 *200*
45:5 *200*
45:6–7 *200*
45:7 *199, 200, 201*
45:12 *207*
45:18 *2, 207*
46:10 *208*
47:7–8 *221*
49:4 *2*
49:14 *207*
49:16 *208*
50:4–9 *71*
51:9–11 *138*
51:9 *137*
52:13–53:12 *71*
51:13 *207*
53 *143*
53:1 *207*
54 *20*
54:1–8 *208*
54:3 *20*
54:17 *212*
55:1–13 *205, 206, 207*
55:1–5 *206*
55:6–9 *206*
55:10–11 *206, 208*
55:11 *205, 207, 209*
55:12–13 *206*
57:3 *20*
59:20–21 *95*
60:6–8 *29*
61:1 *9*
62:4–5 *208*

3:6–10 *34*
9:9–10 *117*
12:1–9 *233*
12:10 *142*
14:1–15 *233*
14:9 *233*
14:16 *233*

Malachi
2:2 *245*
3 *242, 243, 244, 245*
3:8–10 *241*
3:8 *242, 243*
3:10 *243*
14 *242*
15 *243*

Matthew
1:18–25 *19*
5 *92*
5:13–16 *132*
5:17 *92*
5:21–48 *93*
5:21–22 *92*
5:27–30 *80*
5:31–32 *92*
5:32 *80*
5:33–37 *92*
5:43–47 *145*
5:44–47 *148*
6:2–3 *88*
6:2 *245*
6:15 *73*
7:15 *123*
10:22 *73*
11:13 *92*
12:6 *47*
12:41 *239*
15:19 *80*
17:2 *47*
19:18–19 *92*
19:19 *80*
19:21 *88*
19:28 *117*
22:39 *80*
24:11 *123*
24:24 *123*
27:35 *142*
27:39 *141*
27:43 *141*

27:46 *141*

Mark
7:14–23 *61*
7:15–19 *92*
7:19 *79*
10:45 *17*
12:31 *80*
15:29 *141*
15:34 *141*

Luke
1:27–34 *19*
6:27–29 *148*
6:27–28 *145*
10:17–19 *197*
13:1–9 *190*
14:13 *88*
16:19–31 *153*
23:34 *142, 148*
23:35 *141*
24:25–27 *144*
44–47 *144*

John
1:3 *4*
1:14–18 *35*
1:14 *44*
2:17 *143*
2:19–22 *47*
3:16 *211*
4:23–24 *48*
7:37–39 *98*
11:25–26 *155*
13:17–20 *143*
13:18 *143*
14:15–23 *73*
14:17 *98*
15:10 *87*
15:25 *143*
19:24 *142*
19:28–29 *143*
19:34–37 *142*
43:14 *87*

Acts
2:38 *131*
3:13–19 *54*
3:14 *54*
3:17 *54*

Subject Index